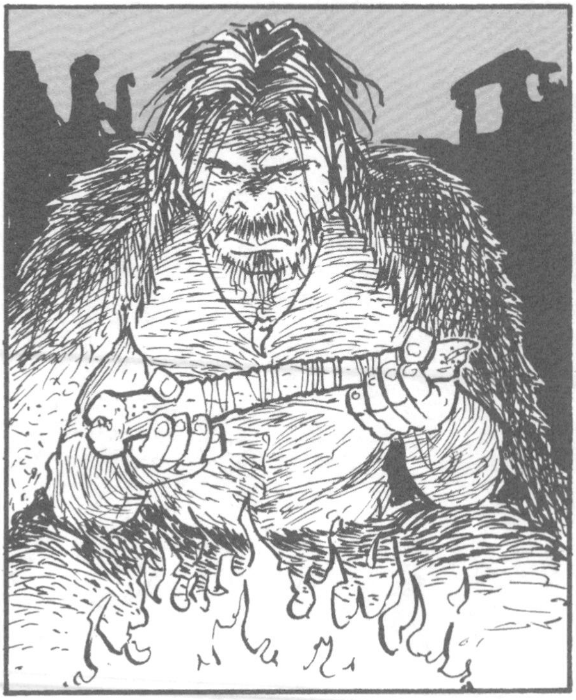

Publisher

Robyn Moore

Color

Brian Miller

abstractstudiocomics.com

mail@abstractstudiocomics.com

Terry Moore's Echo: COLLIDER published by Abstract Studio, Inc. P. O. Box 271487, Houston, Texas 77277-1487.

ECHO
COLLIDER

by
Terry Moore

If there must be trouble let it be in my day,
that my child may have peace.
—Thomas Paine

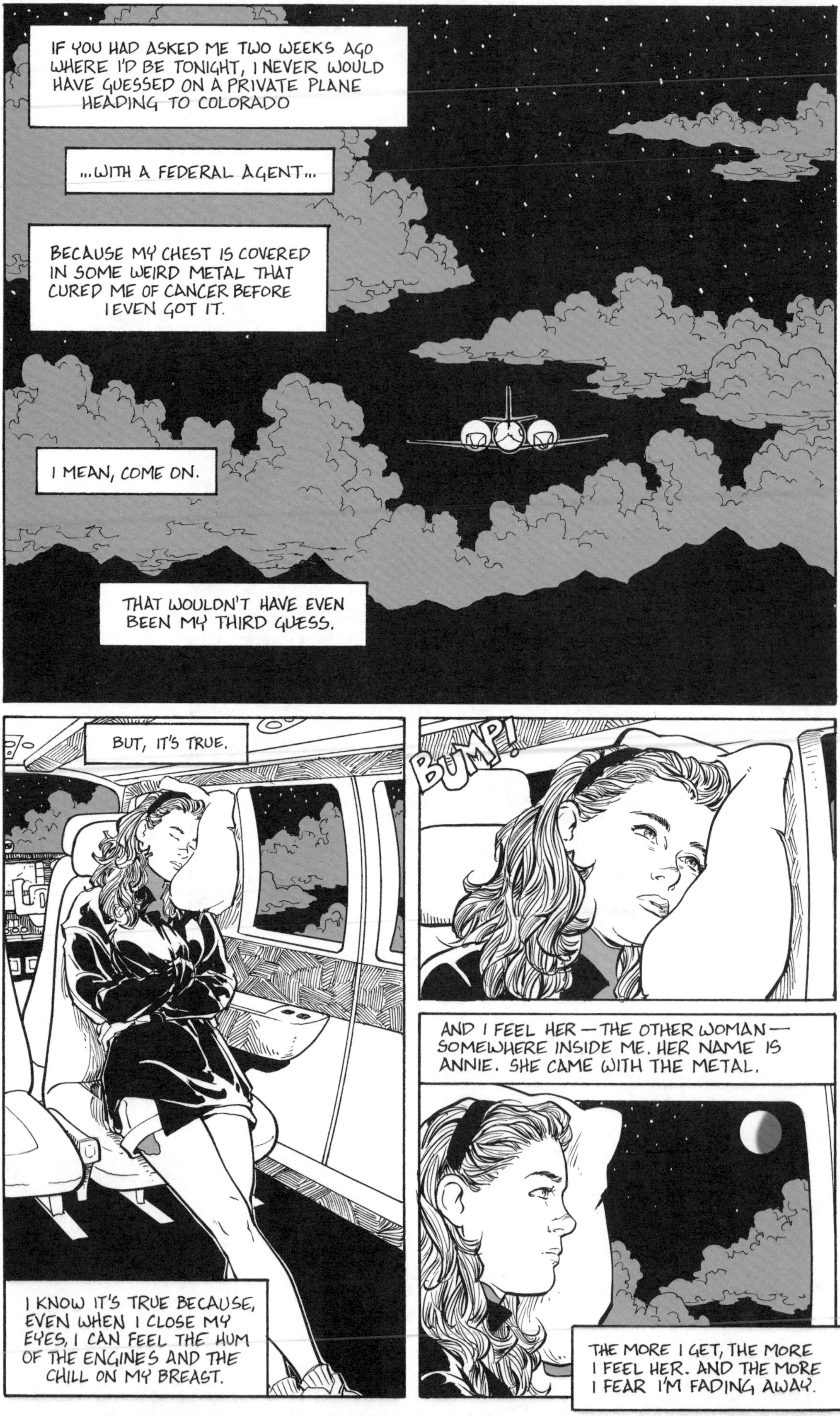
IF YOU HAD ASKED ME TWO WEEKS AGO WHERE I'D BE TONIGHT, I NEVER WOULD HAVE GUESSED ON A PRIVATE PLANE HEADING TO COLORADO
...WITH A FEDERAL AGENT...
BECAUSE MY CHEST IS COVERED IN SOME WEIRD METAL THAT CURED ME OF CANCER BEFORE I EVEN GOT IT.
I MEAN, COME ON.
THAT WOULDN'T HAVE EVEN BEEN MY THIRD GUESS.
BUT, IT'S TRUE.
I KNOW IT'S TRUE BECAUSE, EVEN WHEN I CLOSE MY EYES, I CAN FEEL THE HUM OF THE ENGINES AND THE CHILL ON MY BREAST.
BUMP!
AND I FEEL HER—THE OTHER WOMAN—SOMEWHERE INSIDE ME. HER NAME IS ANNIE. SHE CAME WITH THE METAL.
THE MORE I GET, THE MORE I FEEL HER. AND THE MORE I FEAR I'M FADING AWAY.

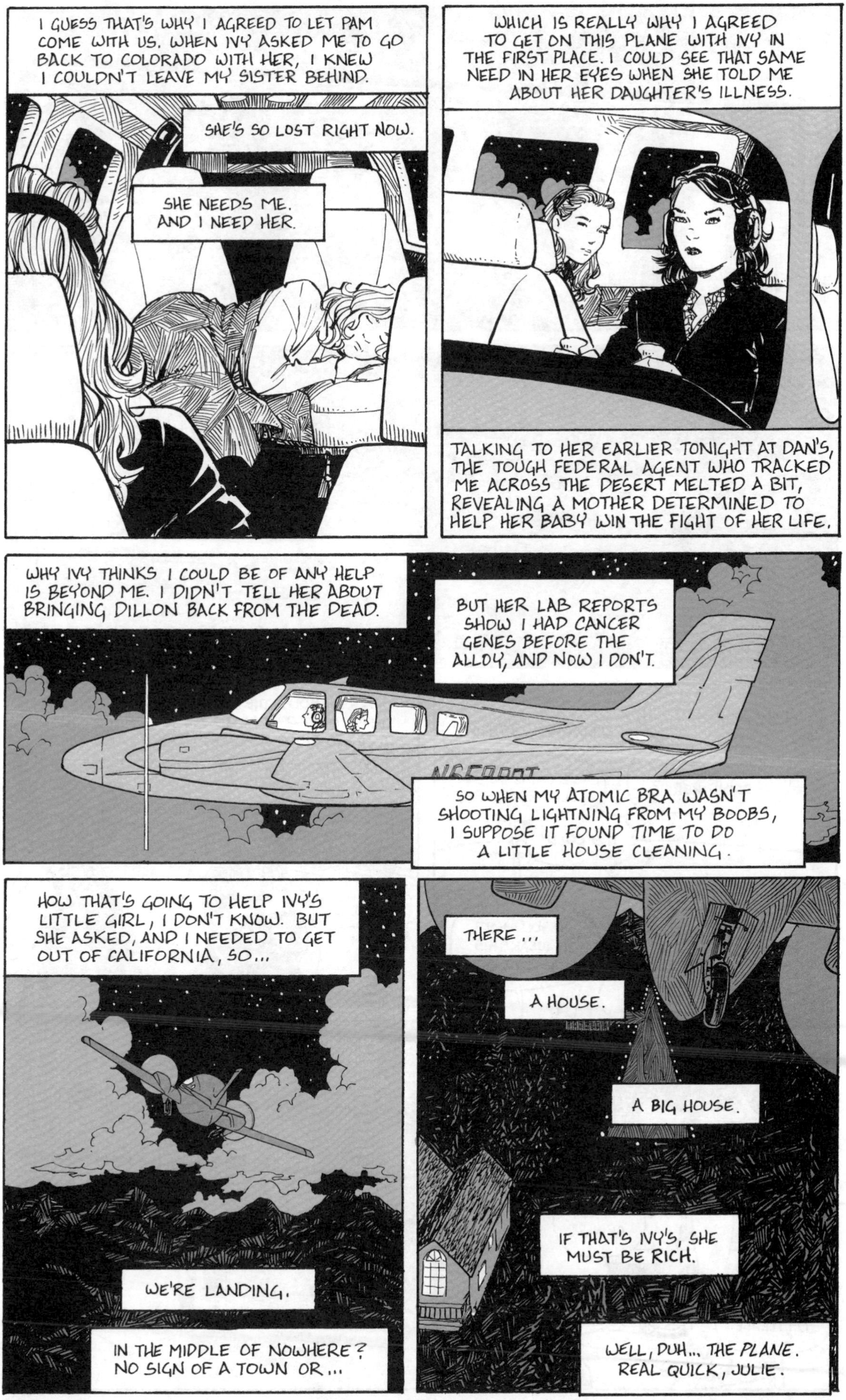
I GUESS THAT'S WHY I AGREED TO LET PAM COME WITH US. WHEN IVY ASKED ME TO GO BACK TO COLORADO WITH HER, I KNEW I COULDN'T LEAVE MY SISTER BEHIND.
SHE'S SO LOST RIGHT NOW.
SHE NEEDS ME. AND I NEED HER.
WHICH IS REALLY WHY I AGREED TO GET ON THIS PLANE WITH IVY IN THE FIRST PLACE. I COULD SEE THAT SAME NEED IN HER EYES WHEN SHE TOLD ME ABOUT HER DAUGHTER'S ILLNESS.
TALKING TO HER EARLIER TONIGHT AT DAN'S, THE TOUGH FEDERAL AGENT WHO TRACKED ME ACROSS THE DESERT MELTED A BIT, REVEALING A MOTHER DETERMINED TO HELP HER BABY WIN THE FIGHT OF HER LIFE.
WHY IVY THINKS I COULD BE OF ANY HELP IS BEYOND ME. I DIDN'T TELL HER ABOUT BRINGING DILLON BACK FROM THE DEAD.
BUT HER LAB REPORTS SHOW I HAD CANCER GENES BEFORE THE ALLOY, AND NOW I DON'T.
SO WHEN MY ATOMIC BRA WASN'T SHOOTING LIGHTNING FROM MY BOOBS, I SUPPOSE IT FOUND TIME TO DO A LITTLE HOUSE CLEANING.
HOW THAT'S GOING TO HELP IVY'S LITTLE GIRL, I DON'T KNOW. BUT SHE ASKED, AND I NEEDED TO GET OUT OF CALIFORNIA, SO...
WE'RE LANDING.
IN THE MIDDLE OF NOWHERE? NO SIGN OF A TOWN OR...
THERE...
A HOUSE.
A BIG HOUSE.
IF THAT'S IVY'S, SHE MUST BE RICH.
WELL, DUH... THE *PLANE*. REAL QUICK, JULIE.

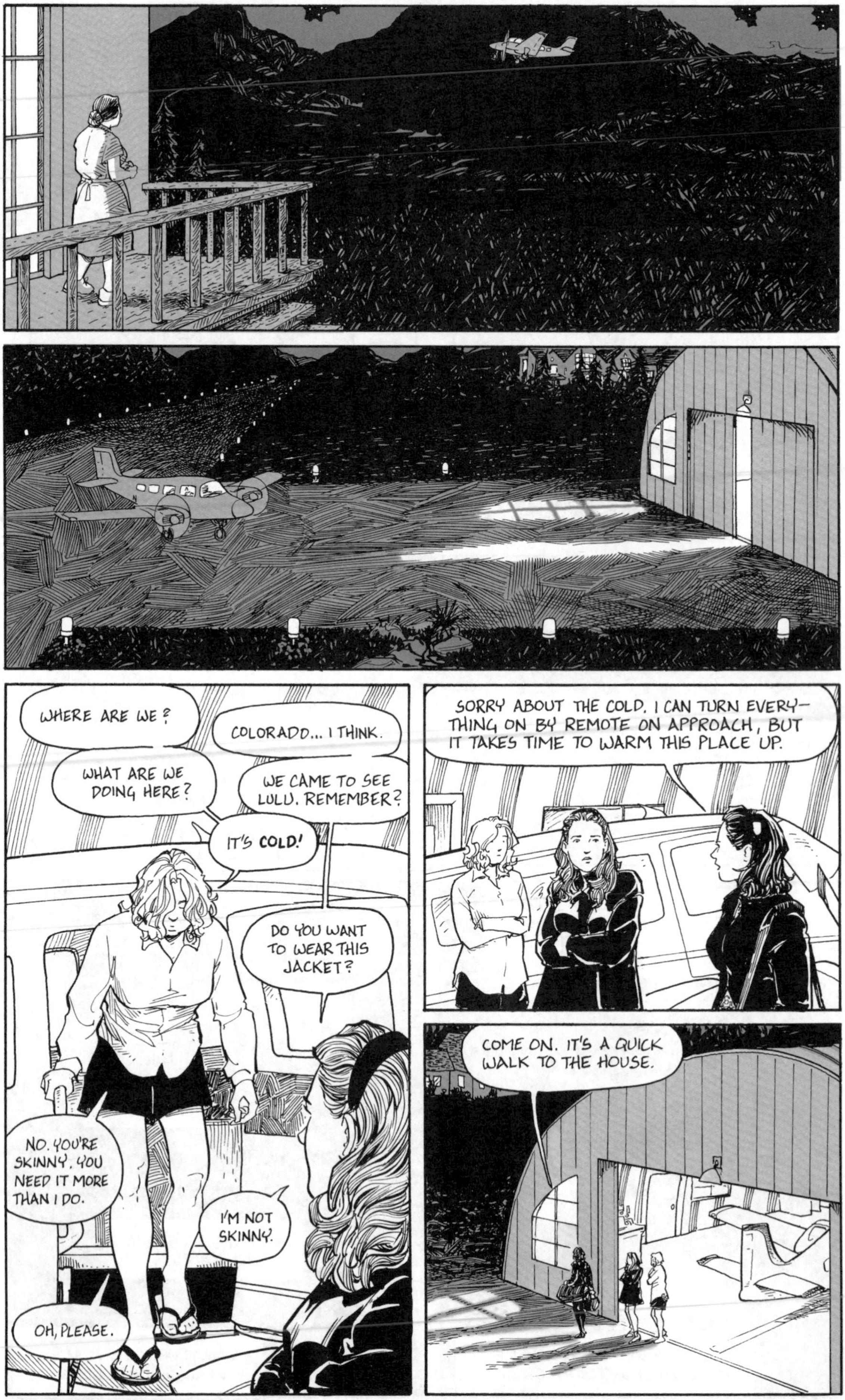
WHERE ARE WE?
COLORADO... I THINK.
WHAT ARE WE DOING HERE?
WE CAME TO SEE LULU. REMEMBER?
IT'S **COLD!**
DO YOU WANT TO WEAR THIS JACKET?
NO. YOU'RE SKINNY. YOU NEED IT MORE THAN I DO.
I'M NOT SKINNY.
OH, PLEASE.
SORRY ABOUT THE COLD. I CAN TURN EVERYTHING ON BY REMOTE ON APPROACH, BUT IT TAKES TIME TO WARM THIS PLACE UP.
COME ON. IT'S A QUICK WALK TO THE HOUSE.

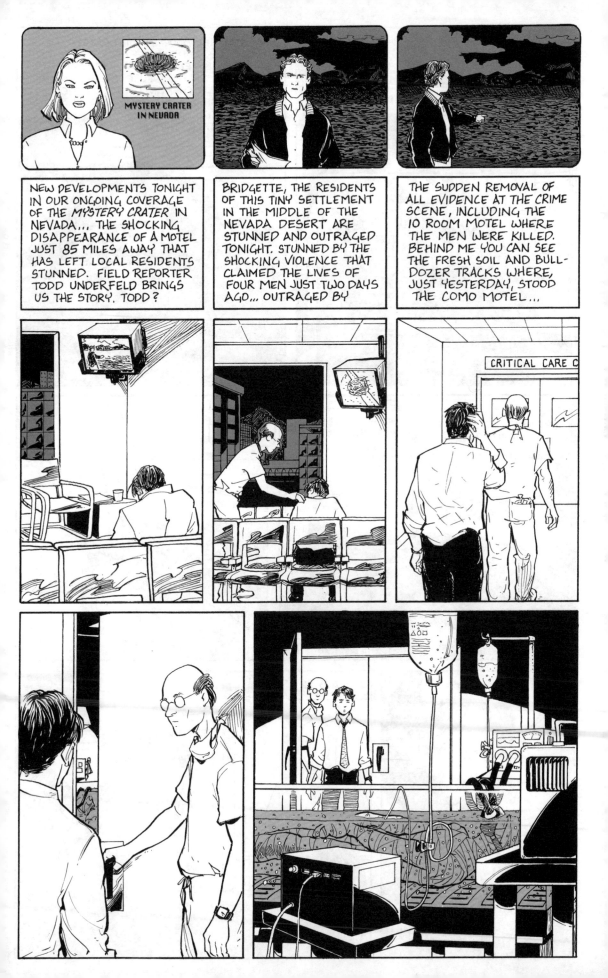

NEW DEVELOPMENTS TONIGHT IN OUR ONGOING COVERAGE OF THE *MYSTERY CRATER* IN NEVADA... THE SHOCKING DISAPPEARANCE OF A MOTEL JUST 85 MILES AWAY THAT HAS LEFT LOCAL RESIDENTS STUNNED. FIELD REPORTER TODD UNDERFELD BRINGS US THE STORY. TODD?

BRIDGETTE, THE RESIDENTS OF THIS TINY SETTLEMENT IN THE MIDDLE OF THE NEVADA DESERT ARE STUNNED AND OUTRAGED TONIGHT. STUNNED BY THE SHOCKING VIOLENCE THAT CLAIMED THE LIVES OF FOUR MEN JUST TWO DAYS AGO... OUTRAGED BY

THE SUDDEN REMOVAL OF ALL EVIDENCE AT THE CRIME SCENE, INCLUDING THE 10 ROOM MOTEL WHERE THE MEN WERE KILLED. BEHIND ME YOU CAN SEE THE FRESH SOIL AND BULL-DOZER TRACKS WHERE, JUST YESTERDAY, STOOD THE COMO MOTEL...

MYSTERY CRATER IN NEVADA

CRITICAL CARE C

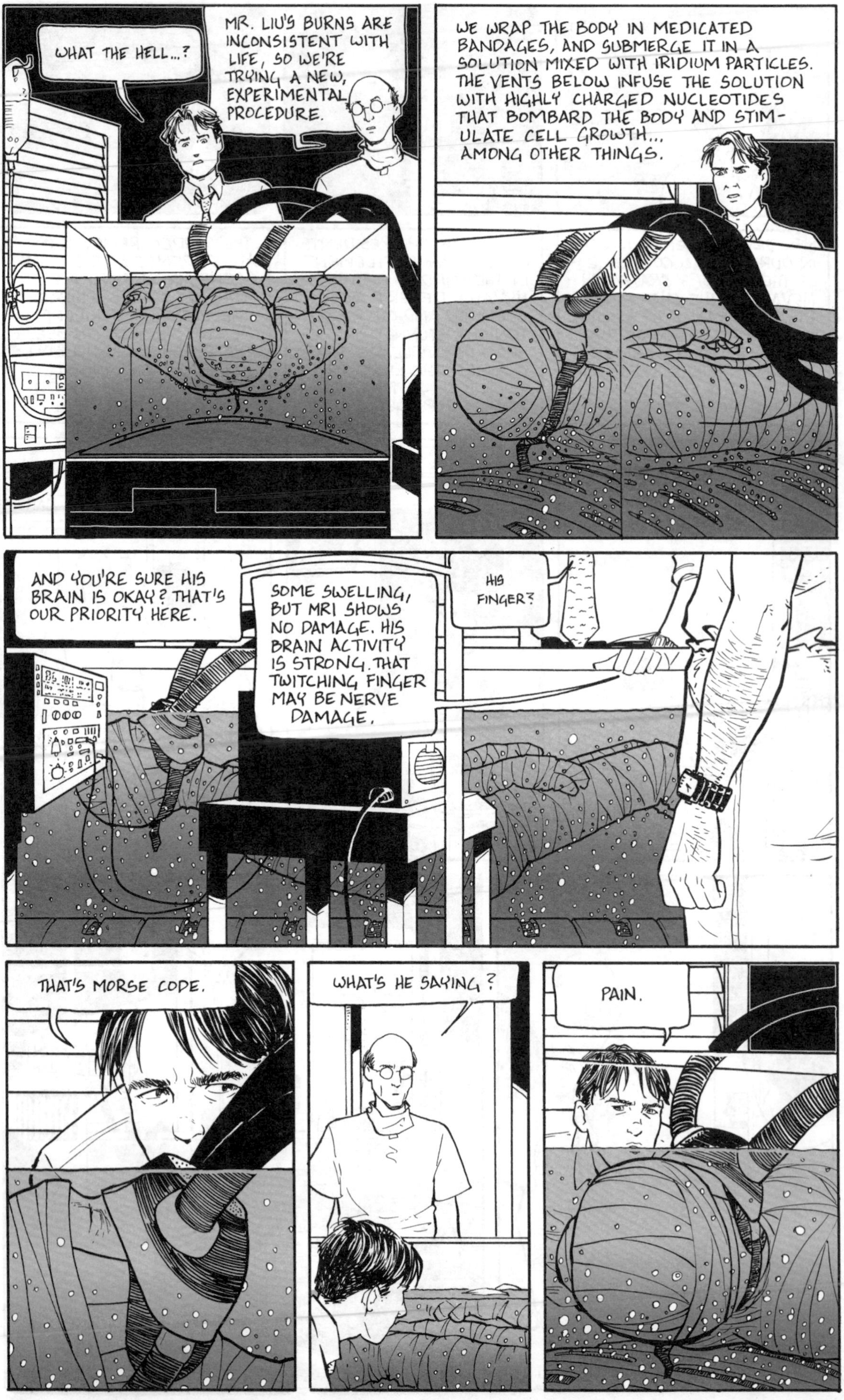
WHAT THE HELL...?
MR. LIU'S BURNS ARE INCONSISTENT WITH LIFE, SO WE'RE TRYING A NEW, EXPERIMENTAL PROCEDURE.
WE WRAP THE BODY IN MEDICATED BANDAGES, AND SUBMERGE IT IN A SOLUTION MIXED WITH IRIDIUM PARTICLES. THE VENTS BELOW INFUSE THE SOLUTION WITH HIGHLY CHARGED NUCLEOTIDES THAT BOMBARD THE BODY AND STIMULATE CELL GROWTH... AMONG OTHER THINGS.
AND YOU'RE SURE HIS BRAIN IS OKAY? THAT'S OUR PRIORITY HERE.
SOME SWELLING, BUT MRI SHOWS NO DAMAGE. HIS BRAIN ACTIVITY IS STRONG. THAT TWITCHING FINGER MAY BE NERVE DAMAGE.
HIS FINGER?
THAT'S MORSE CODE.
WHAT'S HE SAYING?
PAIN.

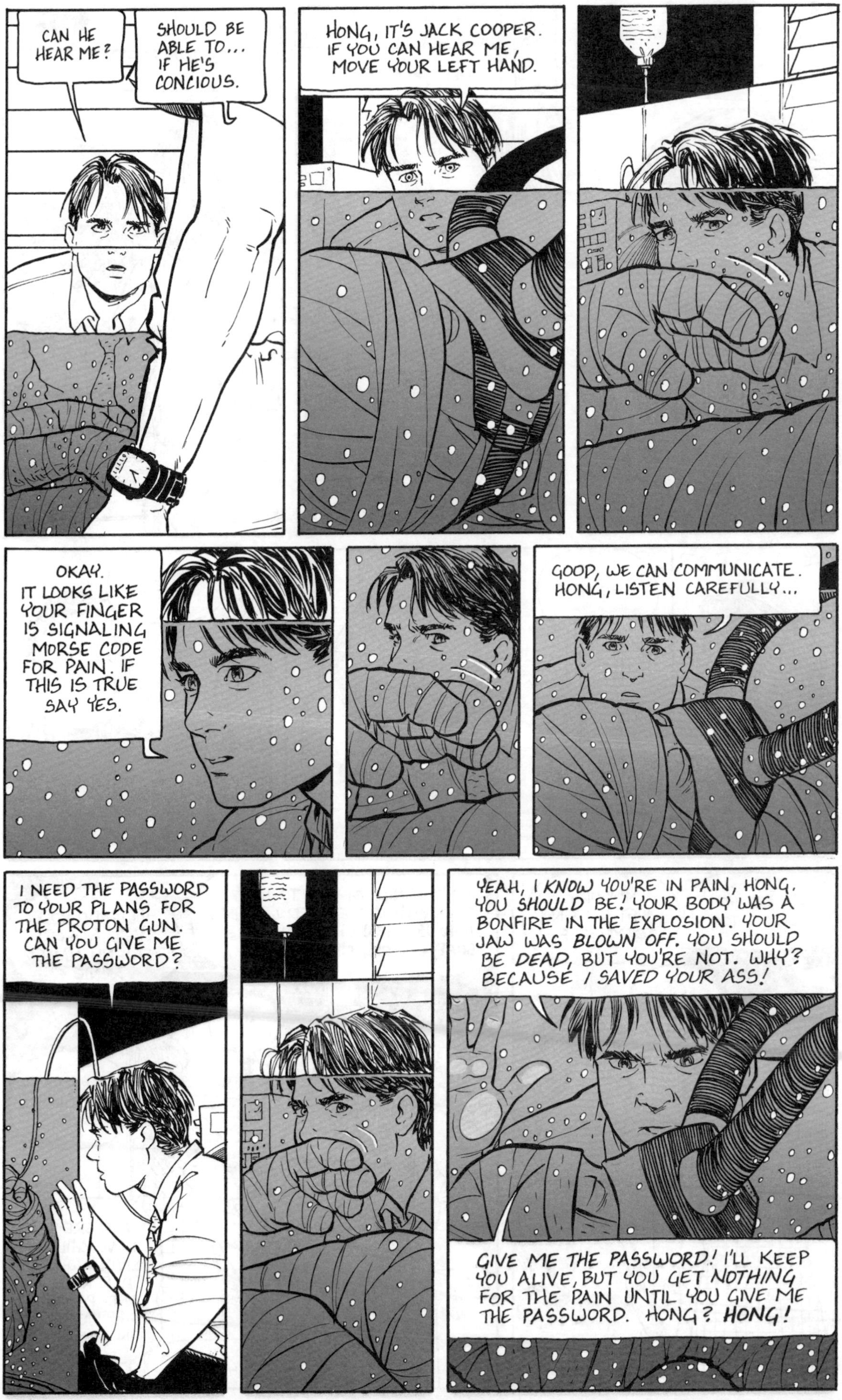
CAN HE HEAR ME?
SHOULD BE ABLE TO... IF HE'S CONCIOUS.
HONG, IT'S JACK COOPER. IF YOU CAN HEAR ME, MOVE YOUR LEFT HAND.
OKAY. IT LOOKS LIKE YOUR FINGER IS SIGNALING MORSE CODE FOR PAIN. IF THIS IS TRUE SAY YES.
GOOD, WE CAN COMMUNICATE. HONG, LISTEN CAREFULLY...
I NEED THE PASSWORD TO YOUR PLANS FOR THE PROTON GUN. CAN YOU GIVE ME THE PASSWORD?
YEAH, I KNOW YOU'RE IN PAIN, HONG. YOU SHOULD BE! YOUR BODY WAS A BONFIRE IN THE EXPLOSION. YOUR JAW WAS BLOWN OFF. YOU SHOULD BE DEAD, BUT YOU'RE NOT. WHY? BECAUSE I SAVED YOUR ASS!
GIVE ME THE PASSWORD! I'LL KEEP YOU ALIVE, BUT YOU GET NOTHING FOR THE PAIN UNTIL YOU GIVE ME THE PASSWORD. HONG? HONG!

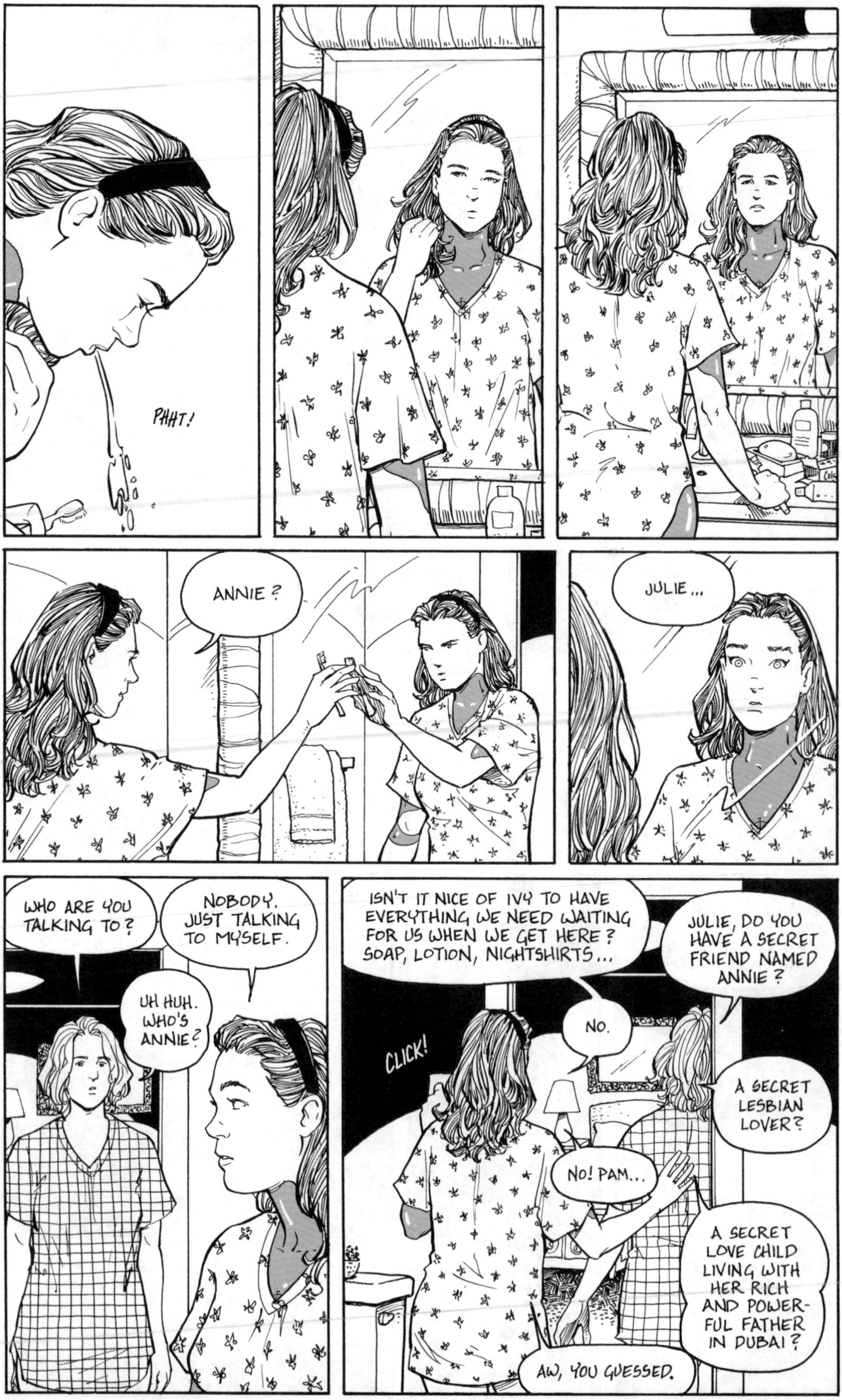
PHHT!
ANNIE?
JULIE...
WHO ARE YOU TALKING TO?
NOBODY. JUST TALKING TO MYSELF.
UH HUH. WHO'S ANNIE?
ISN'T IT NICE OF IVY TO HAVE EVERYTHING WE NEED WAITING FOR US WHEN WE GET HERE? SOAP, LOTION, NIGHTSHIRTS...
JULIE, DO YOU HAVE A SECRET FRIEND NAMED ANNIE?
NO.
CLICK!
A SECRET LESBIAN LOVER?
NO! PAM...
A SECRET LOVE CHILD LIVING WITH HER RICH AND POWERFUL FATHER IN DUBAI?
AW, YOU GUESSED.

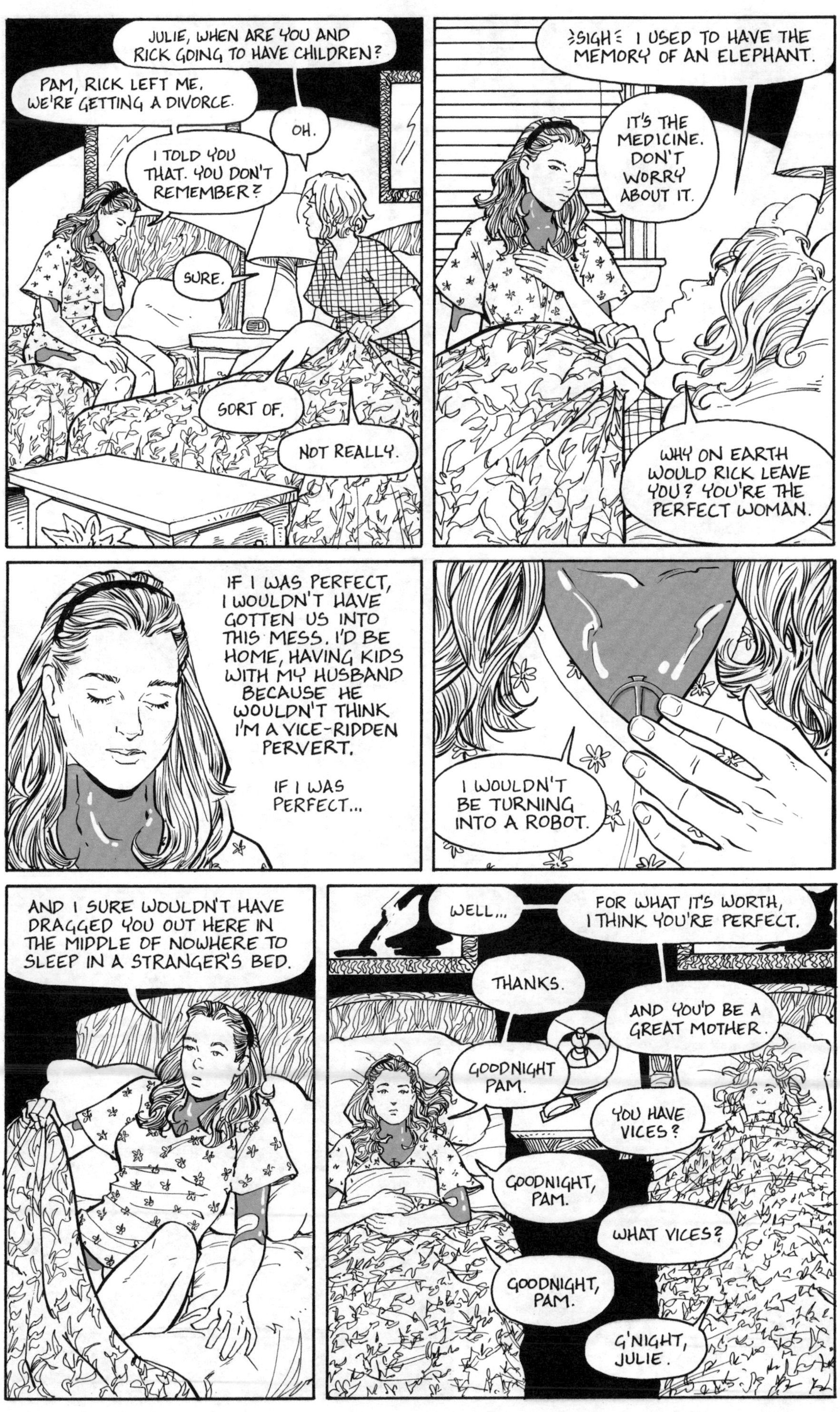
JULIE, WHEN ARE YOU AND RICK GOING TO HAVE CHILDREN?
PAM, RICK LEFT ME. WE'RE GETTING A DIVORCE.
OH.
I TOLD YOU THAT. YOU DON'T REMEMBER?
SURE.
SORT OF.
NOT REALLY.
≶SIGH≷ I USED TO HAVE THE MEMORY OF AN ELEPHANT.
IT'S THE MEDICINE. DON'T WORRY ABOUT IT.
WHY ON EARTH WOULD RICK LEAVE YOU? YOU'RE THE PERFECT WOMAN.
IF I WAS PERFECT, I WOULDN'T HAVE GOTTEN US INTO THIS MESS. I'D BE HOME, HAVING KIDS WITH MY HUSBAND BECAUSE HE WOULDN'T THINK I'M A VICE-RIDDEN PERVERT.
IF I WAS PERFECT...
I WOULDN'T BE TURNING INTO A ROBOT.
AND I SURE WOULDN'T HAVE DRAGGED YOU OUT HERE IN THE MIDDLE OF NOWHERE TO SLEEP IN A STRANGER'S BED.
WELL...
FOR WHAT IT'S WORTH, I THINK YOU'RE PERFECT.
THANKS.
AND YOU'D BE A GREAT MOTHER.
GOODNIGHT PAM.
YOU HAVE VICES?
GOODNIGHT, PAM.
WHAT VICES?
GOODNIGHT, PAM.
G'NIGHT, JULIE.

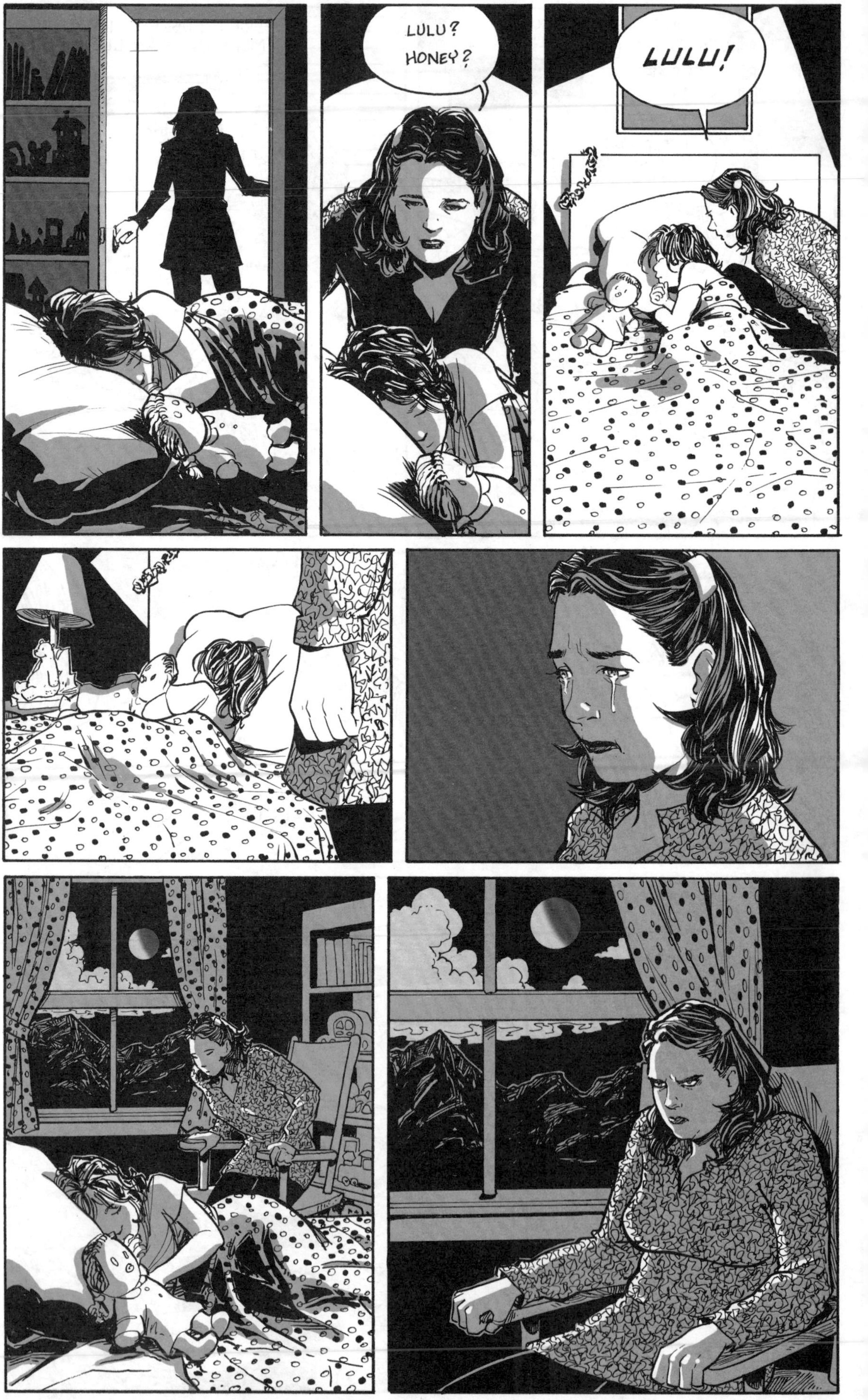
LULU?
HONEY?
LULU!

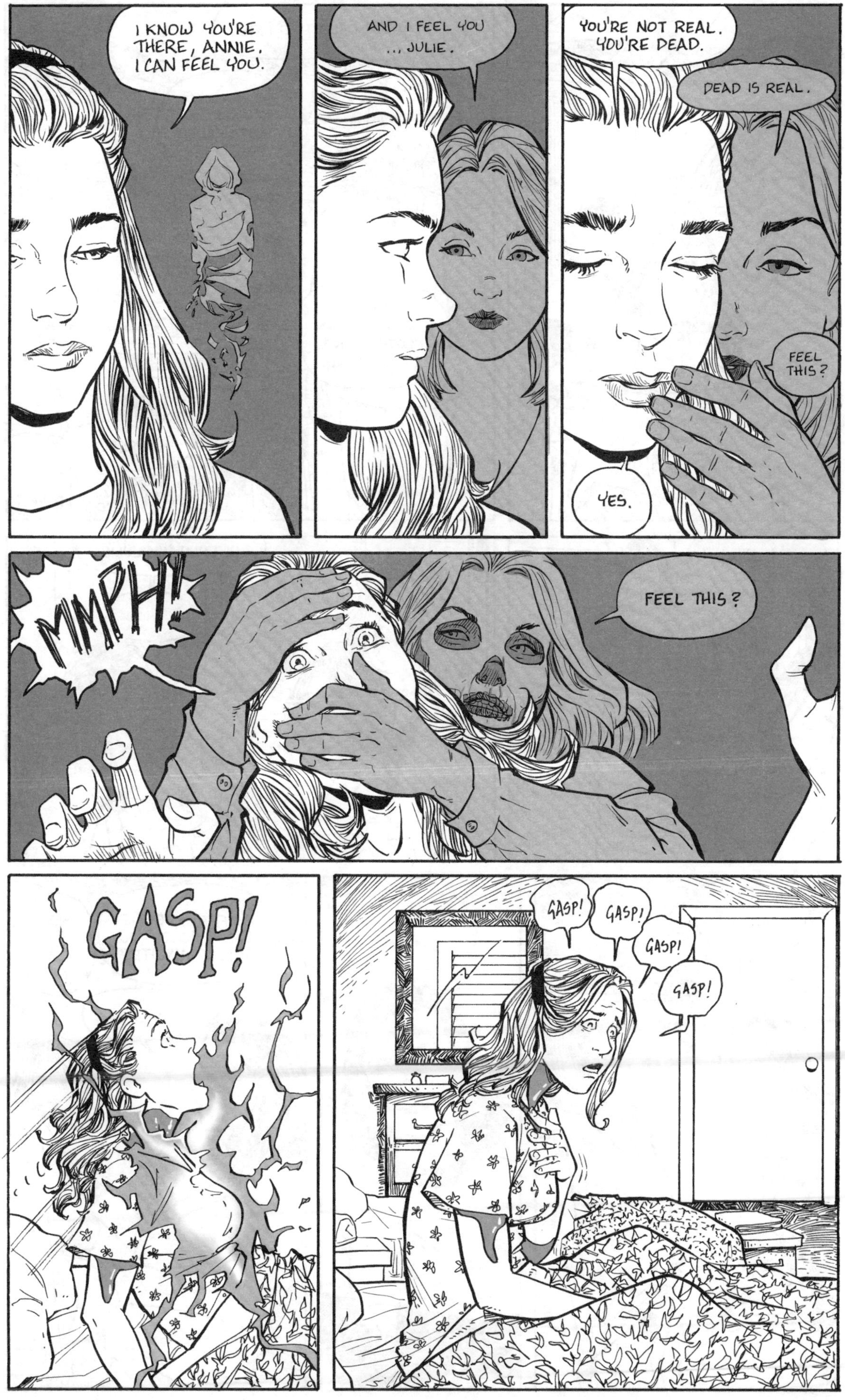
I KNOW YOU'RE THERE, ANNIE, I CAN FEEL YOU.
AND I FEEL YOU ..., JULIE.
YOU'RE NOT REAL. YOU'RE DEAD.
DEAD IS REAL.
FEEL THIS?
YES.
MMPH!
FEEL THIS?
GASP!
GASP!
GASP!
GASP!
GASP!

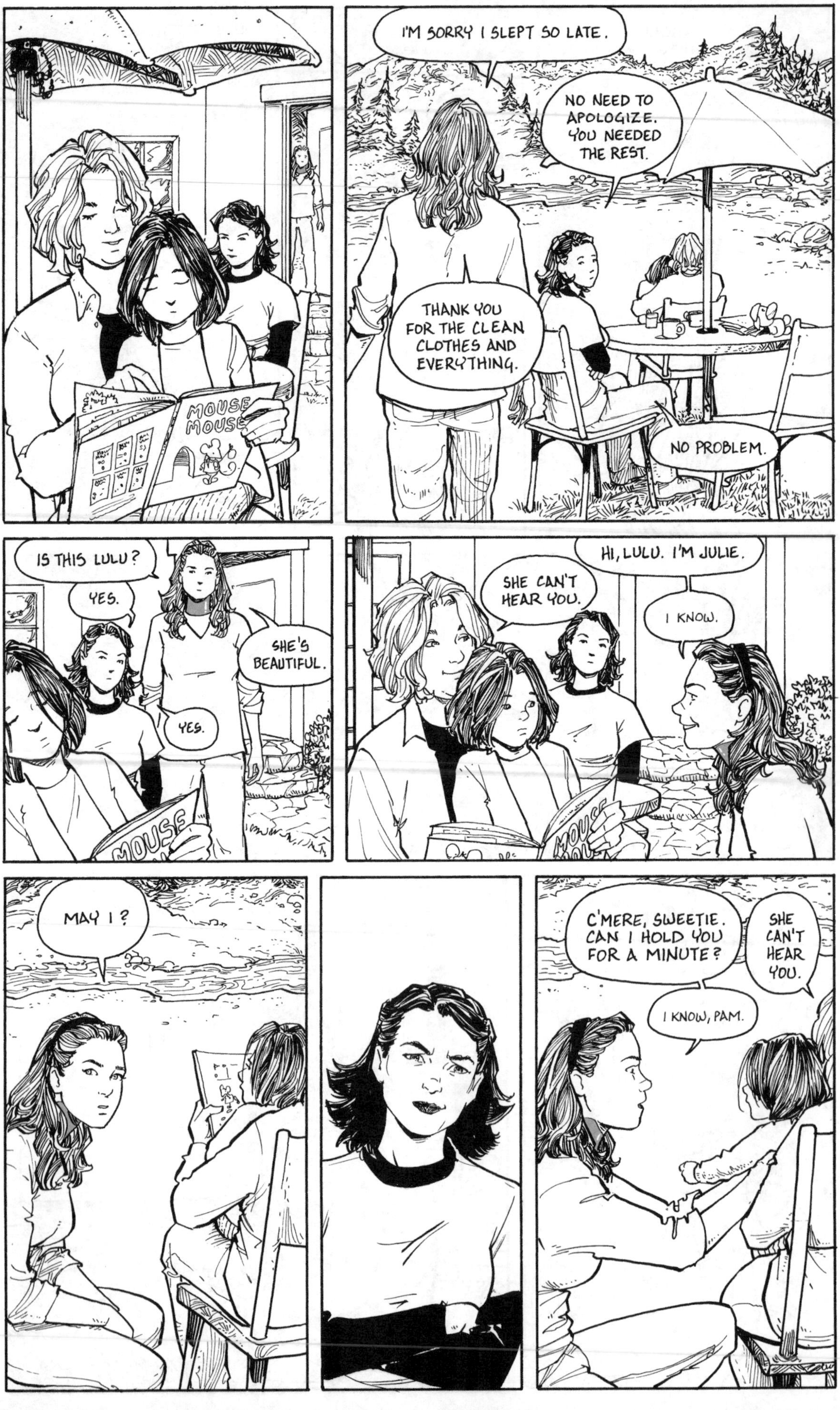

I'M SORRY I SLEPT SO LATE.
NO NEED TO APOLOGIZE. YOU NEEDED THE REST.
THANK YOU FOR THE CLEAN CLOTHES AND EVERYTHING.
NO PROBLEM.
IS THIS LULU?
YES.
SHE'S BEAUTIFUL.
YES.
HI, LULU. I'M JULIE.
SHE CAN'T HEAR YOU.
I KNOW.
MAY I?
C'MERE, SWEETIE. CAN I HOLD YOU FOR A MINUTE?
SHE CAN'T HEAR YOU.
I KNOW, PAM.

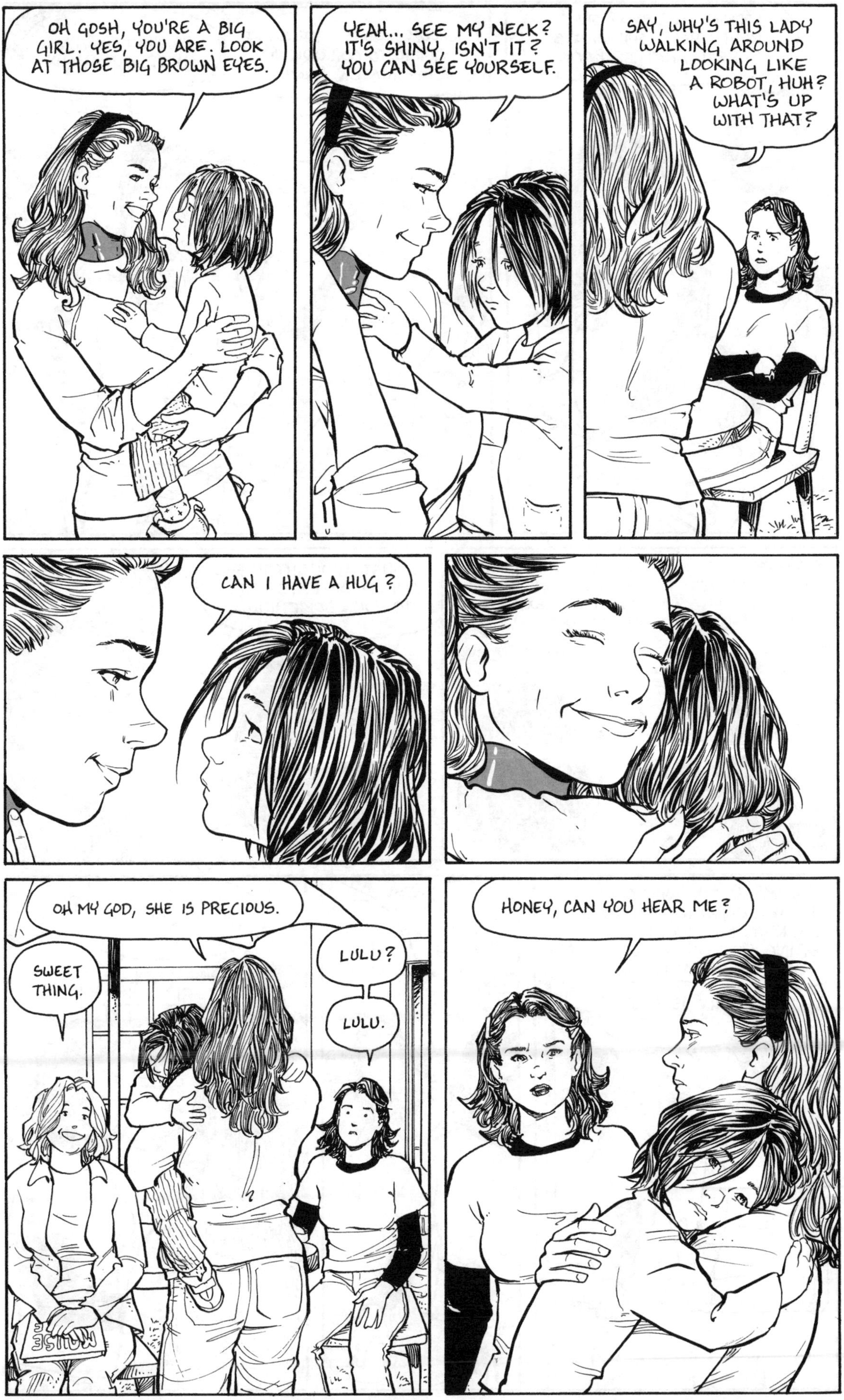
OH GOSH, YOU'RE A BIG GIRL. YES, YOU ARE. LOOK AT THOSE BIG BROWN EYES.
YEAH... SEE MY NECK? IT'S SHINY, ISN'T IT? YOU CAN SEE YOURSELF.
SAY, WHY'S THIS LADY WALKING AROUND LOOKING LIKE A ROBOT, HUH? WHAT'S UP WITH THAT?
CAN I HAVE A HUG?
OH MY GOD, SHE IS PRECIOUS.
SWEET THING.
LULU?
LULU.
HONEY, CAN YOU HEAR ME?

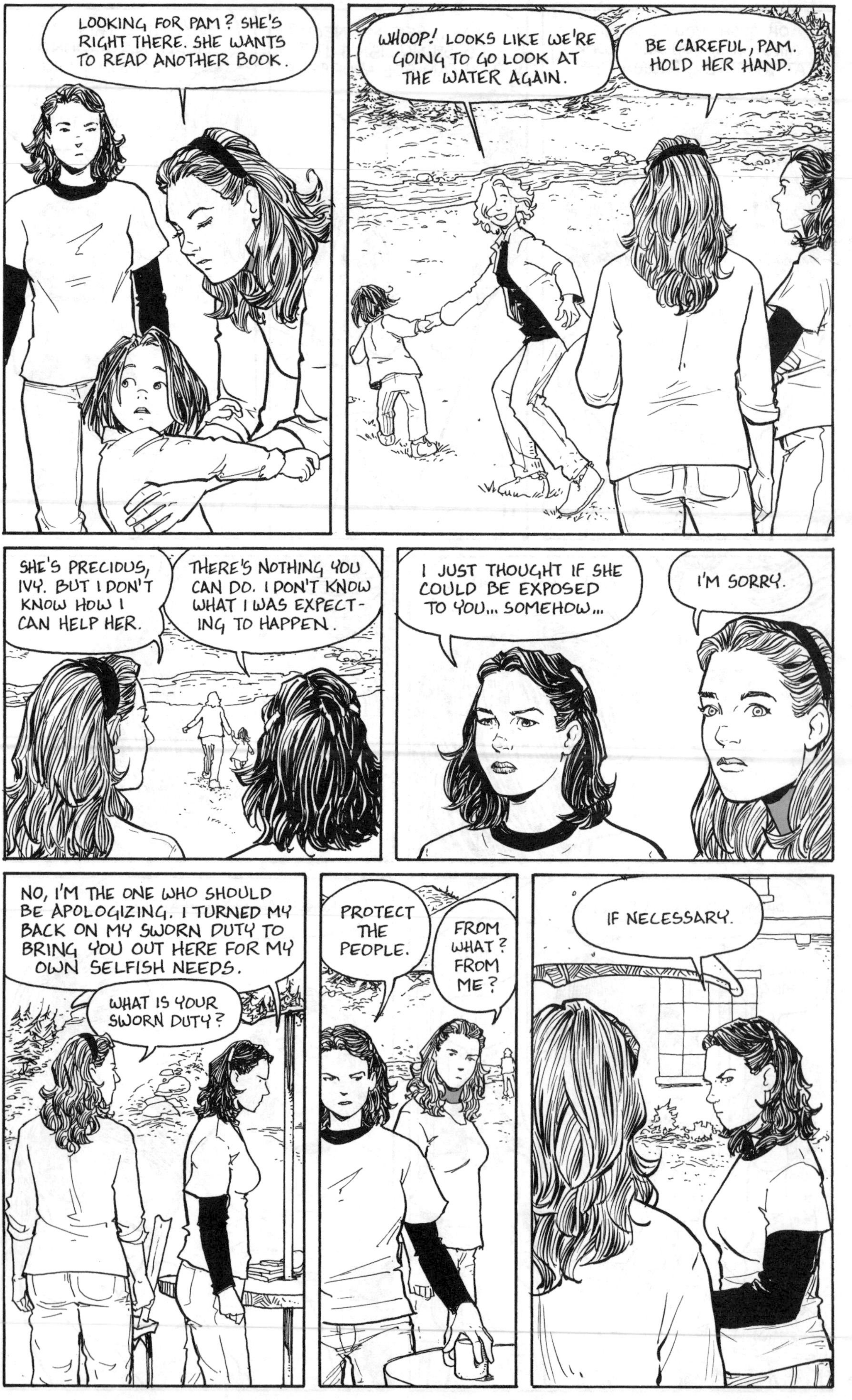
LOOKING FOR PAM? SHE'S RIGHT THERE. SHE WANTS TO READ ANOTHER BOOK.
WHOOP! LOOKS LIKE WE'RE GOING TO GO LOOK AT THE WATER AGAIN.
BE CAREFUL, PAM. HOLD HER HAND.
SHE'S PRECIOUS, IVY. BUT I DON'T KNOW HOW I CAN HELP HER.
THERE'S NOTHING YOU CAN DO. I DON'T KNOW WHAT I WAS EXPECT-ING TO HAPPEN.
I JUST THOUGHT IF SHE COULD BE EXPOSED TO YOU... SOMEHOW...
I'M SORRY.
NO, I'M THE ONE WHO SHOULD BE APOLOGIZING. I TURNED MY BACK ON MY SWORN DUTY TO BRING YOU OUT HERE FOR MY OWN SELFISH NEEDS.
WHAT IS YOUR SWORN DUTY?
PROTECT THE PEOPLE.
FROM WHAT? FROM ME?
IF NECESSARY.

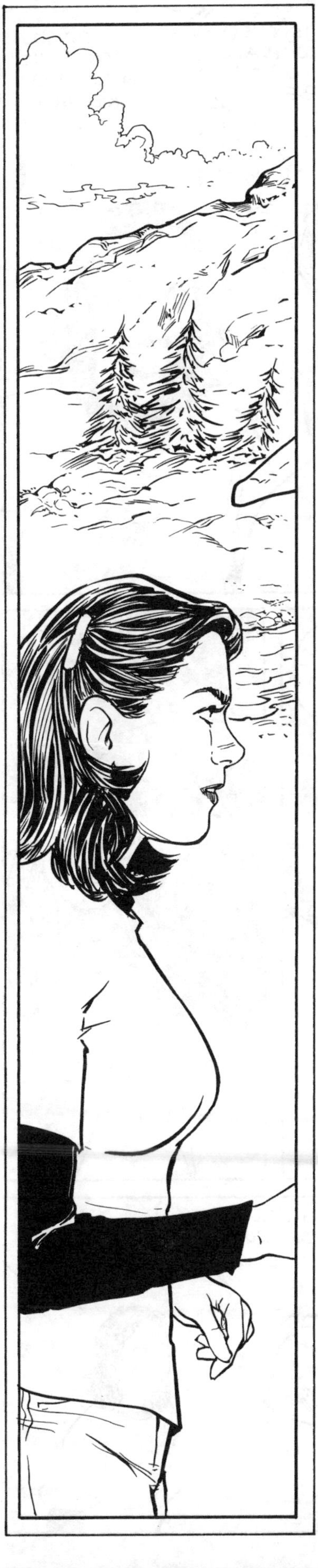

JULIE, DO YOU KNOW SIMON ZIMMERMAN?

NO.

HE POSTED THE WEBSITE MOONLAKECONSPIRACY.COM. WE FOUND HIS BODY RIPPED TO SHREDS IN HIS HOUSE IN TALUPA. KNOW ANYTHING ABOUT THAT?

NO.

THE FOUR BODIES AT THE MOTEL... KNOW ANYTHING ABOUT THAT?

I... I SAW IT HAPPEN. HE KILLED THEM. CAIN.

THE OTHER MAN, WITH THE ALLOY.

YES.

THE MOTEL OFFICE WAS DESTROYED...

I DID THAT. THE ALLOY ATTACKED HIM.

DID IT KILL HIM?

NO. HE FOLLOWED US.

THE HOLE IN THE HIGHWAY.

HE FOUND US. I DON'T KNOW HOW, BUT HE...

SO YOUR ALLOY ATTACKED HIM... ON THE HIGHWAY.

YES.

IS HE DEAD NOW?

I DON'T KNOW. I DOUBT IT. THE ALLOY DIDN'T KILL HIM. I KNOW THAT. HE KEPT COMING. HE CAUGHT US. HE SAID HIS NAME WAS CAIN, AND HE WANTED ME TO KILL HIM. THEN HE TOUCHED ME, AND... AND IT'S LIKE WE WERE HIT BY LIGHTNING. WHEN I CAME TO, I DRAGGED DILLON TO THE TRUCK AND FLOORED IT. CAIN WAS... HE WAS CRAZY, LAUGHING LIKE HE WAS DRUNK OR SOMETHING. HE TRIED TO STOP ME, SO I HIT HIM WITH THE TRUCK AND DIDN'T LOOK BACK. THAT'S THE LAST I SAW OF HIM.

ANYTHING ELSE?

I THINK I HAVE HIS ALLOY.

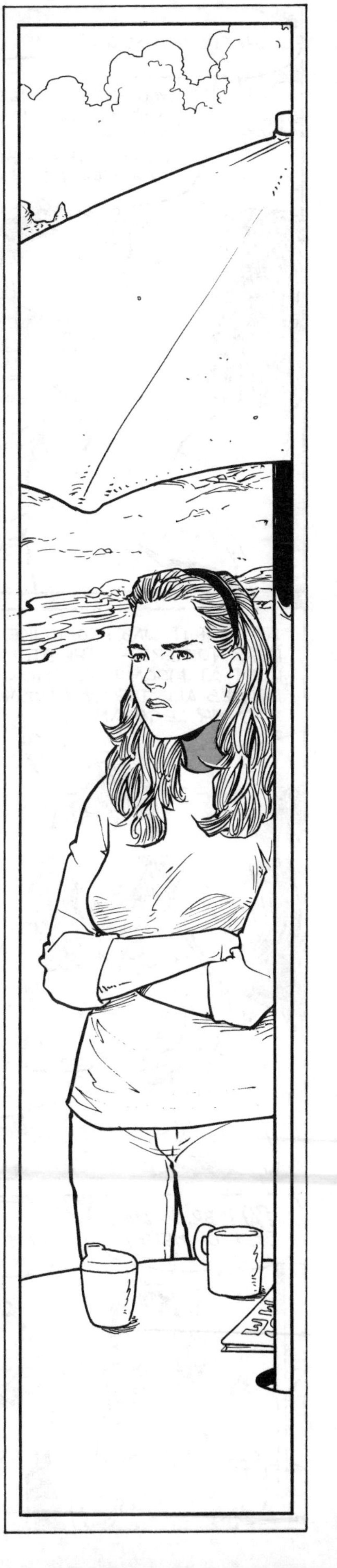

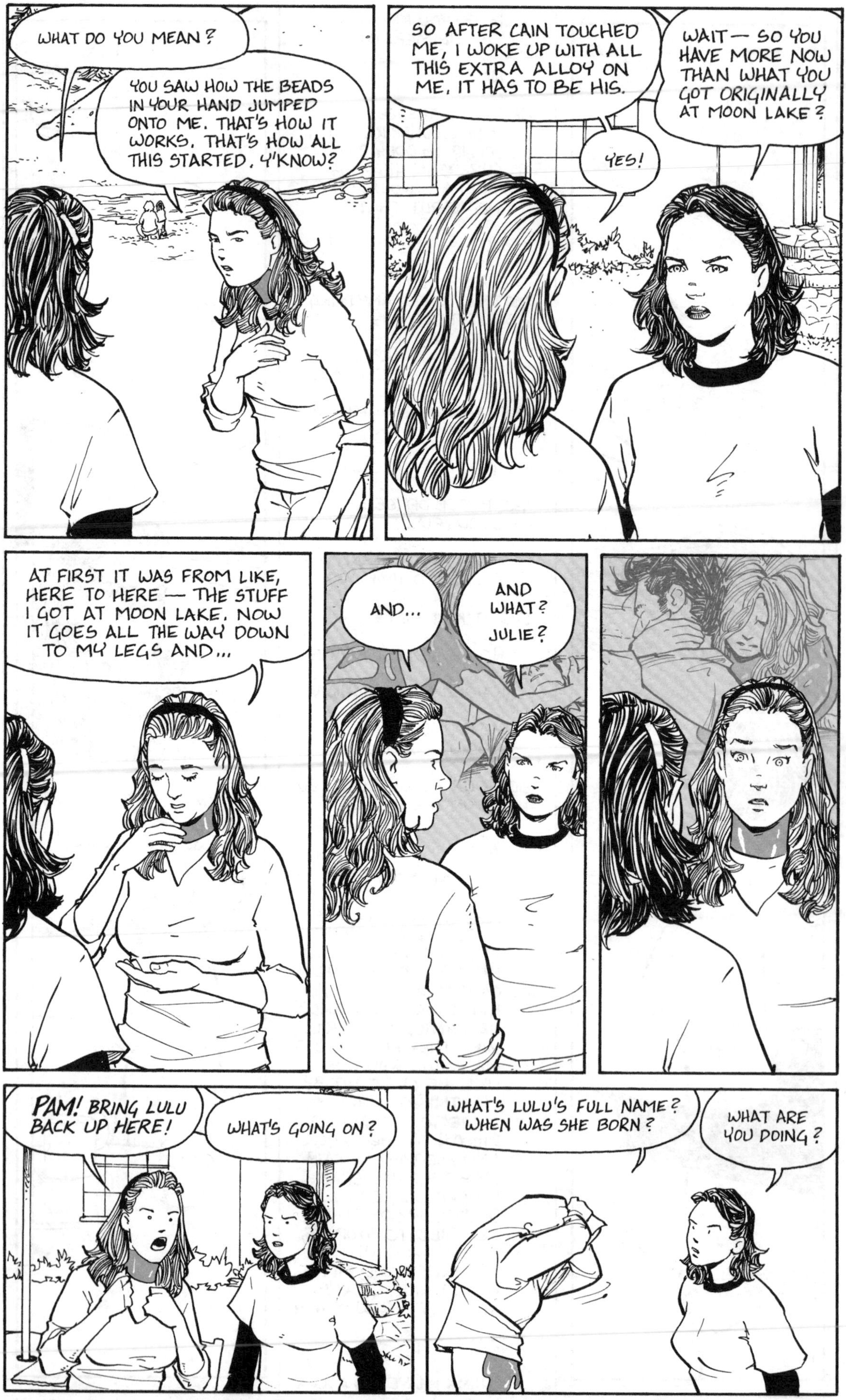
WHAT DO YOU MEAN?
YOU SAW HOW THE BEADS IN YOUR HAND JUMPED ONTO ME. THAT'S HOW IT WORKS. THAT'S HOW ALL THIS STARTED, Y'KNOW?
SO AFTER CAIN TOUCHED ME, I WOKE UP WITH ALL THIS EXTRA ALLOY ON ME, IT HAS TO BE HIS.
WAIT— SO YOU HAVE MORE NOW THAN WHAT YOU GOT ORIGINALLY AT MOON LAKE?
YES!
AT FIRST IT WAS FROM LIKE, HERE TO HERE — THE STUFF I GOT AT MOON LAKE. NOW IT GOES ALL THE WAY DOWN TO MY LEGS AND...
AND...
AND WHAT?
JULIE?
PAM! BRING LULU BACK UP HERE!
WHAT'S GOING ON?
WHAT'S LULU'S FULL NAME? WHEN WAS SHE BORN?
WHAT ARE YOU DOING?

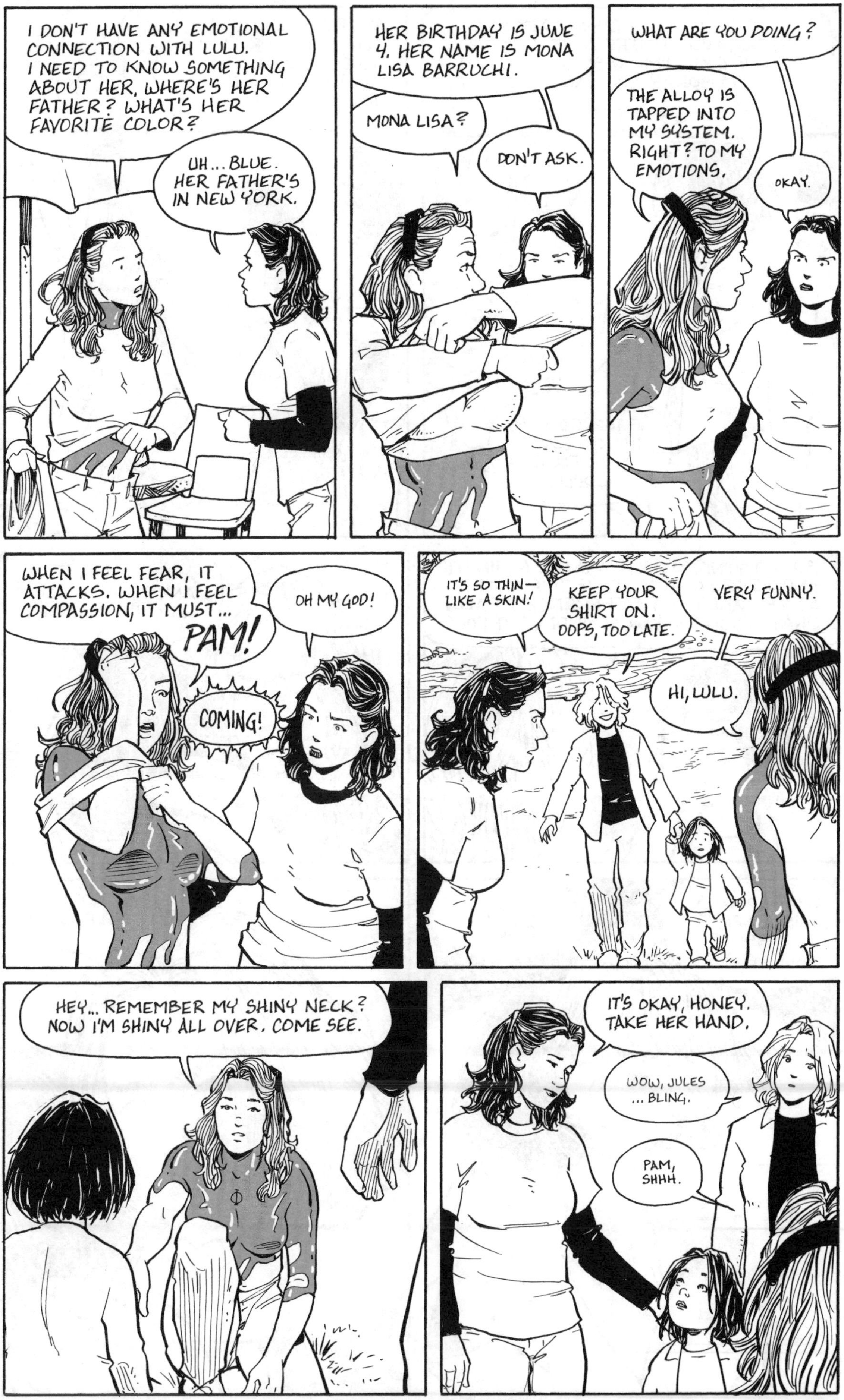
I DON'T HAVE ANY EMOTIONAL CONNECTION WITH LULU. I NEED TO KNOW SOMETHING ABOUT HER, WHERE'S HER FATHER? WHAT'S HER FAVORITE COLOR?
UH... BLUE. HER FATHER'S IN NEW YORK.
HER BIRTHDAY IS JUNE 4. HER NAME IS MONA LISA BARRUCHI.
MONA LISA?
DON'T ASK.
WHAT ARE YOU DOING?
THE ALLOY IS TAPPED INTO MY SYSTEM. RIGHT? TO MY EMOTIONS.
OKAY.
WHEN I FEEL FEAR, IT ATTACKS. WHEN I FEEL COMPASSION, IT MUST...
PAM!
OH MY GOD!
COMING!
IT'S SO THIN— LIKE A SKIN!
KEEP YOUR SHIRT ON. OOPS, TOO LATE.
VERY FUNNY.
HI, LULU.
HEY... REMEMBER MY SHINY NECK? NOW I'M SHINY ALL OVER. COME SEE.
IT'S OKAY, HONEY. TAKE HER HAND.
WOW, JULES ... BLING.
PAM, SHHH.

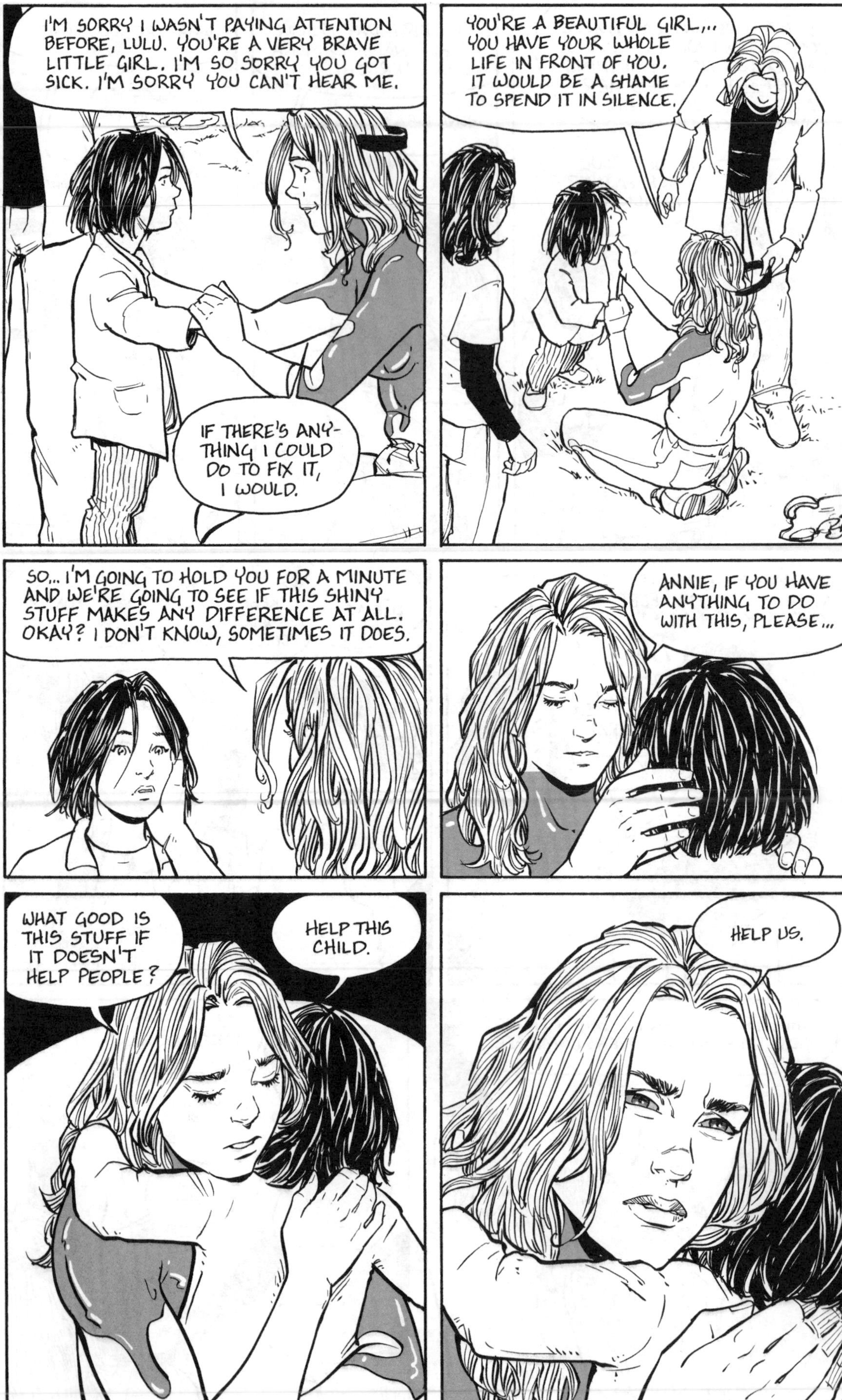
I'M SORRY I WASN'T PAYING ATTENTION BEFORE, LULU. YOU'RE A VERY BRAVE LITTLE GIRL. I'M SO SORRY YOU GOT SICK. I'M SORRY YOU CAN'T HEAR ME.
IF THERE'S ANY-THING I COULD DO TO FIX IT, I WOULD.
YOU'RE A BEAUTIFUL GIRL,.. YOU HAVE YOUR WHOLE LIFE IN FRONT OF YOU. IT WOULD BE A SHAME TO SPEND IT IN SILENCE.
SO... I'M GOING TO HOLD YOU FOR A MINUTE AND WE'RE GOING TO SEE IF THIS SHINY STUFF MAKES ANY DIFFERENCE AT ALL. OKAY? I DON'T KNOW, SOMETIMES IT DOES.
ANNIE, IF YOU HAVE ANYTHING TO DO WITH THIS, PLEASE...
WHAT GOOD IS THIS STUFF IF IT DOESN'T HELP PEOPLE?
HELP THIS CHILD.
HELP US.

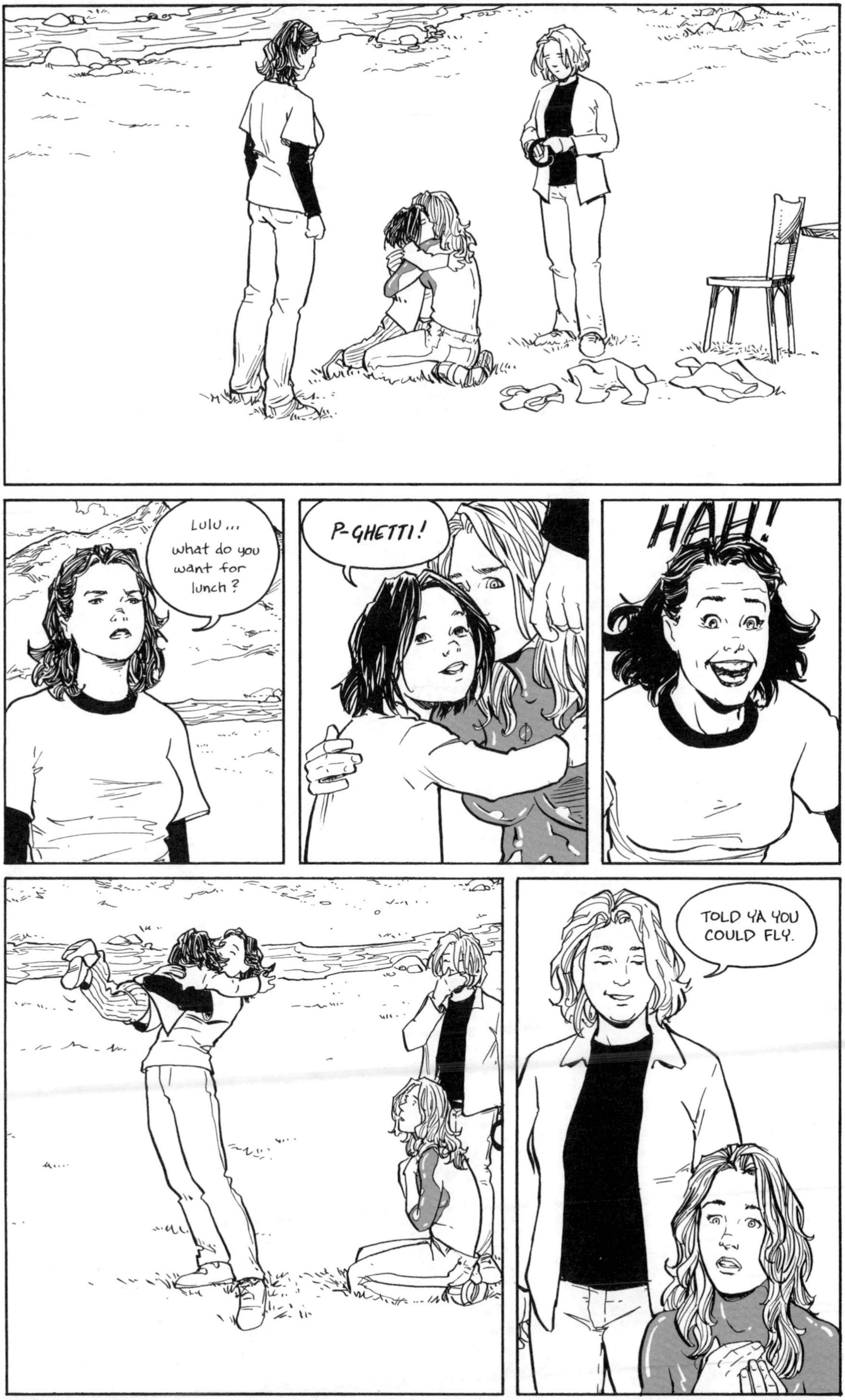
LULU...
what do you
want for
lunch?
P-GHETTI!
HAH!
TOLD YA YOU
COULD FLY.

The greatest challenge we face in
science is the scientist himself.
—William Dumfries

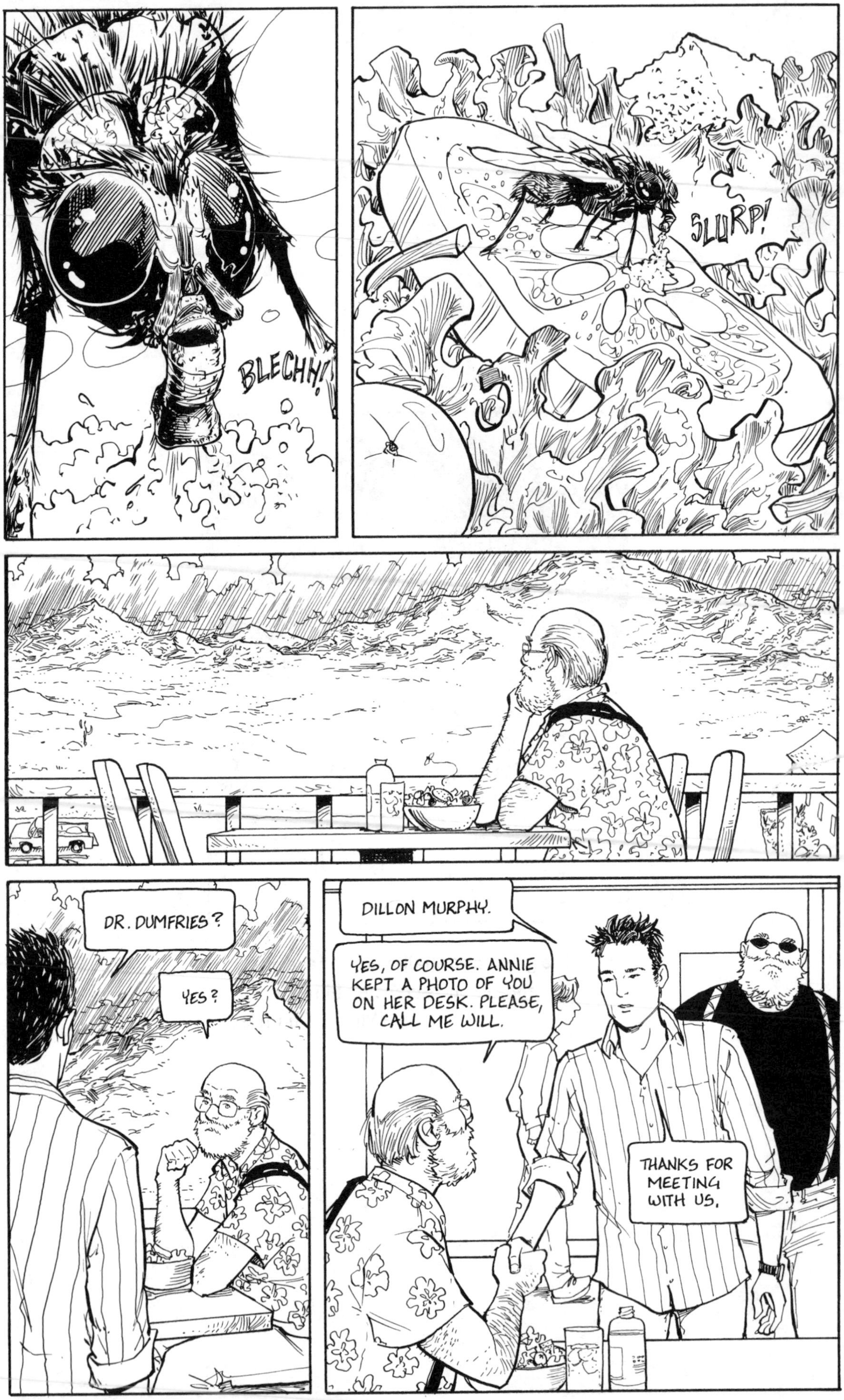
BLECHH!
SLURP!
DR. DUMFRIES?
YES?
DILLON MURPHY.
YES, OF COURSE. ANNIE KEPT A PHOTO OF YOU ON HER DESK. PLEASE, CALL ME WILL.
THANKS FOR MEETING WITH US.

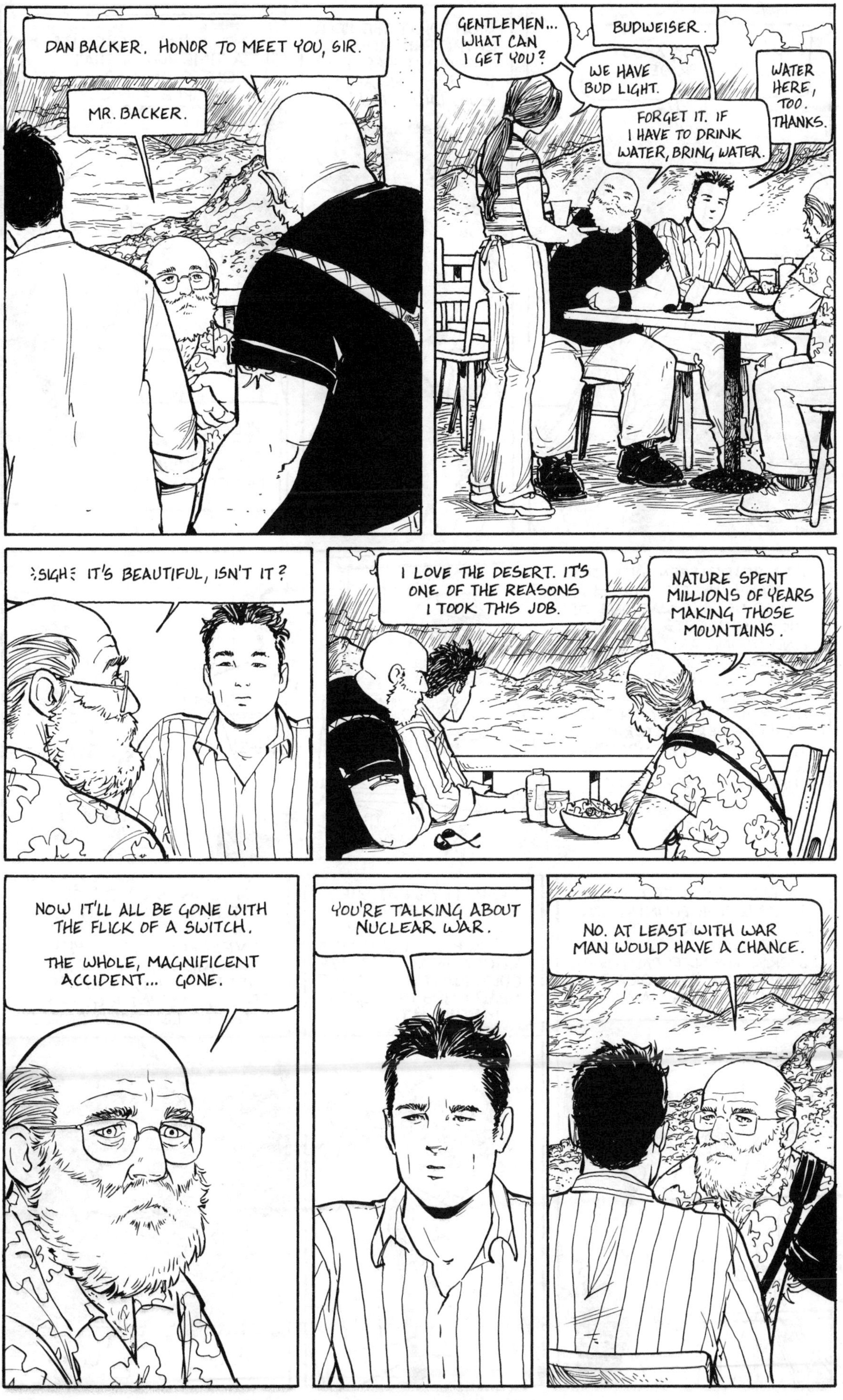
DAN BACKER. HONOR TO MEET YOU, SIR.
MR. BACKER.
GENTLEMEN... WHAT CAN I GET YOU?
BUDWEISER.
WE HAVE BUD LIGHT.
FORGET IT. IF I HAVE TO DRINK WATER, BRING WATER.
WATER HERE, TOO. THANKS.
:SIGH: IT'S BEAUTIFUL, ISN'T IT?
I LOVE THE DESERT. IT'S ONE OF THE REASONS I TOOK THIS JOB.
NATURE SPENT MILLIONS OF YEARS MAKING THOSE MOUNTAINS.
NOW IT'LL ALL BE GONE WITH THE FLICK OF A SWITCH.
THE WHOLE, MAGNIFICENT ACCIDENT... GONE.
YOU'RE TALKING ABOUT NUCLEAR WAR.
NO. AT LEAST WITH WAR MAN WOULD HAVE A CHANCE.

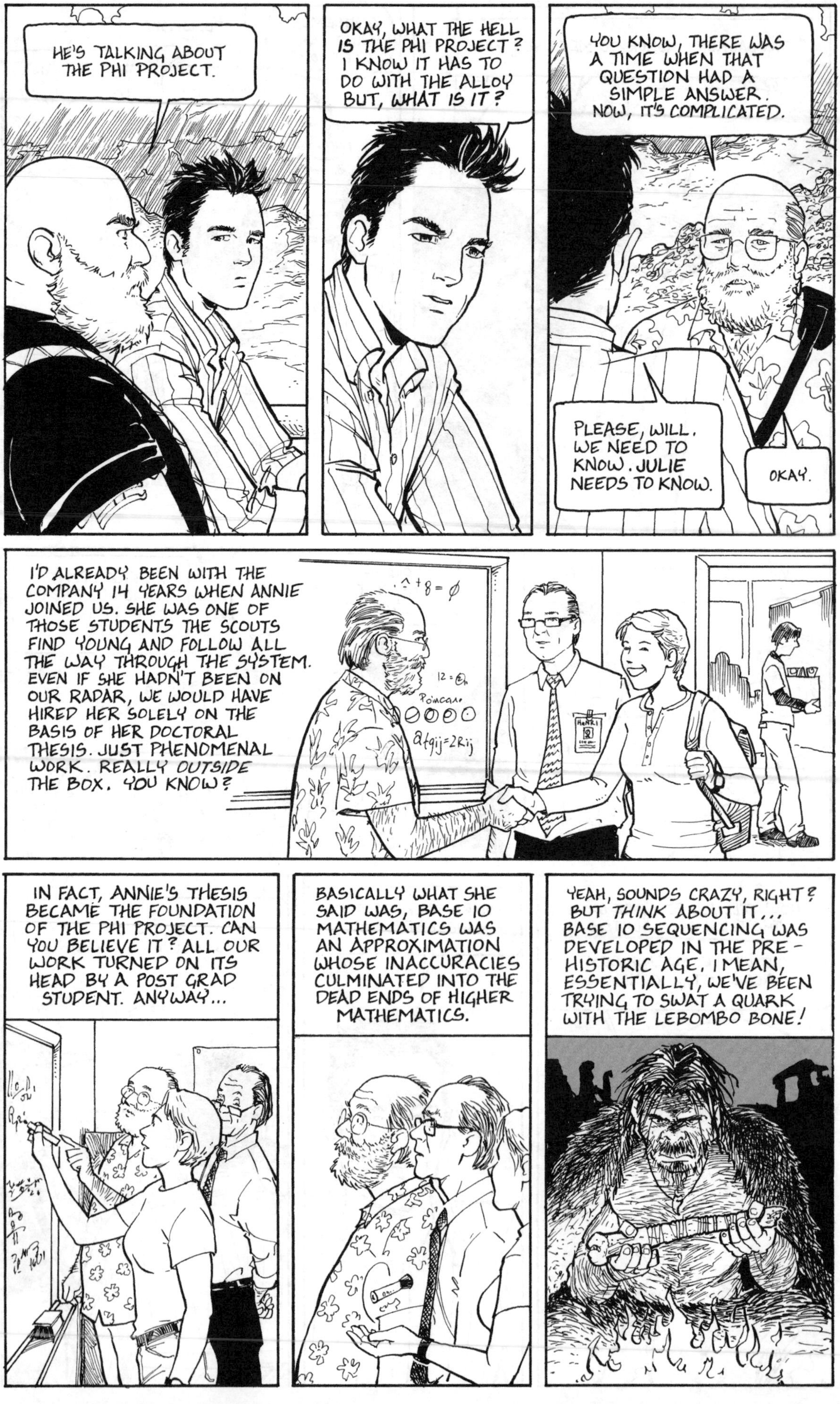
HE'S TALKING ABOUT THE PHI PROJECT.
OKAY, WHAT THE HELL IS THE PHI PROJECT? I KNOW IT HAS TO DO WITH THE ALLOY BUT, WHAT IS IT?
YOU KNOW, THERE WAS A TIME WHEN THAT QUESTION HAD A SIMPLE ANSWER. NOW, IT'S COMPLICATED.
PLEASE, WILL. WE NEED TO KNOW. JULIE NEEDS TO KNOW.
OKAY.
I'D ALREADY BEEN WITH THE COMPANY 14 YEARS WHEN ANNIE JOINED US. SHE WAS ONE OF THOSE STUDENTS THE SCOUTS FIND YOUNG AND FOLLOW ALL THE WAY THROUGH THE SYSTEM. EVEN IF SHE HADN'T BEEN ON OUR RADAR, WE WOULD HAVE HIRED HER SOLELY ON THE BASIS OF HER DOCTORAL THESIS. JUST PHENOMENAL WORK. REALLY *OUTSIDE* THE BOX. YOU KNOW?
IN FACT, ANNIE'S THESIS BECAME THE FOUNDATION OF THE PHI PROJECT. CAN YOU BELIEVE IT? ALL OUR WORK TURNED ON ITS HEAD BY A POST GRAD STUDENT. ANYWAY...
BASICALLY WHAT SHE SAID WAS, BASE 10 MATHEMATICS WAS AN APPROXIMATION WHOSE INACCURACIES CULMINATED INTO THE DEAD ENDS OF HIGHER MATHEMATICS.
YEAH, SOUNDS CRAZY, RIGHT? BUT *THINK* ABOUT IT... BASE 10 SEQUENCING WAS DEVELOPED IN THE PRE-HISTORIC AGE, I MEAN, ESSENTIALLY, WE'VE BEEN TRYING TO SWAT A QUARK WITH THE LEBOMBO BONE!

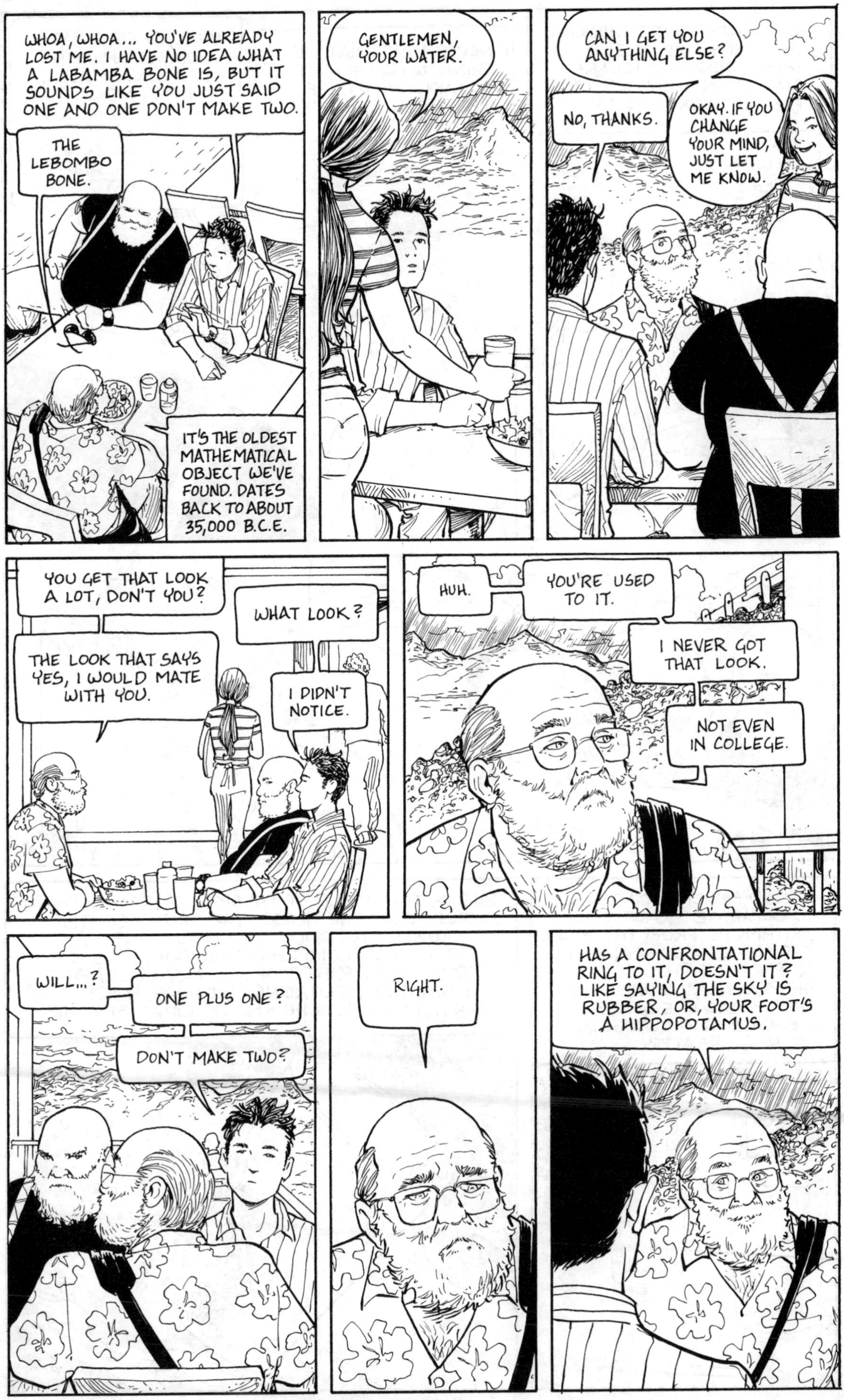
WHOA, WHOA... YOU'VE ALREADY LOST ME. I HAVE NO IDEA WHAT A LABAMBA BONE IS, BUT IT SOUNDS LIKE YOU JUST SAID ONE AND ONE DON'T MAKE TWO.
THE LEBOMBO BONE.
IT'S THE OLDEST MATHEMATICAL OBJECT WE'VE FOUND. DATES BACK TO ABOUT 35,000 B.C.E.
GENTLEMEN, YOUR WATER.
CAN I GET YOU ANYTHING ELSE?
NO, THANKS.
OKAY. IF YOU CHANGE YOUR MIND, JUST LET ME KNOW.
YOU GET THAT LOOK A LOT, DON'T YOU?
WHAT LOOK?
THE LOOK THAT SAYS YES, I WOULD MATE WITH YOU.
I DIDN'T NOTICE.
HUH.
YOU'RE USED TO IT.
I NEVER GOT THAT LOOK.
NOT EVEN IN COLLEGE.
WILL...?
ONE PLUS ONE?
DON'T MAKE TWO?
RIGHT.
HAS A CONFRONTATIONAL RING TO IT, DOESN'T IT? LIKE SAYING THE SKY IS RUBBER, OR, YOUR FOOT'S A HIPPOPOTAMUS.

OR, PERHAPS YOU'RE THINKING IT SOUNDS LIKE ONE OF THOSE THINGS SCHOLARS SAY WHEN THEY GET TOO FAR UP THEIR OWN ASS.

NEVER MIND WHAT WE THINK, WILL. WE WANT TO KNOW ABOUT THE PHI PROJECT AND WHAT YOU WERE THINKING.

WELL, AT FIRST WE THOUGHT ANNIE'S IDEA WAS SMALL ... NOTHING MORE THAN A LOGIC TRICK. KIDS LOVE THAT STUFF. YOU KNOW, ZENO'S DICHOTOMY AND ALL THAT.

ANYHOO...

ANNIE'S SALIENT POINT WAS TO SEPARATE PRACTICAL ARITHMETIC FROM THE MORE STRINGENT REQUIREMENTS OF PARTICLE PHYSICS. IN THE PRACTICAL WORLD, ONE GLASS PLUS ONE GLASS EQUALS TWO GLASSES. YAY... REALITY.

BUT, IN THE WORLD OF PHYSICS, THERE'S NOTHING ONE ABOUT THE GLASS. THE TRUTH IS, IT'S ACTUALLY A GROUPING OF BILLIONS OF MOLECULES COMPRISED OF TRILLIONS OF ATOMS COMPRISED OF AN INCALCULABLE NUMBER OF NEUTRONS, PROTONS, POINT PARTICLES AND WHO KNOWS WHAT BEYOND.

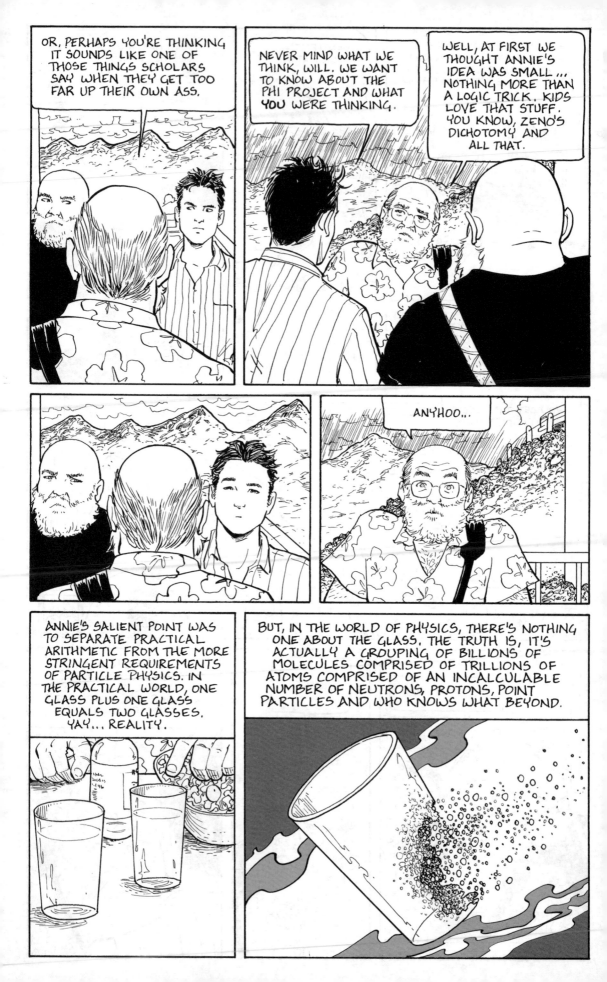

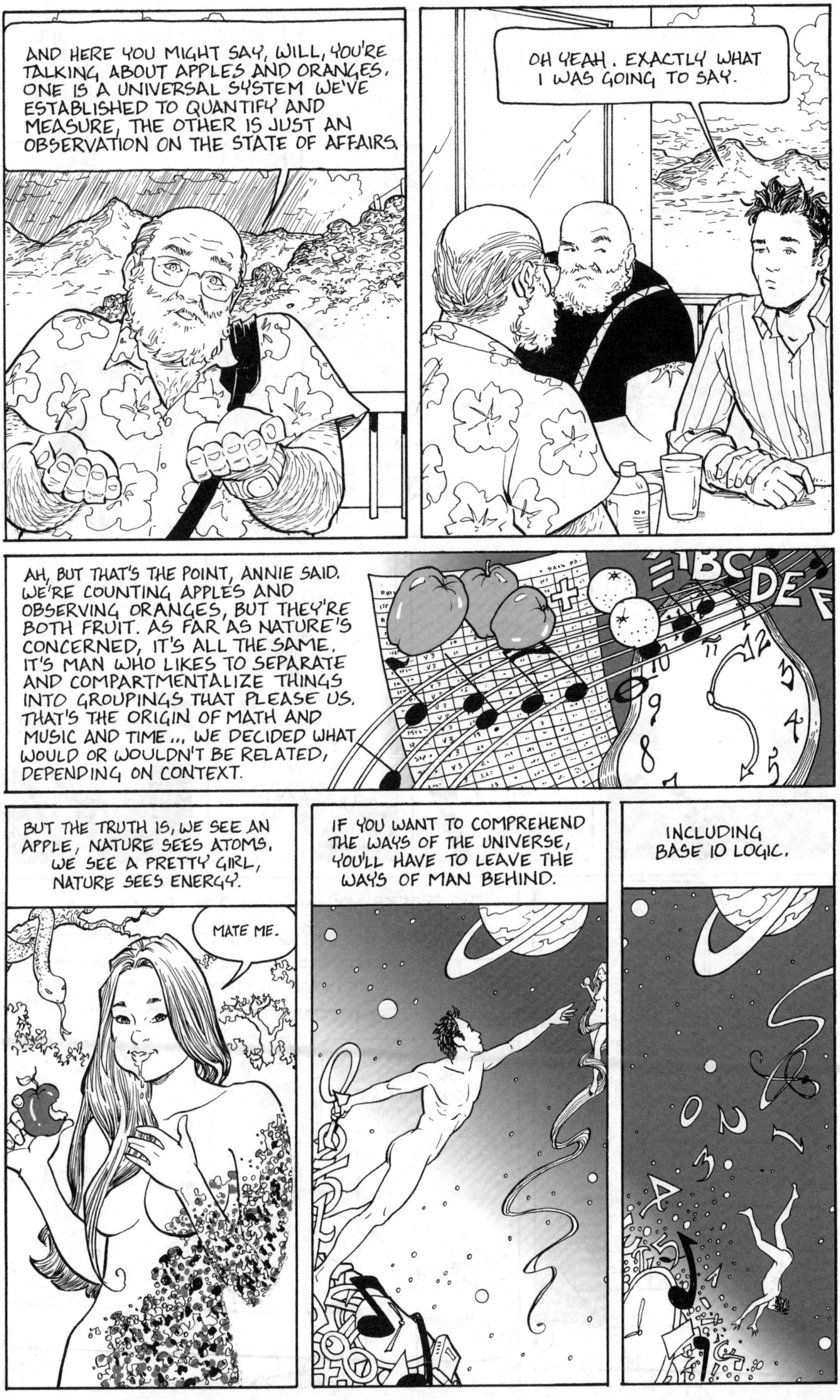
AND HERE YOU MIGHT SAY, WILL, YOU'RE TALKING ABOUT APPLES AND ORANGES. ONE IS A UNIVERSAL SYSTEM WE'VE ESTABLISHED TO QUANTIFY AND MEASURE, THE OTHER IS JUST AN OBSERVATION ON THE STATE OF AFFAIRS.
OH YEAH. EXACTLY WHAT I WAS GOING TO SAY.
AH, BUT THAT'S THE POINT, ANNIE SAID. WE'RE COUNTING APPLES AND OBSERVING ORANGES, BUT THEY'RE BOTH FRUIT. AS FAR AS NATURE'S CONCERNED, IT'S ALL THE SAME. IT'S MAN WHO LIKES TO SEPARATE AND COMPARTMENTALIZE THINGS INTO GROUPINGS THAT PLEASE US. THAT'S THE ORIGIN OF MATH AND MUSIC AND TIME... WE DECIDED WHAT WOULD OR WOULDN'T BE RELATED, DEPENDING ON CONTEXT.
BUT THE TRUTH IS, WE SEE AN APPLE, NATURE SEES ATOMS. WE SEE A PRETTY GIRL, NATURE SEES ENERGY.
MATE ME.
IF YOU WANT TO COMPREHEND THE WAYS OF THE UNIVERSE, YOU'LL HAVE TO LEAVE THE WAYS OF MAN BEHIND.
INCLUDING BASE 10 LOGIC.

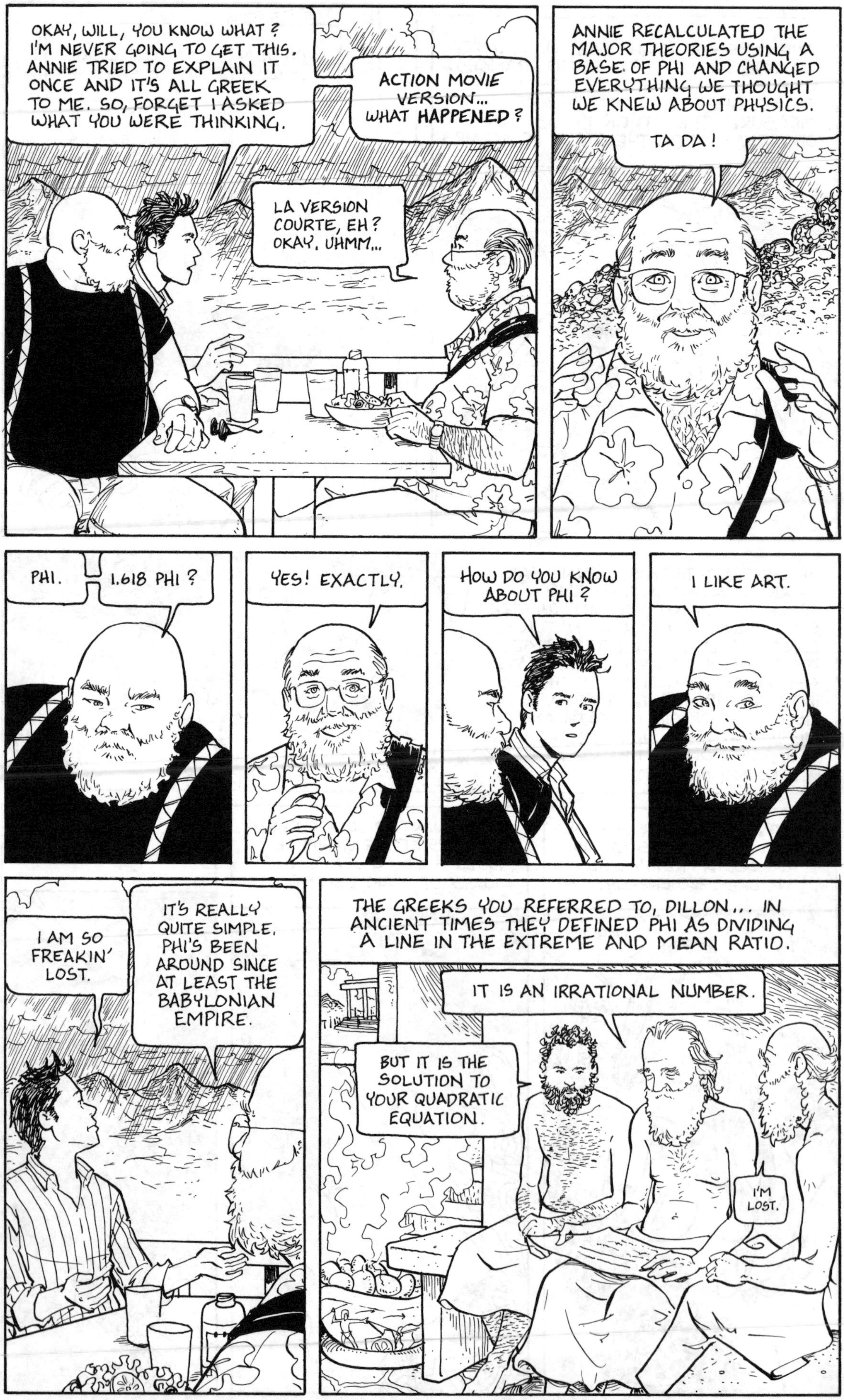
OKAY, WILL, YOU KNOW WHAT? I'M NEVER GOING TO GET THIS. ANNIE TRIED TO EXPLAIN IT ONCE AND IT'S ALL GREEK TO ME. SO, FORGET I ASKED WHAT YOU WERE THINKING.
ACTION MOVIE VERSION... WHAT **HAPPENED**?
LA VERSION COURTE, EH? OKAY, UHMM...
ANNIE RECALCULATED THE MAJOR THEORIES USING A BASE OF PHI AND CHANGED EVERYTHING WE THOUGHT WE KNEW ABOUT PHYSICS.
TA DA!
PHI.
1.618 PHI?
YES! EXACTLY.
HOW DO YOU KNOW ABOUT PHI?
I LIKE ART.
I AM SO FREAKIN' LOST.
IT'S REALLY QUITE SIMPLE. PHI'S BEEN AROUND SINCE AT LEAST THE BABYLONIAN EMPIRE.
THE GREEKS YOU REFERRED TO, DILLON... IN ANCIENT TIMES THEY DEFINED PHI AS DIVIDING A LINE IN THE EXTREME AND MEAN RATIO.
IT IS AN IRRATIONAL NUMBER.
BUT IT IS THE SOLUTION TO YOUR QUADRATIC EQUATION.
I'M LOST.

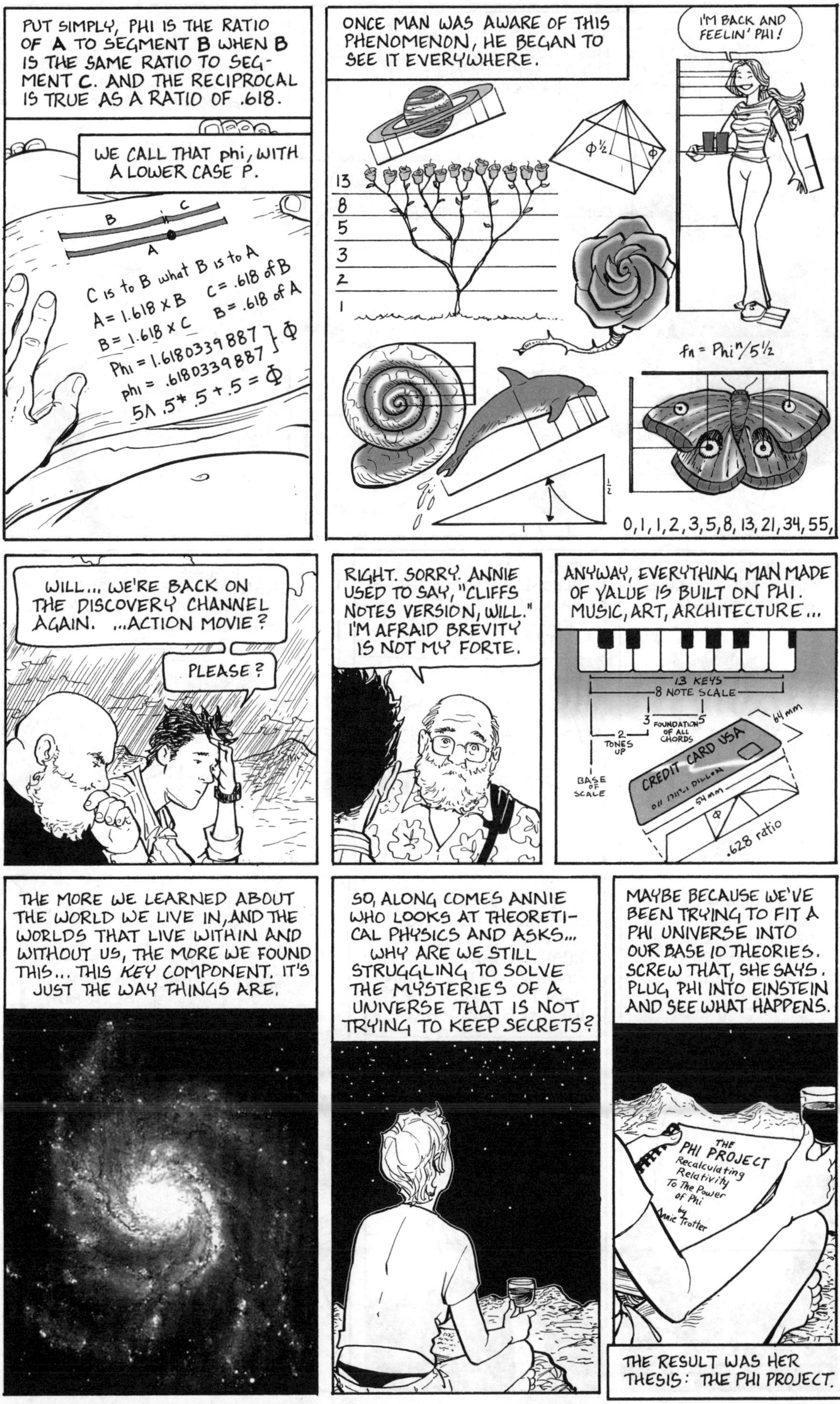
PUT SIMPLY, PHI IS THE RATIO OF A TO SEGMENT B WHEN B IS THE SAME RATIO TO SEGMENT C. AND THE RECIPROCAL IS TRUE AS A RATIO OF .618.
WE CALL THAT phi, WITH A LOWER CASE P.
B
C
A
C is to B what B is to A
A = 1.618 x B C = .618 of B
B = 1.618 x C B = .618 of A
Phi = 1.6180339887
phi = .6180339887
5^.5*.5+.5 = Φ
ONCE MAN WAS AWARE OF THIS PHENOMENON, HE BEGAN TO SEE IT EVERYWHERE.
I'M BACK AND FEELIN' PHI!
13
8
5
3
2
1
fn = Phi^n/5^1/2
0,1,1,2,3,5,8,13,21,34,55,
WILL... WE'RE BACK ON THE DISCOVERY CHANNEL AGAIN. ...ACTION MOVIE?
PLEASE?
RIGHT. SORRY. ANNIE USED TO SAY, "CLIFFS NOTES VERSION, WILL." I'M AFRAID BREVITY IS NOT MY FORTE.
ANYWAY, EVERYTHING MAN MADE OF VALUE IS BUILT ON PHI. MUSIC, ART, ARCHITECTURE...
13 KEYS
8 NOTE SCALE
3
5
FOUNDATION OF ALL CHORDS
2 TONES UP
BASE OF SCALE
CREDIT CARD USA
64mm
54mm
.628 ratio
THE MORE WE LEARNED ABOUT THE WORLD WE LIVE IN, AND THE WORLDS THAT LIVE WITHIN AND WITHOUT US, THE MORE WE FOUND THIS... THIS KEY COMPONENT. IT'S JUST THE WAY THINGS ARE.
SO, ALONG COMES ANNIE WHO LOOKS AT THEORETICAL PHYSICS AND ASKS... WHY ARE WE STILL STRUGGLING TO SOLVE THE MYSTERIES OF A UNIVERSE THAT IS NOT TRYING TO KEEP SECRETS?
MAYBE BECAUSE WE'VE BEEN TRYING TO FIT A PHI UNIVERSE INTO OUR BASE 10 THEORIES. SCREW THAT, SHE SAYS. PLUG PHI INTO EINSTEIN AND SEE WHAT HAPPENS.
THE PHI PROJECT
Recalculating Relativity To The Power of Phi
by Annie Trotter
THE RESULT WAS HER THESIS: THE PHI PROJECT.

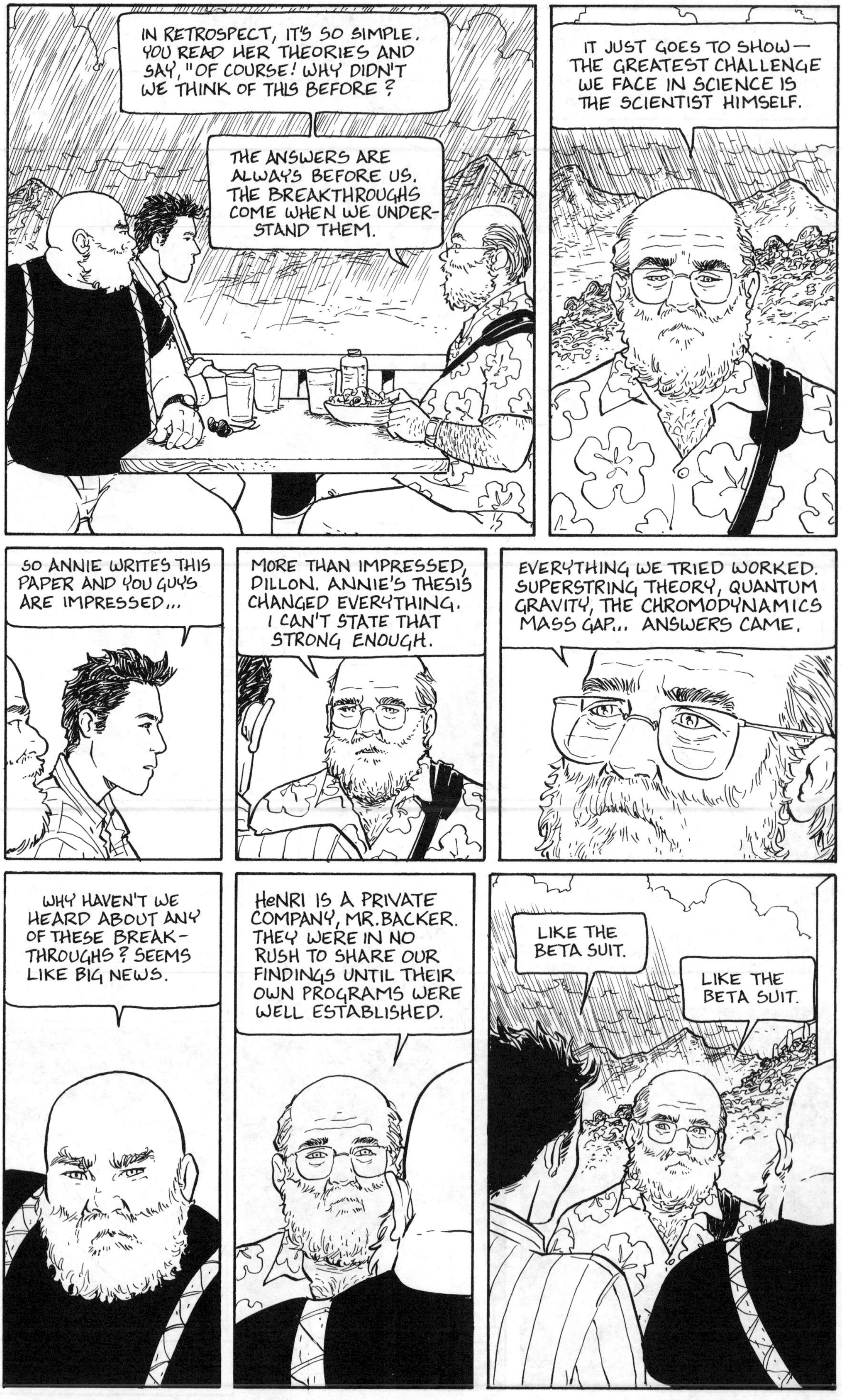
IN RETROSPECT, IT'S SO SIMPLE. YOU READ HER THEORIES AND SAY, "OF COURSE! WHY DIDN'T WE THINK OF THIS BEFORE?
THE ANSWERS ARE ALWAYS BEFORE US. THE BREAKTHROUGHS COME WHEN WE UNDERSTAND THEM.
IT JUST GOES TO SHOW— THE GREATEST CHALLENGE WE FACE IN SCIENCE IS THE SCIENTIST HIMSELF.
SO ANNIE WRITES THIS PAPER AND YOU GUYS ARE IMPRESSED...
MORE THAN IMPRESSED, DILLON. ANNIE'S THESIS CHANGED EVERYTHING. I CAN'T STATE THAT STRONG ENOUGH.
EVERYTHING WE TRIED WORKED. SUPERSTRING THEORY, QUANTUM GRAVITY, THE CHROMODYNAMICS MASS GAP... ANSWERS CAME.
WHY HAVEN'T WE HEARD ABOUT ANY OF THESE BREAKTHROUGHS? SEEMS LIKE BIG NEWS.
HeNRI IS A PRIVATE COMPANY, MR. BACKER. THEY WERE IN NO RUSH TO SHARE OUR FINDINGS UNTIL THEIR OWN PROGRAMS WERE WELL ESTABLISHED.
LIKE THE BETA SUIT.
LIKE THE BETA SUIT.

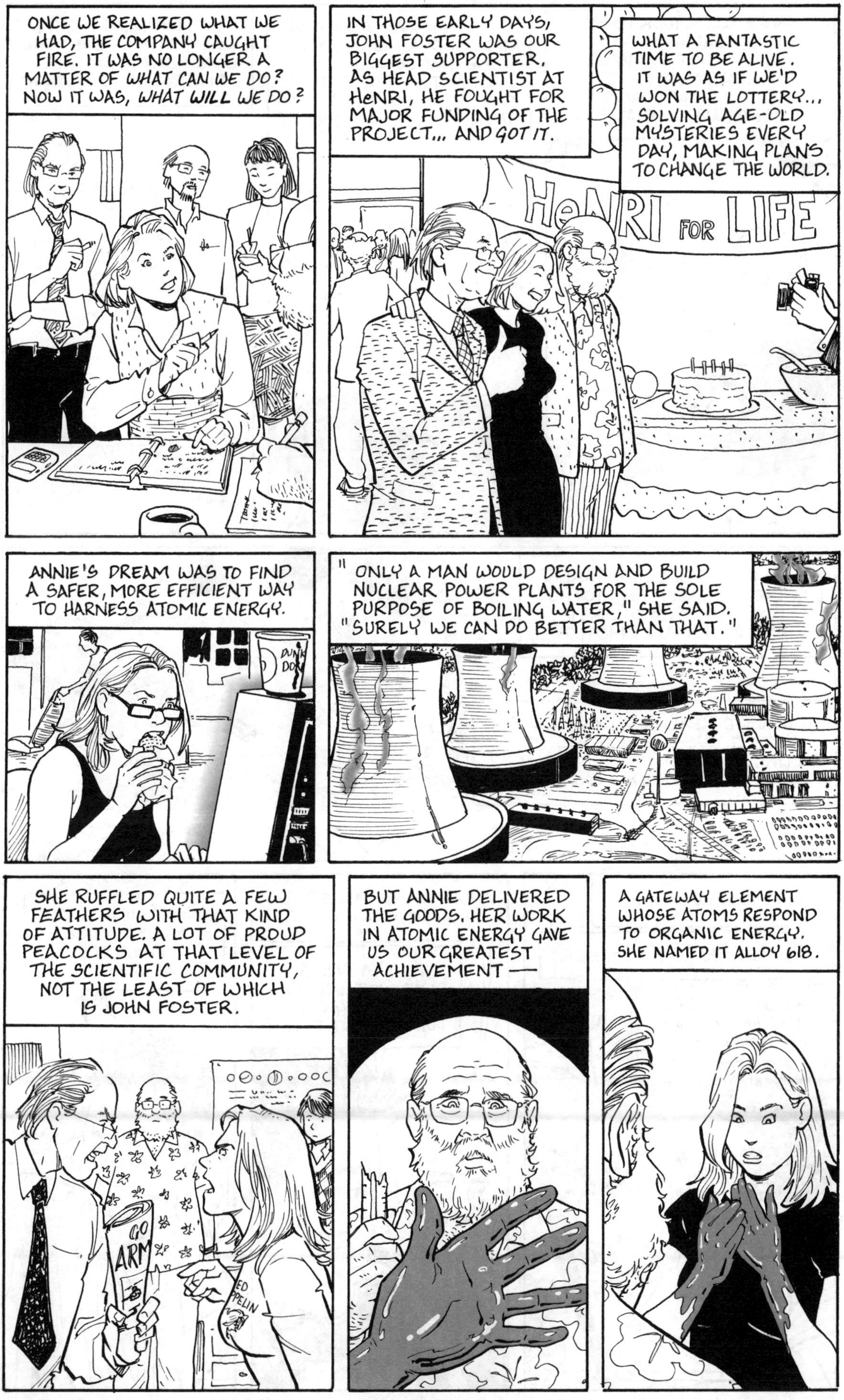
ONCE WE REALIZED WHAT WE HAD, THE COMPANY CAUGHT FIRE. IT WAS NO LONGER A MATTER OF WHAT CAN WE DO? NOW IT WAS, WHAT WILL WE DO?
IN THOSE EARLY DAYS, JOHN FOSTER WAS OUR BIGGEST SUPPORTER. AS HEAD SCIENTIST AT HeNRI, HE FOUGHT FOR MAJOR FUNDING OF THE PROJECT... AND GOT IT.
WHAT A FANTASTIC TIME TO BE ALIVE. IT WAS AS IF WE'D WON THE LOTTERY... SOLVING AGE-OLD MYSTERIES EVERY DAY, MAKING PLANS TO CHANGE THE WORLD.
HeNRI FOR LIFE
ANNIE'S DREAM WAS TO FIND A SAFER, MORE EFFICIENT WAY TO HARNESS ATOMIC ENERGY.
"ONLY A MAN WOULD DESIGN AND BUILD NUCLEAR POWER PLANTS FOR THE SOLE PURPOSE OF BOILING WATER," SHE SAID. "SURELY WE CAN DO BETTER THAN THAT."
SHE RUFFLED QUITE A FEW FEATHERS WITH THAT KIND OF ATTITUDE. A LOT OF PROUD PEACOCKS AT THAT LEVEL OF THE SCIENTIFIC COMMUNITY, NOT THE LEAST OF WHICH IS JOHN FOSTER.
BUT ANNIE DELIVERED THE GOODS. HER WORK IN ATOMIC ENERGY GAVE US OUR GREATEST ACHIEVEMENT —
A GATEWAY ELEMENT WHOSE ATOMS RESPOND TO ORGANIC ENERGY. SHE NAMED IT ALLOY 618.

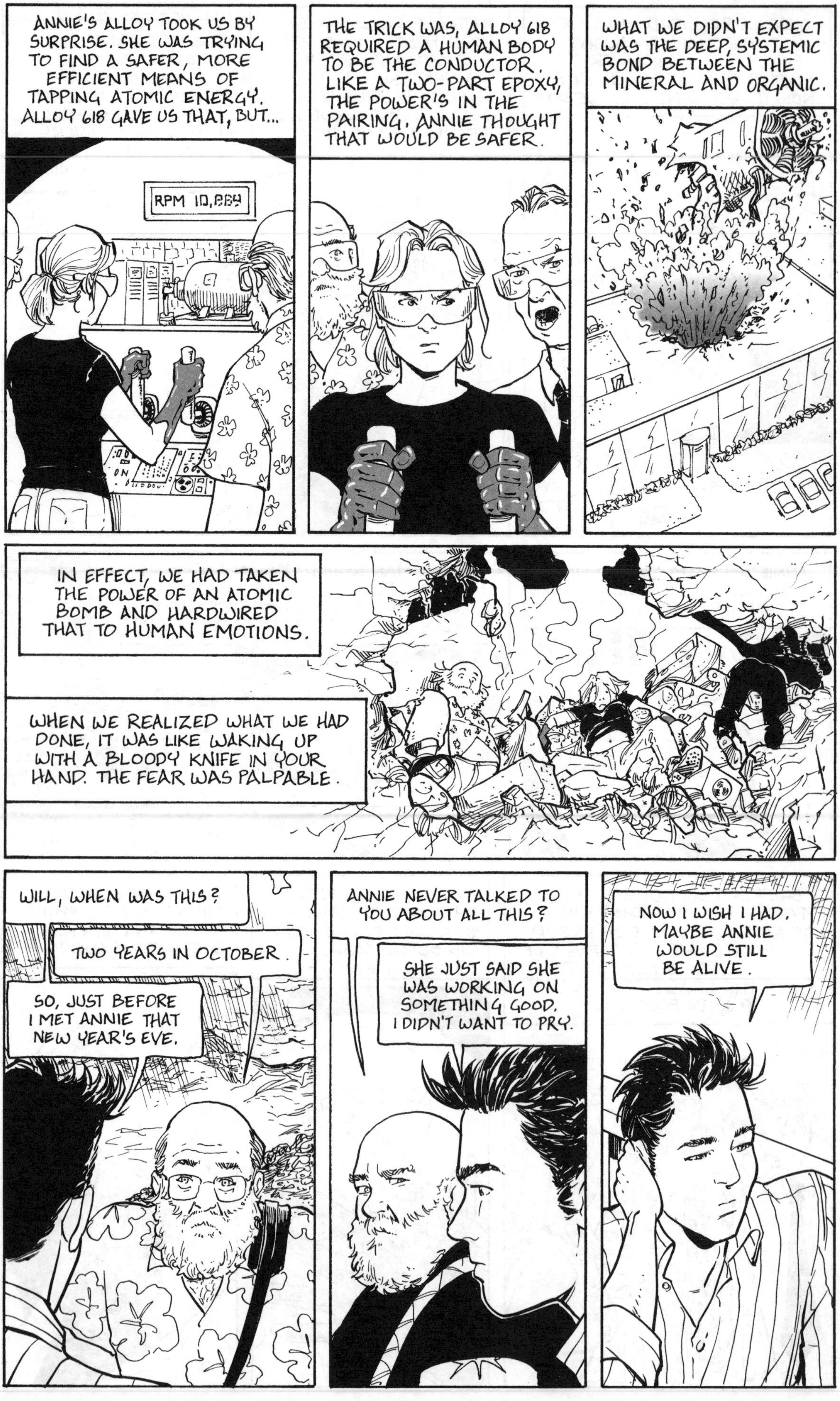
ANNIE'S ALLOY TOOK US BY SURPRISE. SHE WAS TRYING TO FIND A SAFER, MORE EFFICIENT MEANS OF TAPPING ATOMIC ENERGY. ALLOY 618 GAVE US THAT, BUT...
RPM 10,884
THE TRICK WAS, ALLOY 618 REQUIRED A HUMAN BODY TO BE THE CONDUCTOR. LIKE A TWO-PART EPOXY, THE POWER'S IN THE PAIRING. ANNIE THOUGHT THAT WOULD BE SAFER.
WHAT WE DIDN'T EXPECT WAS THE DEEP, SYSTEMIC BOND BETWEEN THE MINERAL AND ORGANIC.
IN EFFECT, WE HAD TAKEN THE POWER OF AN ATOMIC BOMB AND HARDWIRED THAT TO HUMAN EMOTIONS.
WHEN WE REALIZED WHAT WE HAD DONE, IT WAS LIKE WAKING UP WITH A BLOODY KNIFE IN YOUR HAND. THE FEAR WAS PALPABLE.
WILL, WHEN WAS THIS?
TWO YEARS IN OCTOBER.
SO, JUST BEFORE I MET ANNIE THAT NEW YEAR'S EVE.
ANNIE NEVER TALKED TO YOU ABOUT ALL THIS?
SHE JUST SAID SHE WAS WORKING ON SOMETHING GOOD. I DIDN'T WANT TO PRY.
NOW I WISH I HAD. MAYBE ANNIE WOULD STILL BE ALIVE.

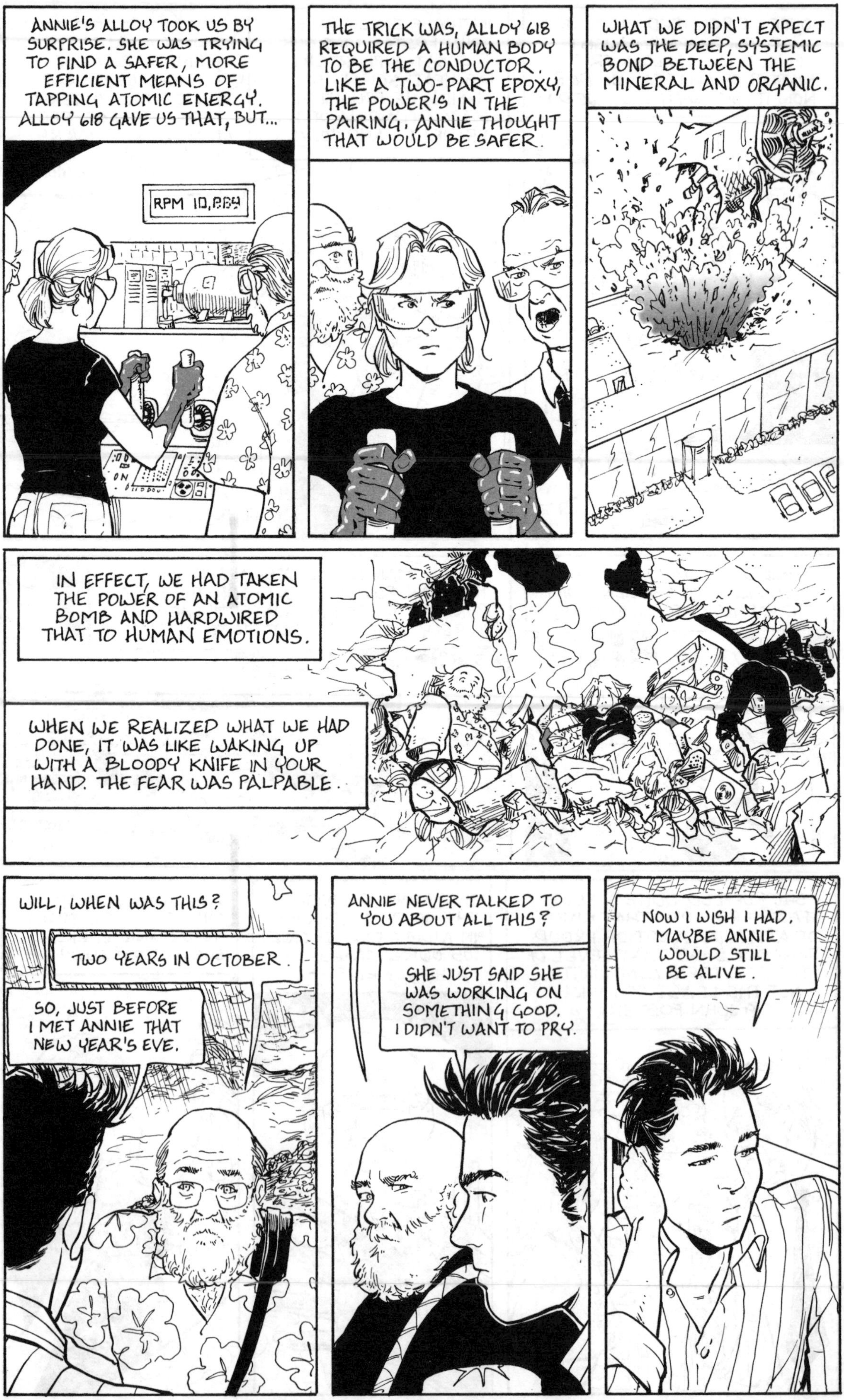
ANNIE'S ALLOY TOOK US BY SURPRISE. SHE WAS TRYING TO FIND A SAFER, MORE EFFICIENT MEANS OF TAPPING ATOMIC ENERGY. ALLOY 618 GAVE US THAT, BUT...
RPM 10,884
THE TRICK WAS, ALLOY 618 REQUIRED A HUMAN BODY TO BE THE CONDUCTOR. LIKE A TWO-PART EPOXY, THE POWER'S IN THE PAIRING. ANNIE THOUGHT THAT WOULD BE SAFER.
WHAT WE DIDN'T EXPECT WAS THE DEEP, SYSTEMIC BOND BETWEEN THE MINERAL AND ORGANIC.
IN EFFECT, WE HAD TAKEN THE POWER OF AN ATOMIC BOMB AND HARDWIRED THAT TO HUMAN EMOTIONS.
WHEN WE REALIZED WHAT WE HAD DONE, IT WAS LIKE WAKING UP WITH A BLOODY KNIFE IN YOUR HAND. THE FEAR WAS PALPABLE.
WILL, WHEN WAS THIS?
TWO YEARS IN OCTOBER.
SO, JUST BEFORE I MET ANNIE THAT NEW YEAR'S EVE.
ANNIE NEVER TALKED TO YOU ABOUT ALL THIS?
SHE JUST SAID SHE WAS WORKING ON SOMETHING GOOD. I DIDN'T WANT TO PRY.
NOW I WISH I HAD. MAYBE ANNIE WOULD STILL BE ALIVE.

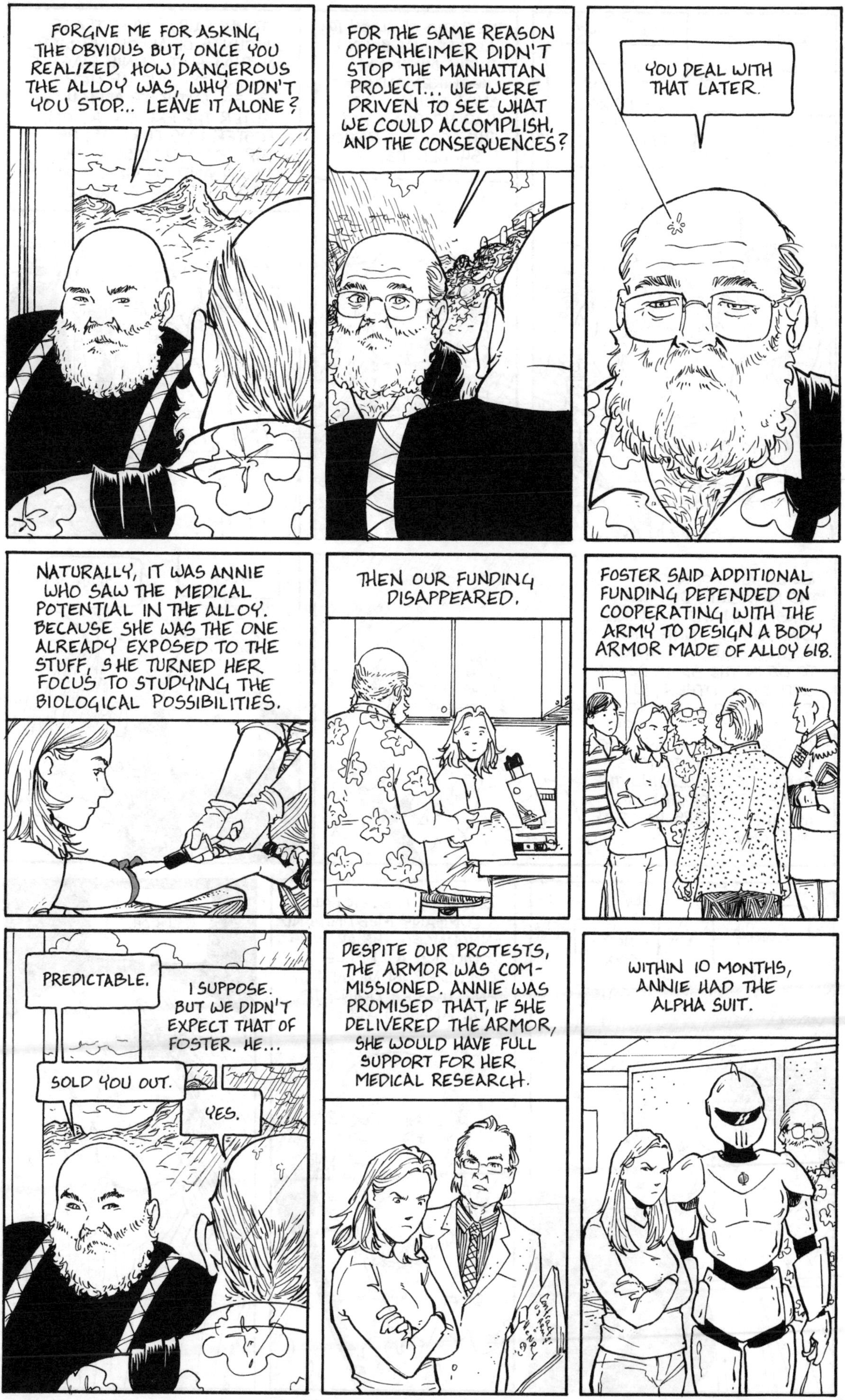
FORGIVE ME FOR ASKING THE OBVIOUS BUT, ONCE YOU REALIZED HOW DANGEROUS THE ALLOY WAS, WHY DIDN'T YOU STOP... LEAVE IT ALONE?
FOR THE SAME REASON OPPENHEIMER DIDN'T STOP THE MANHATTAN PROJECT... WE WERE DRIVEN TO SEE WHAT WE COULD ACCOMPLISH, AND THE CONSEQUENCES?
YOU DEAL WITH THAT LATER.
NATURALLY, IT WAS ANNIE WHO SAW THE MEDICAL POTENTIAL IN THE ALLOY. BECAUSE SHE WAS THE ONE ALREADY EXPOSED TO THE STUFF, SHE TURNED HER FOCUS TO STUDYING THE BIOLOGICAL POSSIBILITIES.
THEN OUR FUNDING DISAPPEARED.
FOSTER SAID ADDITIONAL FUNDING DEPENDED ON COOPERATING WITH THE ARMY TO DESIGN A BODY ARMOR MADE OF ALLOY 618.
PREDICTABLE.
I SUPPOSE. BUT WE DIDN'T EXPECT THAT OF FOSTER. HE...
SOLD YOU OUT.
YES.
DESPITE OUR PROTESTS, THE ARMOR WAS COMMISSIONED. ANNIE WAS PROMISED THAT, IF SHE DELIVERED THE ARMOR, SHE WOULD HAVE FULL SUPPORT FOR HER MEDICAL RESEARCH.
WITHIN 10 MONTHS, ANNIE HAD THE ALPHA SUIT.

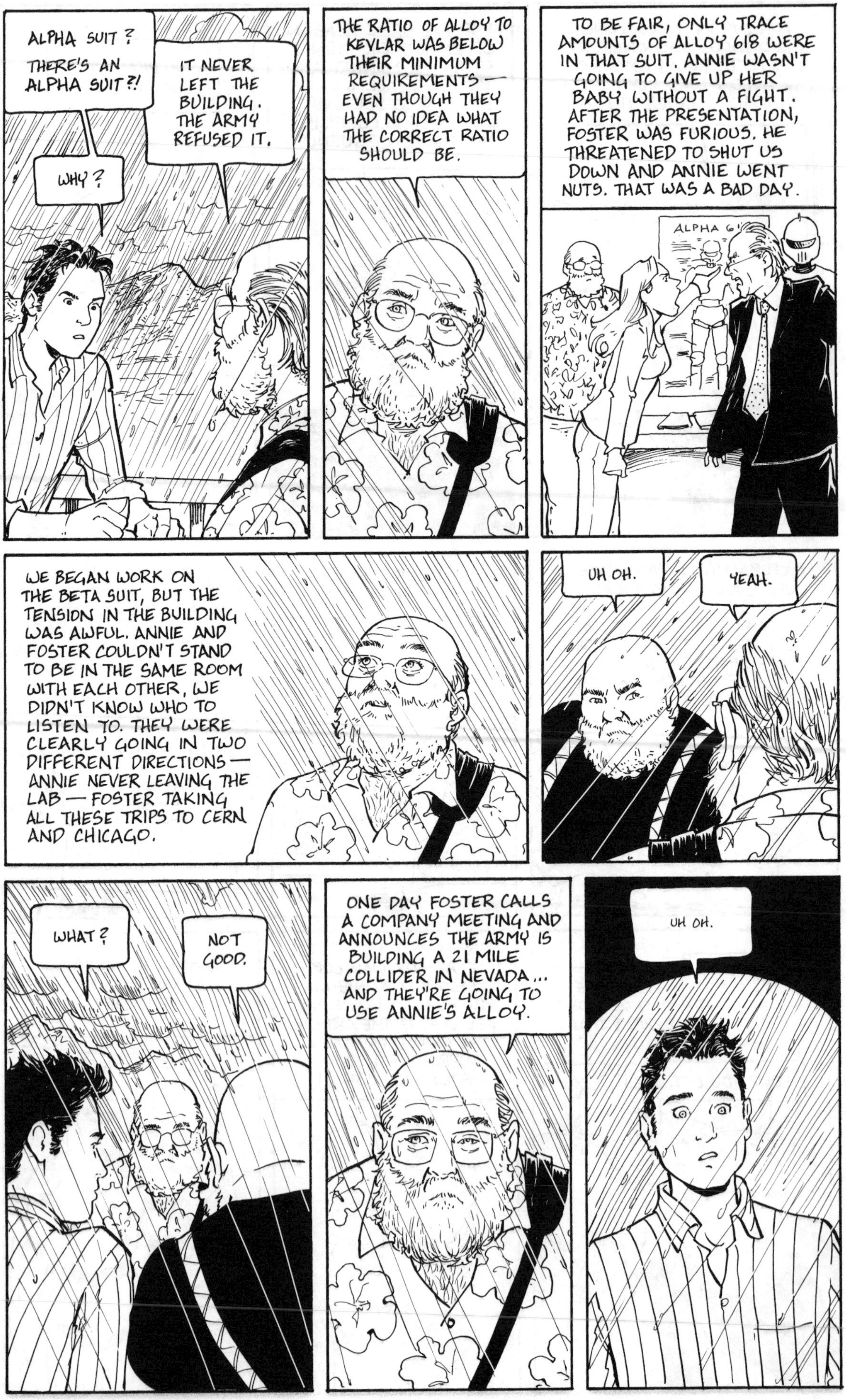
ALPHA SUIT ? THERE'S AN ALPHA SUIT ?!
IT NEVER LEFT THE BUILDING. THE ARMY REFUSED IT.
WHY ?
THE RATIO OF ALLOY TO KEVLAR WAS BELOW THEIR MINIMUM REQUIREMENTS — EVEN THOUGH THEY HAD NO IDEA WHAT THE CORRECT RATIO SHOULD BE.
TO BE FAIR, ONLY TRACE AMOUNTS OF ALLOY 618 WERE IN THAT SUIT. ANNIE WASN'T GOING TO GIVE UP HER BABY WITHOUT A FIGHT. AFTER THE PRESENTATION, FOSTER WAS FURIOUS. HE THREATENED TO SHUT US DOWN AND ANNIE WENT NUTS. THAT WAS A BAD DAY.
WE BEGAN WORK ON THE BETA SUIT, BUT THE TENSION IN THE BUILDING WAS AWFUL. ANNIE AND FOSTER COULDN'T STAND TO BE IN THE SAME ROOM WITH EACH OTHER, WE DIDN'T KNOW WHO TO LISTEN TO. THEY WERE CLEARLY GOING IN TWO DIFFERENT DIRECTIONS — ANNIE NEVER LEAVING THE LAB — FOSTER TAKING ALL THESE TRIPS TO CERN AND CHICAGO.
UH OH.
YEAH.
WHAT ?
NOT GOOD.
ONE DAY FOSTER CALLS A COMPANY MEETING AND ANNOUNCES THE ARMY IS BUILDING A 21 MILE COLLIDER IN NEVADA... AND THEY'RE GOING TO USE ANNIE'S ALLOY.
UH OH.

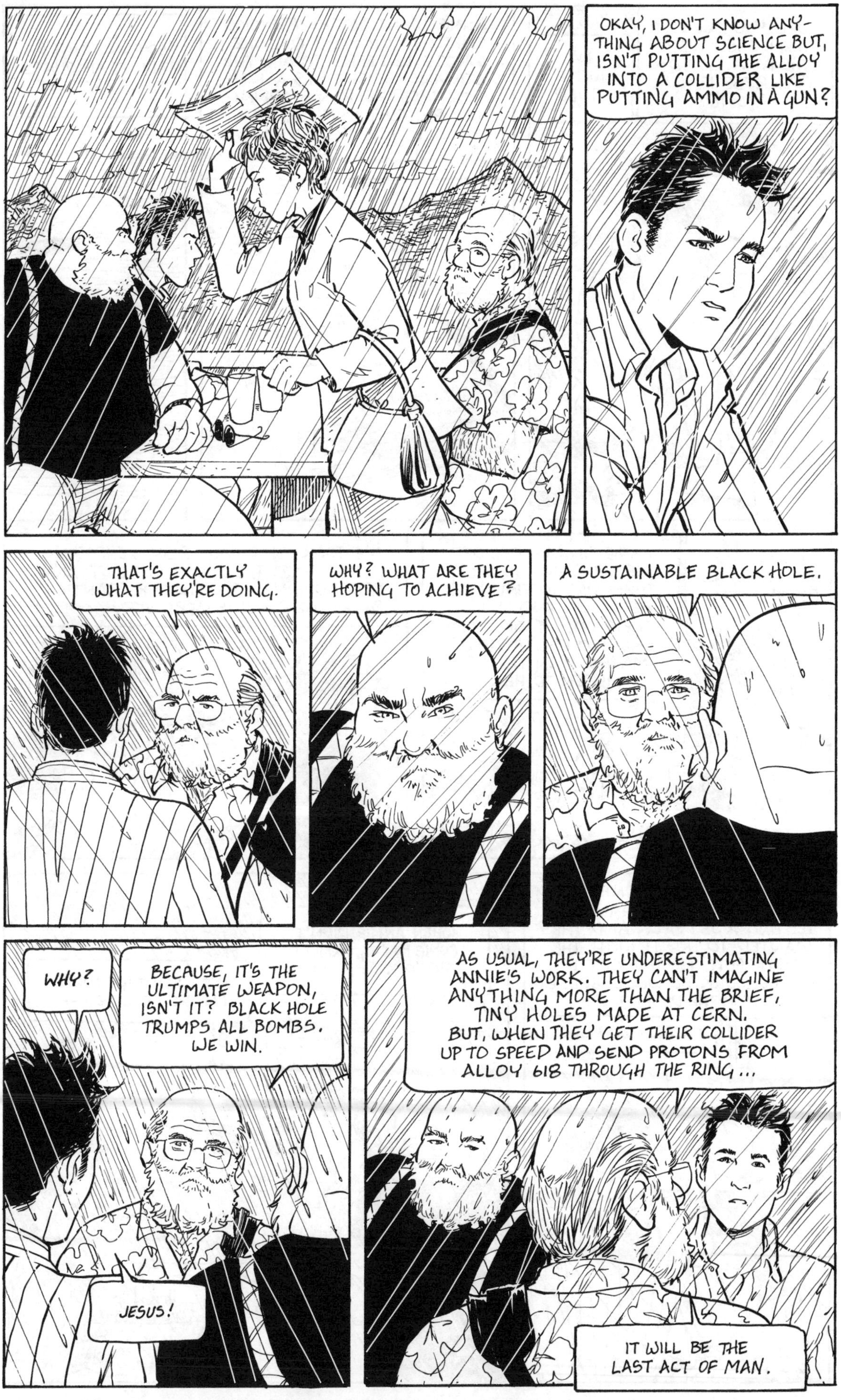
OKAY, I DON'T KNOW ANYTHING ABOUT SCIENCE BUT, ISN'T PUTTING THE ALLOY INTO A COLLIDER LIKE PUTTING AMMO IN A GUN?
THAT'S EXACTLY WHAT THEY'RE DOING.
WHY? WHAT ARE THEY HOPING TO ACHIEVE?
A SUSTAINABLE BLACK HOLE.
WHY?
BECAUSE, IT'S THE ULTIMATE WEAPON, ISN'T IT? BLACK HOLE TRUMPS ALL BOMBS. WE WIN.
JESUS!
AS USUAL, THEY'RE UNDERESTIMATING ANNIE'S WORK. THEY CAN'T IMAGINE ANYTHING MORE THAN THE BRIEF, TINY HOLES MADE AT CERN. BUT, WHEN THEY GET THEIR COLLIDER UP TO SPEED AND SEND PROTONS FROM ALLOY 618 THROUGH THE RING...
IT WILL BE THE LAST ACT OF MAN.

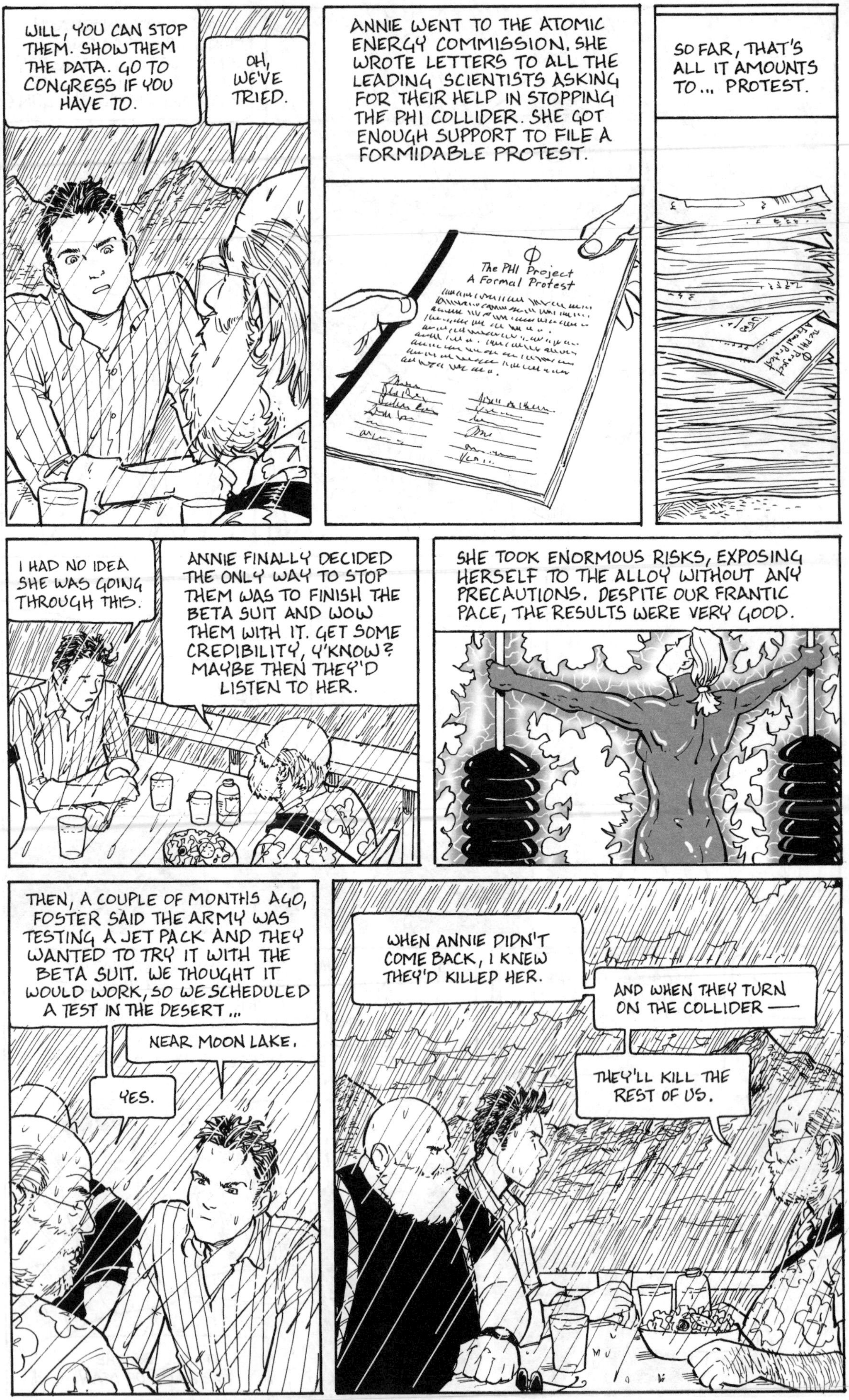
WILL, YOU CAN STOP THEM. SHOW THEM THE DATA. GO TO CONGRESS IF YOU HAVE TO.
OH, WE'VE TRIED.
ANNIE WENT TO THE ATOMIC ENERGY COMMISSION. SHE WROTE LETTERS TO ALL THE LEADING SCIENTISTS ASKING FOR THEIR HELP IN STOPPING THE PHI COLLIDER. SHE GOT ENOUGH SUPPORT TO FILE A FORMIDABLE PROTEST.
The PHI Project
A Formal Protest
SO FAR, THAT'S ALL IT AMOUNTS TO... PROTEST.
I HAD NO IDEA SHE WAS GOING THROUGH THIS.
ANNIE FINALLY DECIDED THE ONLY WAY TO STOP THEM WAS TO FINISH THE BETA SUIT AND WOW THEM WITH IT. GET SOME CREDIBILITY, Y'KNOW? MAYBE THEN THEY'D LISTEN TO HER.
SHE TOOK ENORMOUS RISKS, EXPOSING HERSELF TO THE ALLOY WITHOUT ANY PRECAUTIONS. DESPITE OUR FRANTIC PACE, THE RESULTS WERE VERY GOOD.
THEN, A COUPLE OF MONTHS AGO, FOSTER SAID THE ARMY WAS TESTING A JET PACK AND THEY WANTED TO TRY IT WITH THE BETA SUIT. WE THOUGHT IT WOULD WORK, SO WE SCHEDULED A TEST IN THE DESERT...
NEAR MOON LAKE.
YES.
WHEN ANNIE DIDN'T COME BACK, I KNEW THEY'D KILLED HER.
AND WHEN THEY TURN ON THE COLLIDER —
THEY'LL KILL THE REST OF US.

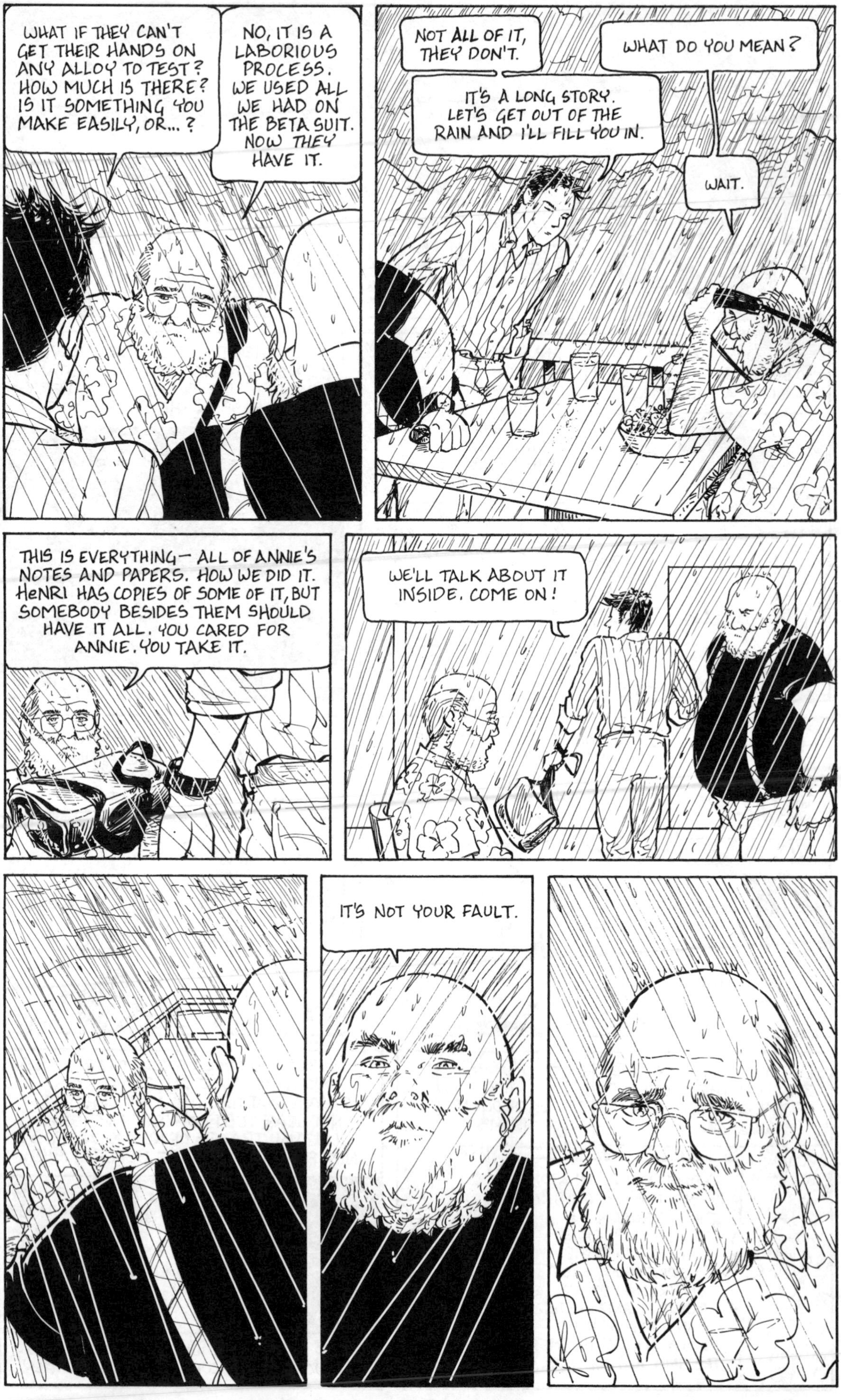
WHAT IF THEY CAN'T GET THEIR HANDS ON ANY ALLOY TO TEST? HOW MUCH IS THERE? IS IT SOMETHING YOU MAKE EASILY, OR...?
NO, IT IS A LABORIOUS PROCESS. WE USED ALL WE HAD ON THE BETA SUIT. NOW THEY HAVE IT.
NOT ALL OF IT, THEY DON'T.
IT'S A LONG STORY. LET'S GET OUT OF THE RAIN AND I'LL FILL YOU IN.
WHAT DO YOU MEAN?
WAIT.
THIS IS EVERYTHING— ALL OF ANNIE'S NOTES AND PAPERS. HOW WE DID IT. HeNRI HAS COPIES OF SOME OF IT, BUT SOMEBODY BESIDES THEM SHOULD HAVE IT ALL. YOU CARED FOR ANNIE. YOU TAKE IT.
WE'LL TALK ABOUT IT INSIDE. COME ON!
IT'S NOT YOUR FAULT.

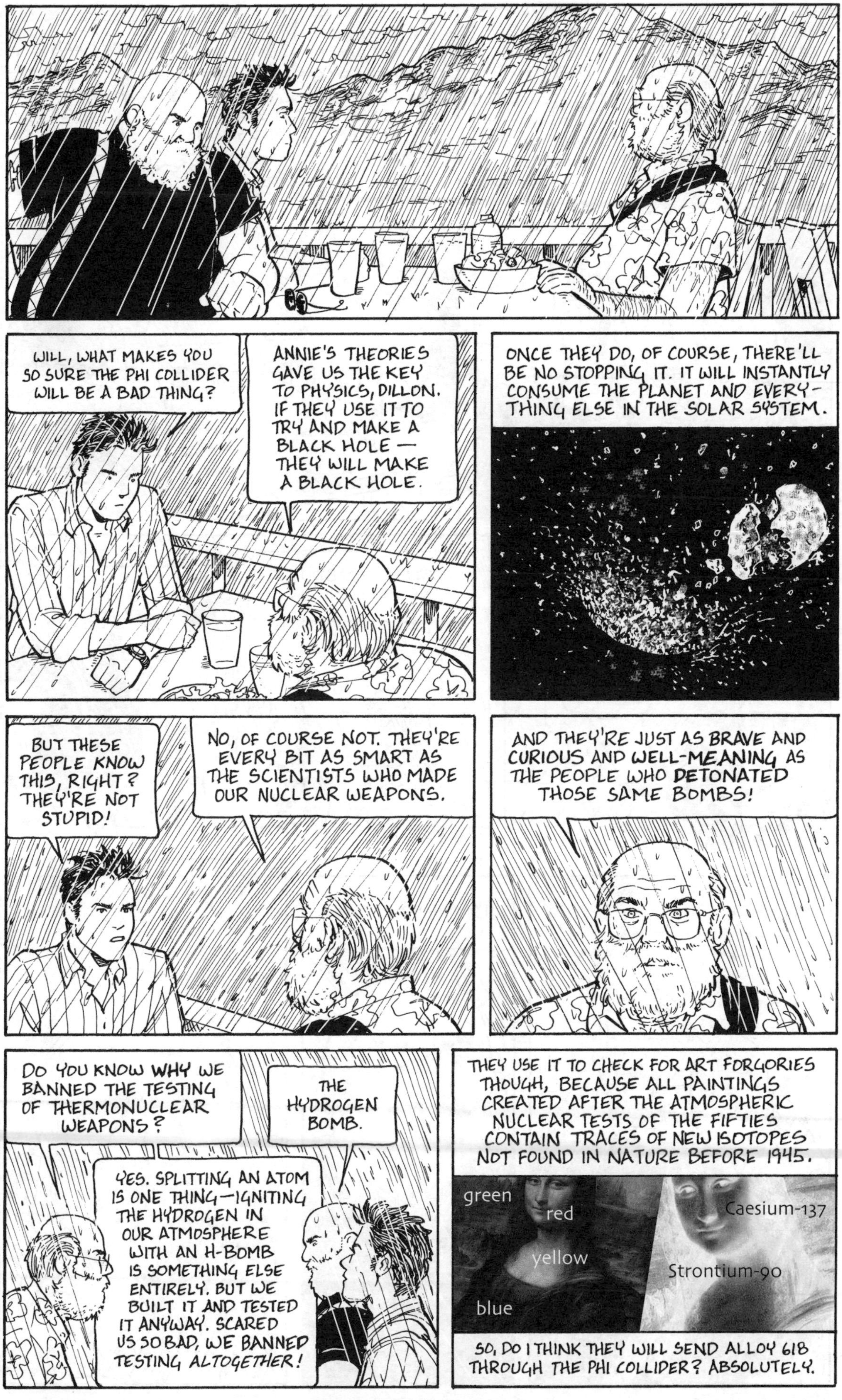
WILL, WHAT MAKES YOU SO SURE THE PHI COLLIDER WILL BE A BAD THING?
ANNIE'S THEORIES GAVE US THE KEY TO PHYSICS, DILLON. IF THEY USE IT TO TRY AND MAKE A BLACK HOLE — THEY WILL MAKE A BLACK HOLE.
ONCE THEY DO, OF COURSE, THERE'LL BE NO STOPPING IT. IT WILL INSTANTLY CONSUME THE PLANET AND EVERYTHING ELSE IN THE SOLAR SYSTEM.
BUT THESE PEOPLE KNOW THIS, RIGHT? THEY'RE NOT STUPID!
NO, OF COURSE NOT. THEY'RE EVERY BIT AS SMART AS THE SCIENTISTS WHO MADE OUR NUCLEAR WEAPONS.
AND THEY'RE JUST AS BRAVE AND CURIOUS AND WELL-MEANING AS THE PEOPLE WHO DETONATED THOSE SAME BOMBS!
DO YOU KNOW WHY WE BANNED THE TESTING OF THERMONUCLEAR WEAPONS?
THE HYDROGEN BOMB.
YES. SPLITTING AN ATOM IS ONE THING—IGNITING THE HYDROGEN IN OUR ATMOSPHERE WITH AN H-BOMB IS SOMETHING ELSE ENTIRELY. BUT WE BUILT IT AND TESTED IT ANYWAY. SCARED US SO BAD, WE BANNED TESTING ALTOGETHER!
THEY USE IT TO CHECK FOR ART FORGERIES THOUGH, BECAUSE ALL PAINTINGS CREATED AFTER THE ATMOSPHERIC NUCLEAR TESTS OF THE FIFTIES CONTAIN TRACES OF NEW ISOTOPES NOT FOUND IN NATURE BEFORE 1945.
green
red
yellow
blue
Caesium-137
Strontium-90
SO, DO I THINK THEY WILL SEND ALLOY 618 THROUGH THE PHI COLLIDER? ABSOLUTELY.

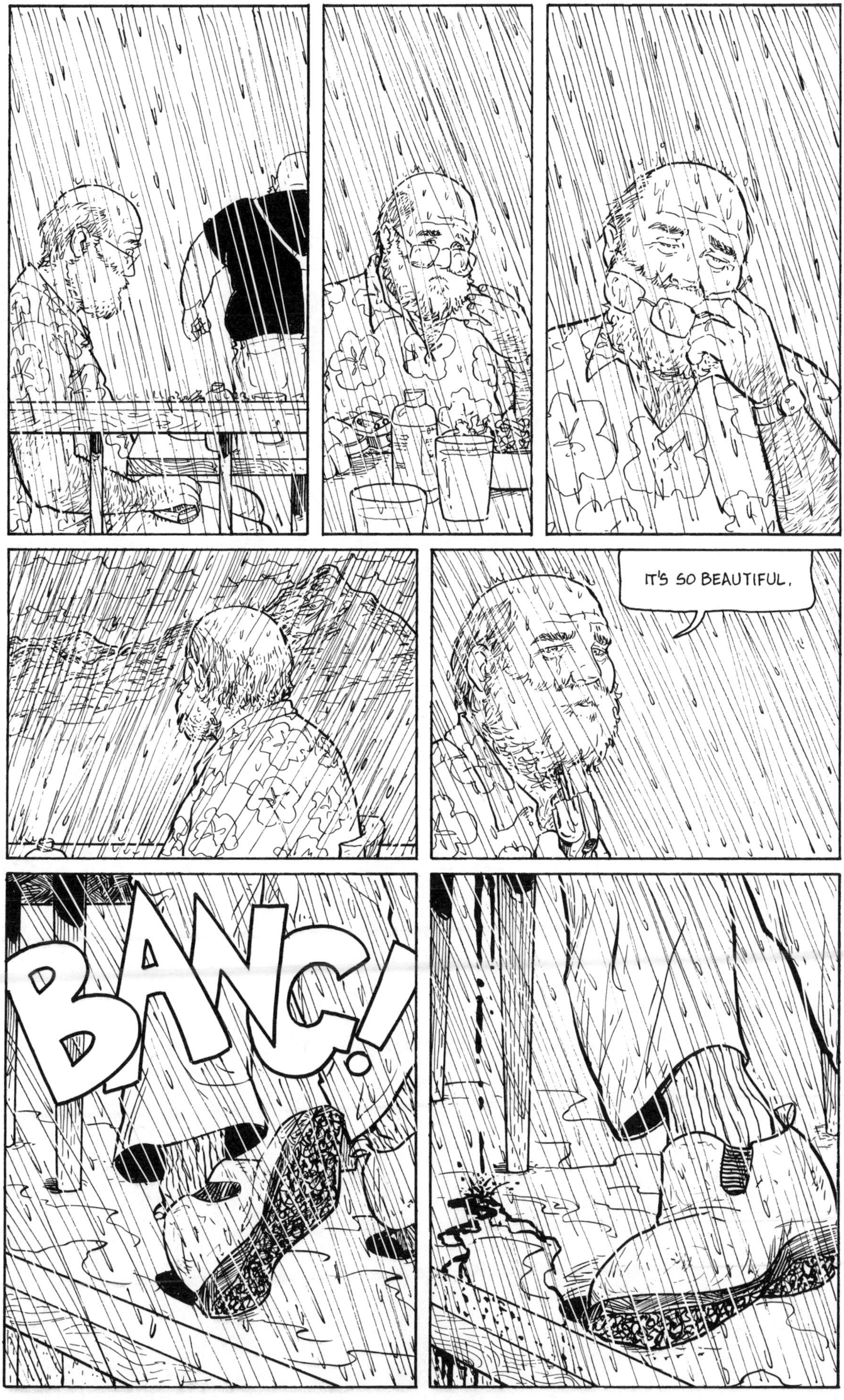
IT'S SO BEAUTIFUL.
BANG!

And He said, "What have you done?
The voice of your brother's blood calls
out to Me from the ground."
Genesis 4:10

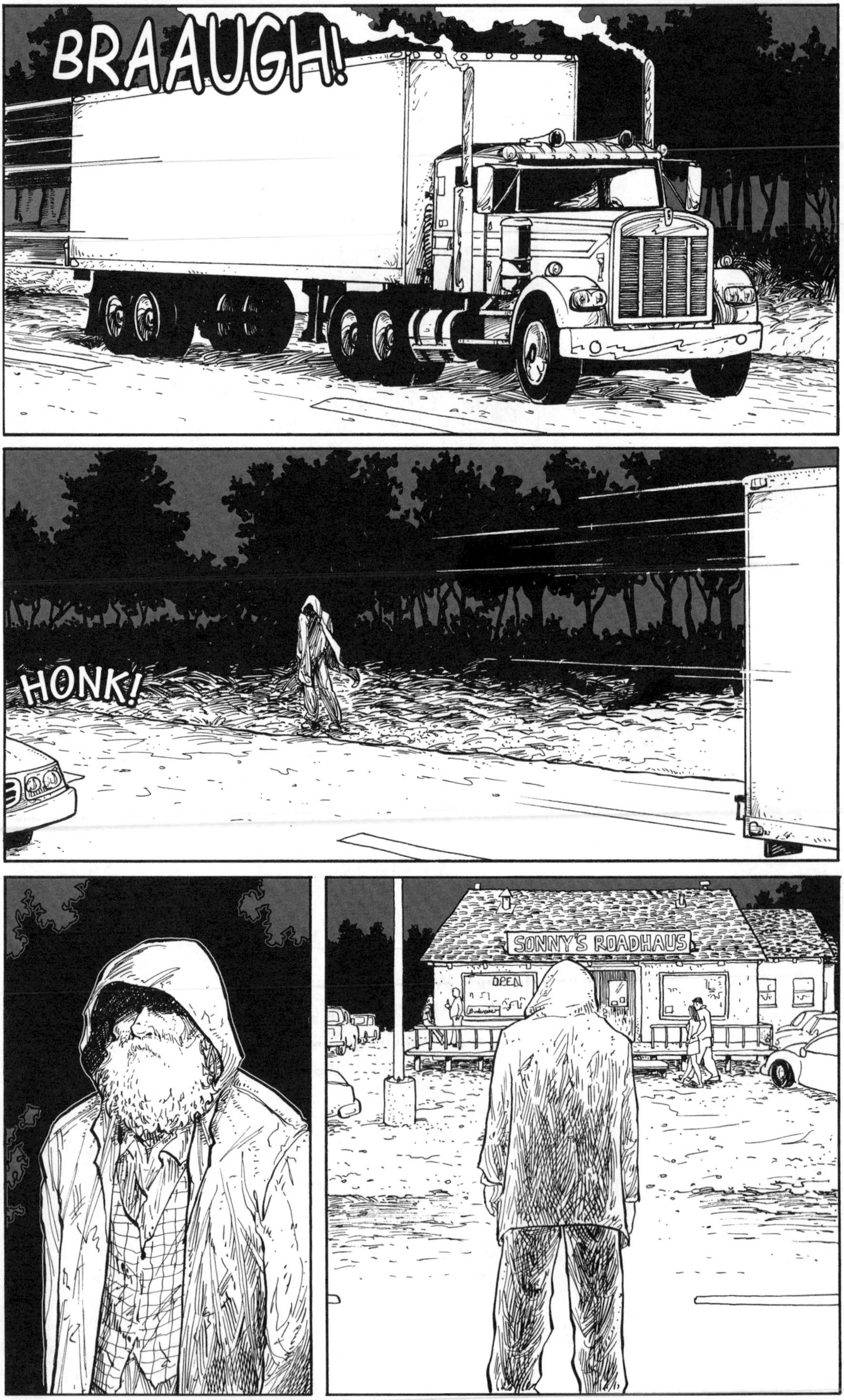
BRAAUGH!
HONK!
SONNY'S ROADHAUS
OPEN

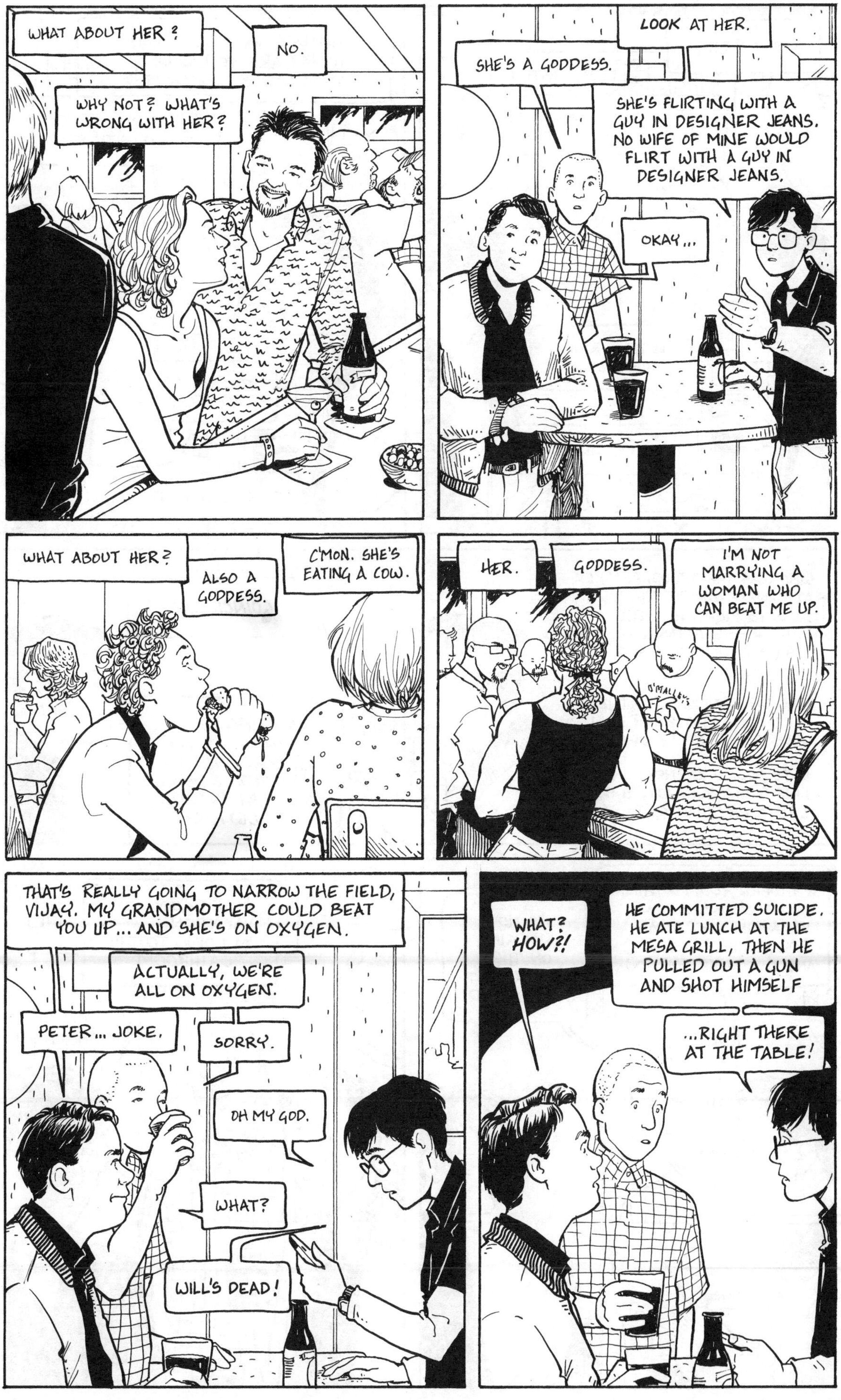
WHAT ABOUT HER?
NO.
WHY NOT? WHAT'S WRONG WITH HER?
LOOK AT HER.
SHE'S A GODDESS.
SHE'S FLIRTING WITH A GUY IN DESIGNER JEANS. NO WIFE OF MINE WOULD FLIRT WITH A GUY IN DESIGNER JEANS.
OKAY...
WHAT ABOUT HER?
ALSO A GODDESS.
C'MON. SHE'S EATING A COW.
HER.
GODDESS.
I'M NOT MARRYING A WOMAN WHO CAN BEAT ME UP.
O'MALLEY'S
THAT'S REALLY GOING TO NARROW THE FIELD, VIJAY. MY GRANDMOTHER COULD BEAT YOU UP... AND SHE'S ON OXYGEN.
ACTUALLY, WE'RE ALL ON OXYGEN.
PETER... JOKE.
SORRY.
OH MY GOD.
WHAT?
WILL'S DEAD!
WHAT? HOW?!
HE COMMITTED SUICIDE. HE ATE LUNCH AT THE MESA GRILL, THEN HE PULLED OUT A GUN AND SHOT HIMSELF
...RIGHT THERE AT THE TABLE!

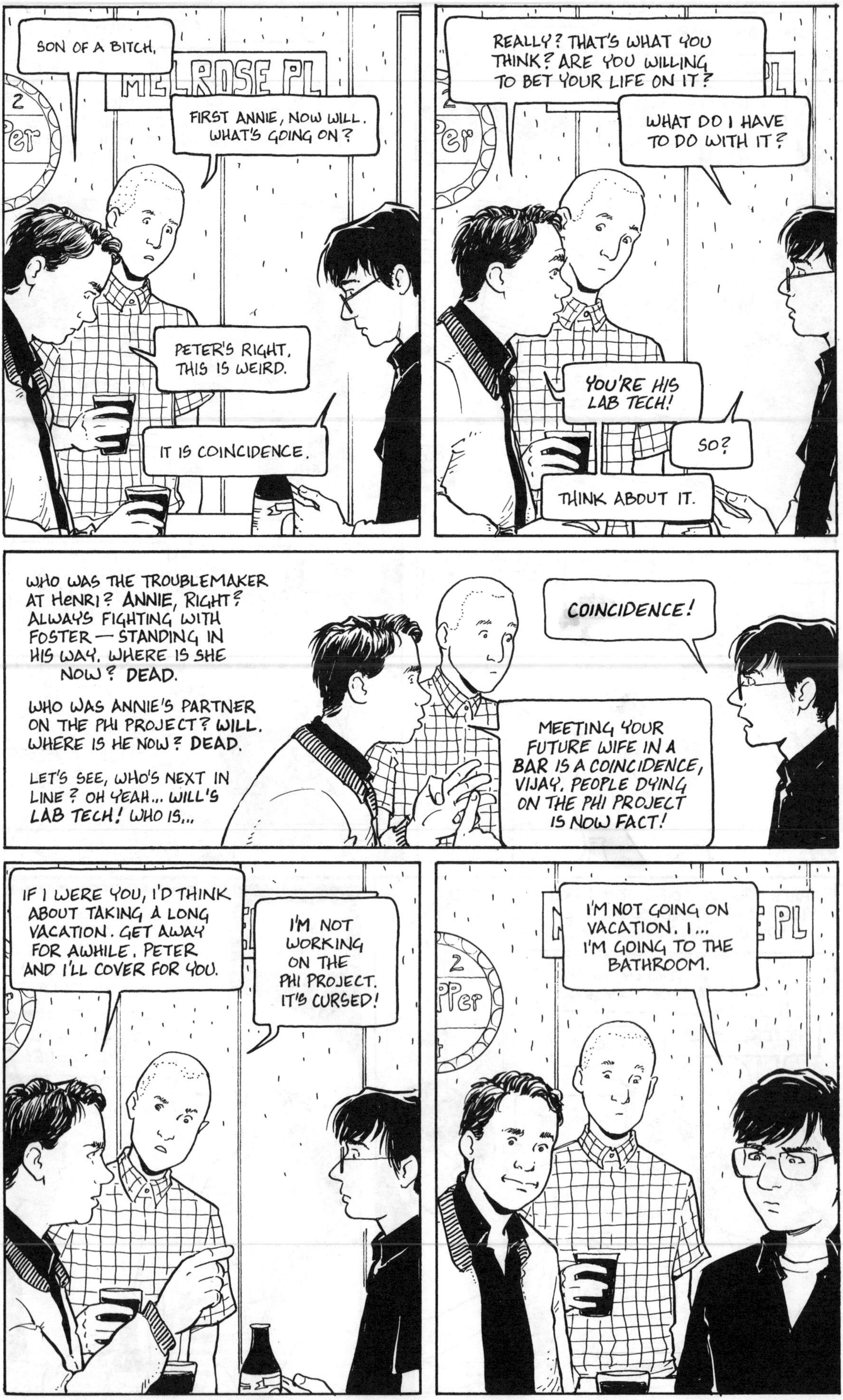
SON OF A BITCH.
MELROSE PL
FIRST ANNIE, NOW WILL. WHAT'S GOING ON?
PETER'S RIGHT. THIS IS WEIRD.
IT IS COINCIDENCE.
REALLY? THAT'S WHAT YOU THINK? ARE YOU WILLING TO BET YOUR LIFE ON IT?
WHAT DO I HAVE TO DO WITH IT?
YOU'RE HIS LAB TECH!
SO?
THINK ABOUT IT.
WHO WAS THE TROUBLEMAKER AT HENRI? ANNIE, RIGHT? ALWAYS FIGHTING WITH FOSTER — STANDING IN HIS WAY. WHERE IS SHE NOW? DEAD.
WHO WAS ANNIE'S PARTNER ON THE PHI PROJECT? WILL. WHERE IS HE NOW? DEAD.
LET'S SEE, WHO'S NEXT IN LINE? OH YEAH... WILL'S LAB TECH! WHO IS...
COINCIDENCE!
MEETING YOUR FUTURE WIFE IN A BAR IS A COINCIDENCE, VIJAY. PEOPLE DYING ON THE PHI PROJECT IS NOW FACT!
IF I WERE YOU, I'D THINK ABOUT TAKING A LONG VACATION. GET AWAY FOR AWHILE. PETER AND I'LL COVER FOR YOU.
I'M NOT WORKING ON THE PHI PROJECT. IT'S CURSED!
I'M NOT GOING ON VACATION. I... I'M GOING TO THE BATHROOM.

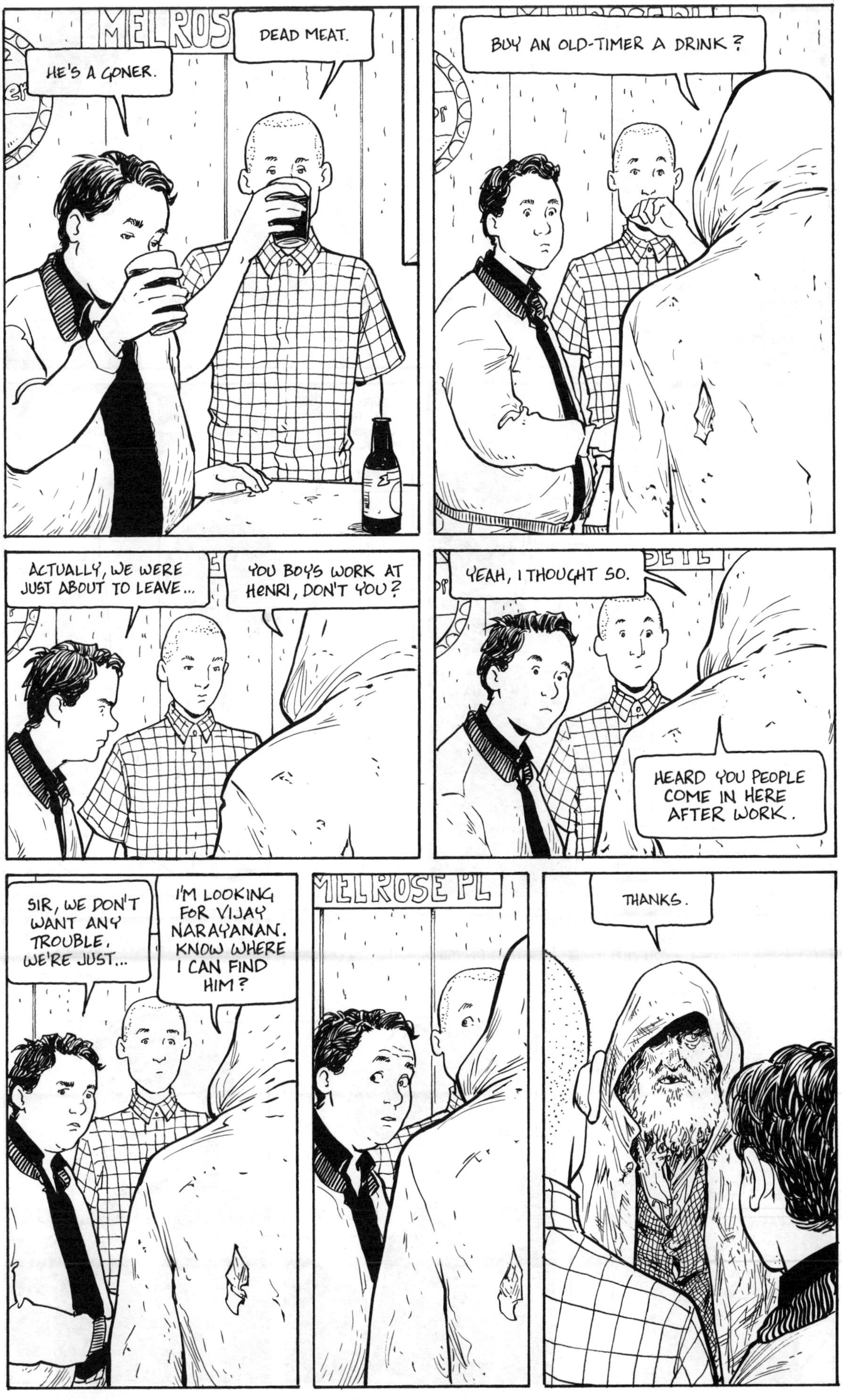
MELROS
HE'S A GONER.
DEAD MEAT.
BUY AN OLD-TIMER A DRINK?
ACTUALLY, WE WERE JUST ABOUT TO LEAVE...
YOU BOYS WORK AT HENRI, DON'T YOU?
YEAH, I THOUGHT SO.
HEARD YOU PEOPLE COME IN HERE AFTER WORK.
SIR, WE DON'T WANT ANY TROUBLE. WE'RE JUST...
I'M LOOKING FOR VIJAY NARAYANAN. KNOW WHERE I CAN FIND HIM?
MELROSE PL
THANKS.

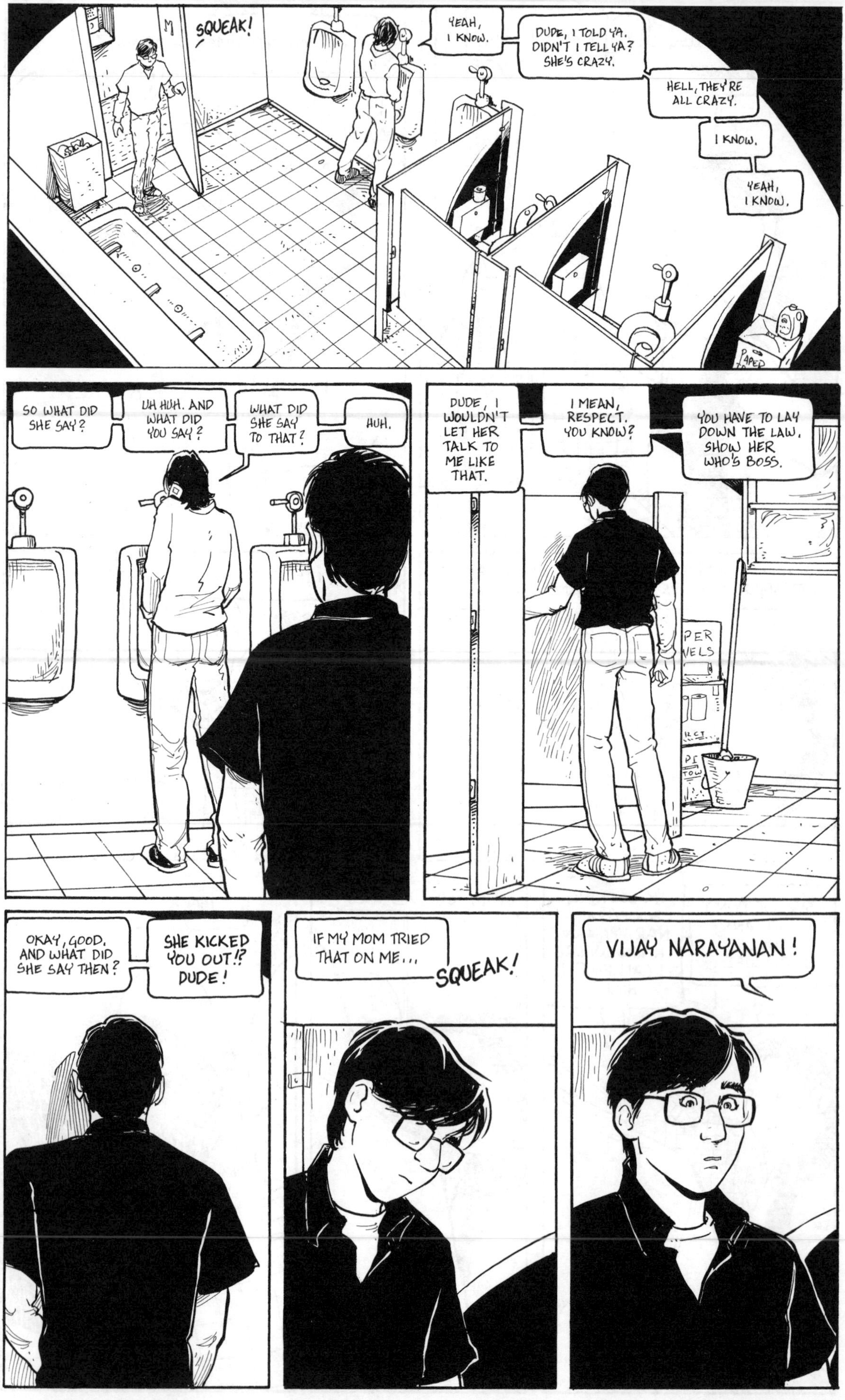
M
SQUEAK!
YEAH, I KNOW.
DUDE, I TOLD YA. DIDN'T I TELL YA? SHE'S CRAZY.
HELL, THEY'RE ALL CRAZY.
I KNOW.
YEAH, I KNOW.
SO WHAT DID SHE SAY?
UH HUH. AND WHAT DID YOU SAY?
WHAT DID SHE SAY TO THAT?
HUH.
DUDE, I WOULDN'T LET HER TALK TO ME LIKE THAT.
I MEAN, RESPECT. YOU KNOW?
YOU HAVE TO LAY DOWN THE LAW. SHOW HER WHO'S BOSS.
OKAY, GOOD. AND WHAT DID SHE SAY THEN?
SHE KICKED YOU OUT!? DUDE!
IF MY MOM TRIED THAT ON ME...
SQUEAK!
VIJAY NARAYANAN!

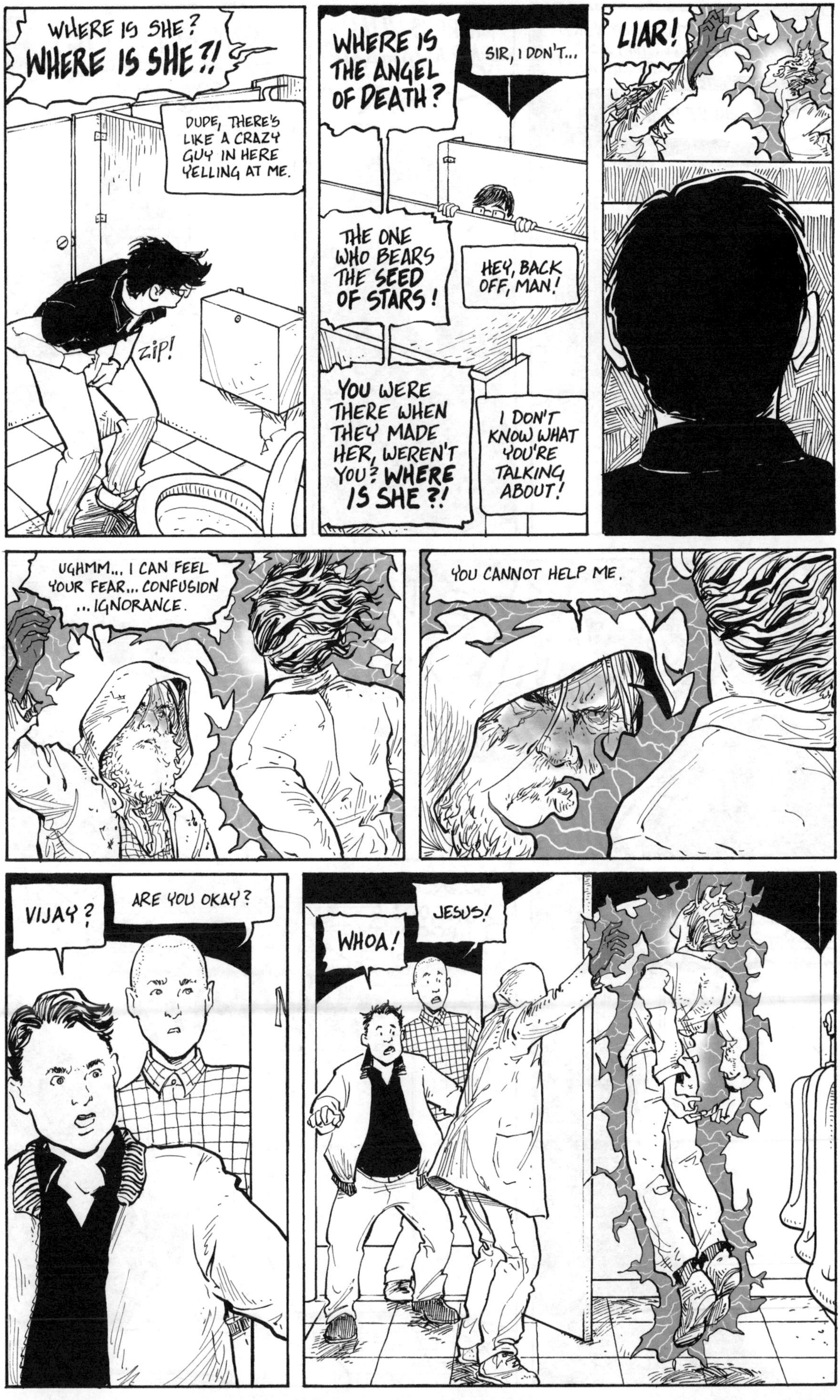
WHERE IS SHE? WHERE IS SHE?!
DUDE, THERE'S LIKE A CRAZY GUY IN HERE YELLING AT ME.
ZIP!
WHERE IS THE ANGEL OF DEATH?
SIR, I DON'T...
THE ONE WHO BEARS THE SEED OF STARS!
HEY, BACK OFF, MAN!
YOU WERE THERE WHEN THEY MADE HER, WEREN'T YOU? WHERE IS SHE?!
I DON'T KNOW WHAT YOU'RE TALKING ABOUT!
LIAR!
UGHMM... I CAN FEEL YOUR FEAR... CONFUSION ...IGNORANCE.
YOU CANNOT HELP ME.
VIJAY?
ARE YOU OKAY?
WHOA!
JESUS!

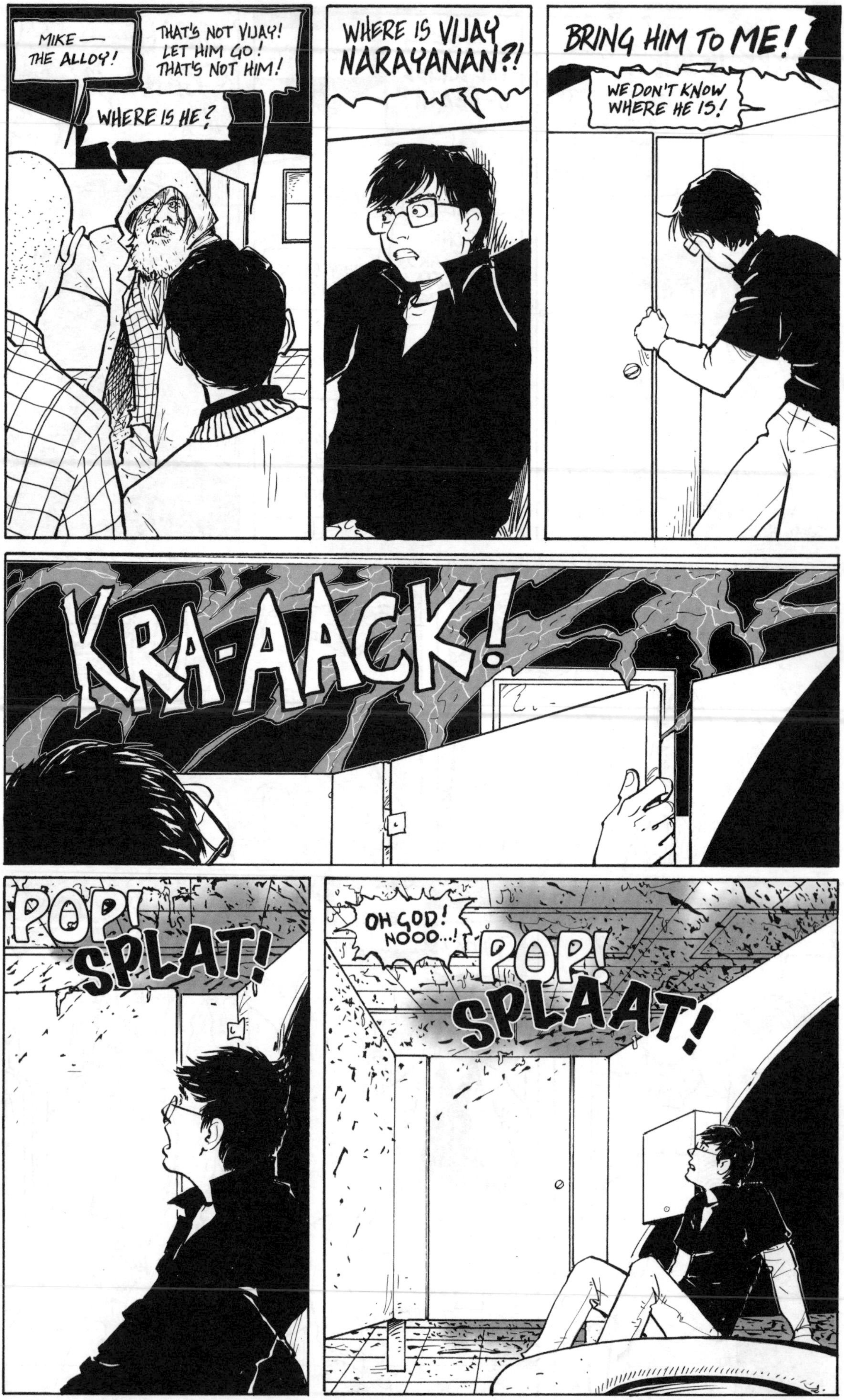
MIKE — THE ALLOY!
THAT'S NOT VIJAY! LET HIM GO! THAT'S NOT HIM!
WHERE IS HE?
WHERE IS VIJAY NARAYANAN?!
BRING HIM TO ME!
WE DON'T KNOW WHERE HE IS!
KRA-AACK!
POP! SPLAT!
OH GOD! NOOO...!
POP! SPLAAT!

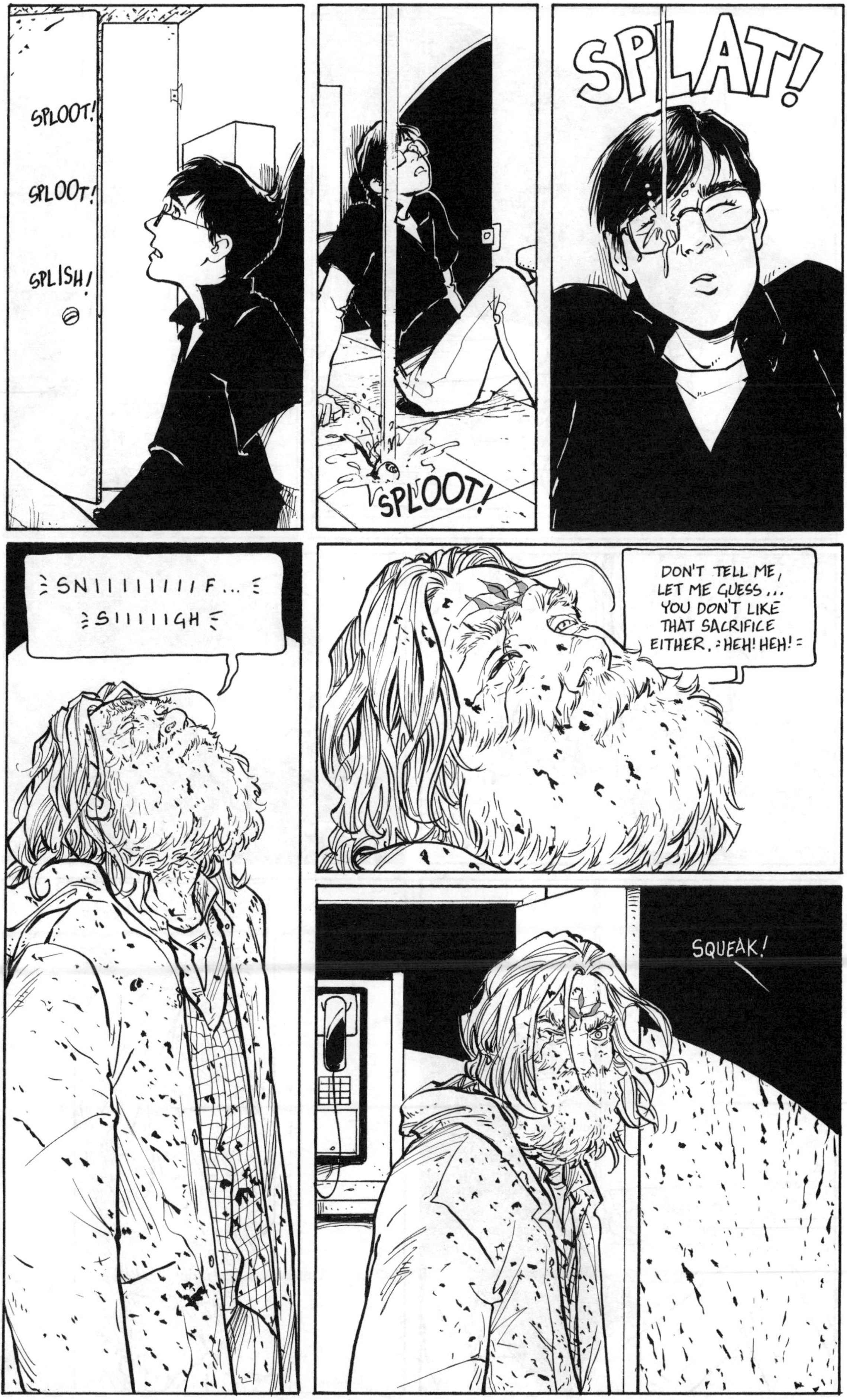
SPLOOT!
SPLOOT!
SPLISH!
SPLOOT!
SPLAT!
SNIIIIIIIIF...
SIIIIIGH
DON'T TELL ME, LET ME GUESS... YOU DON'T LIKE THAT SACRIFICE EITHER. HEH! HEH!
SQUEAK!

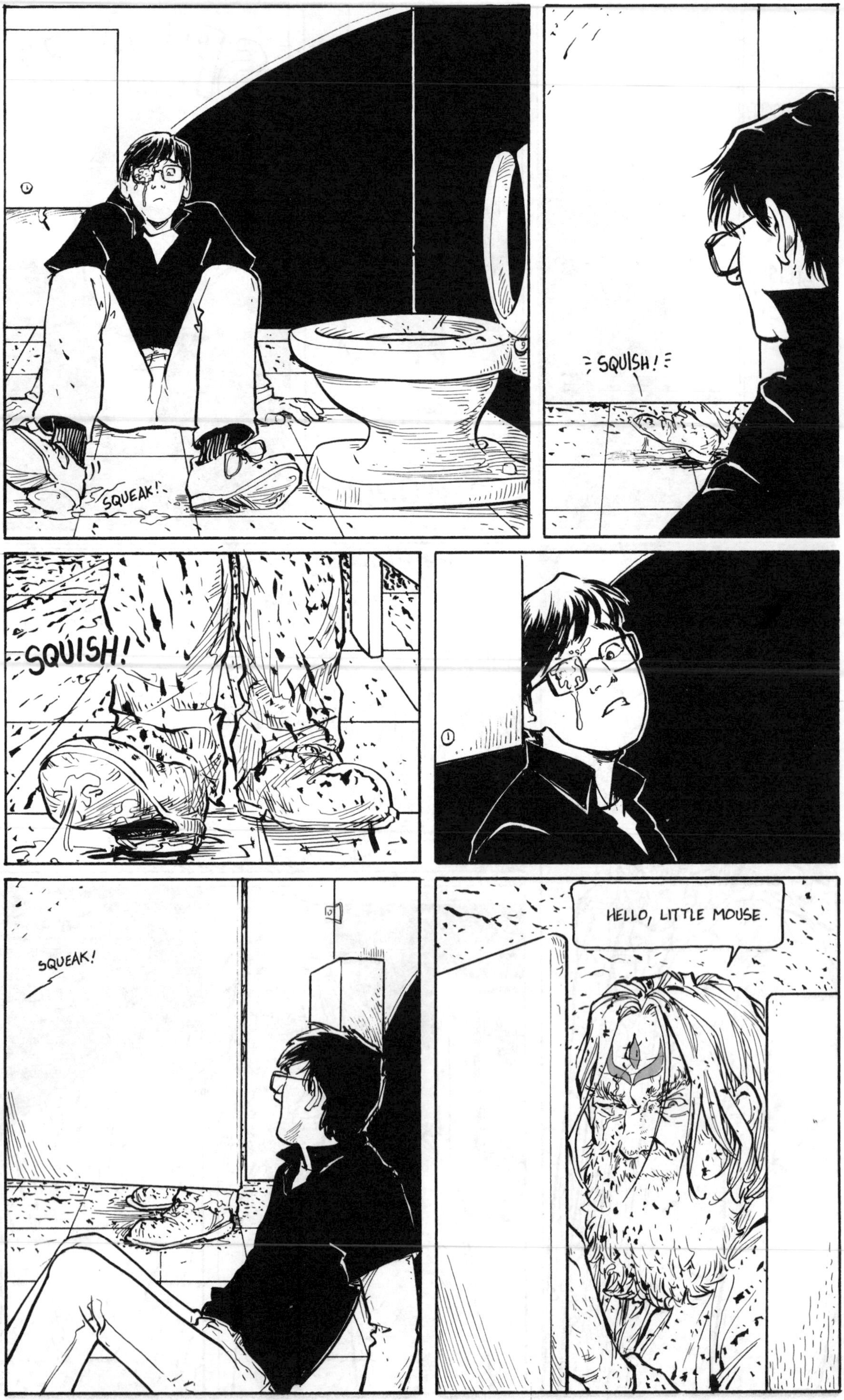
SQUEAK!
SQUISH!
SQUISH!
SQUEAK!
HELLO, LITTLE MOUSE.

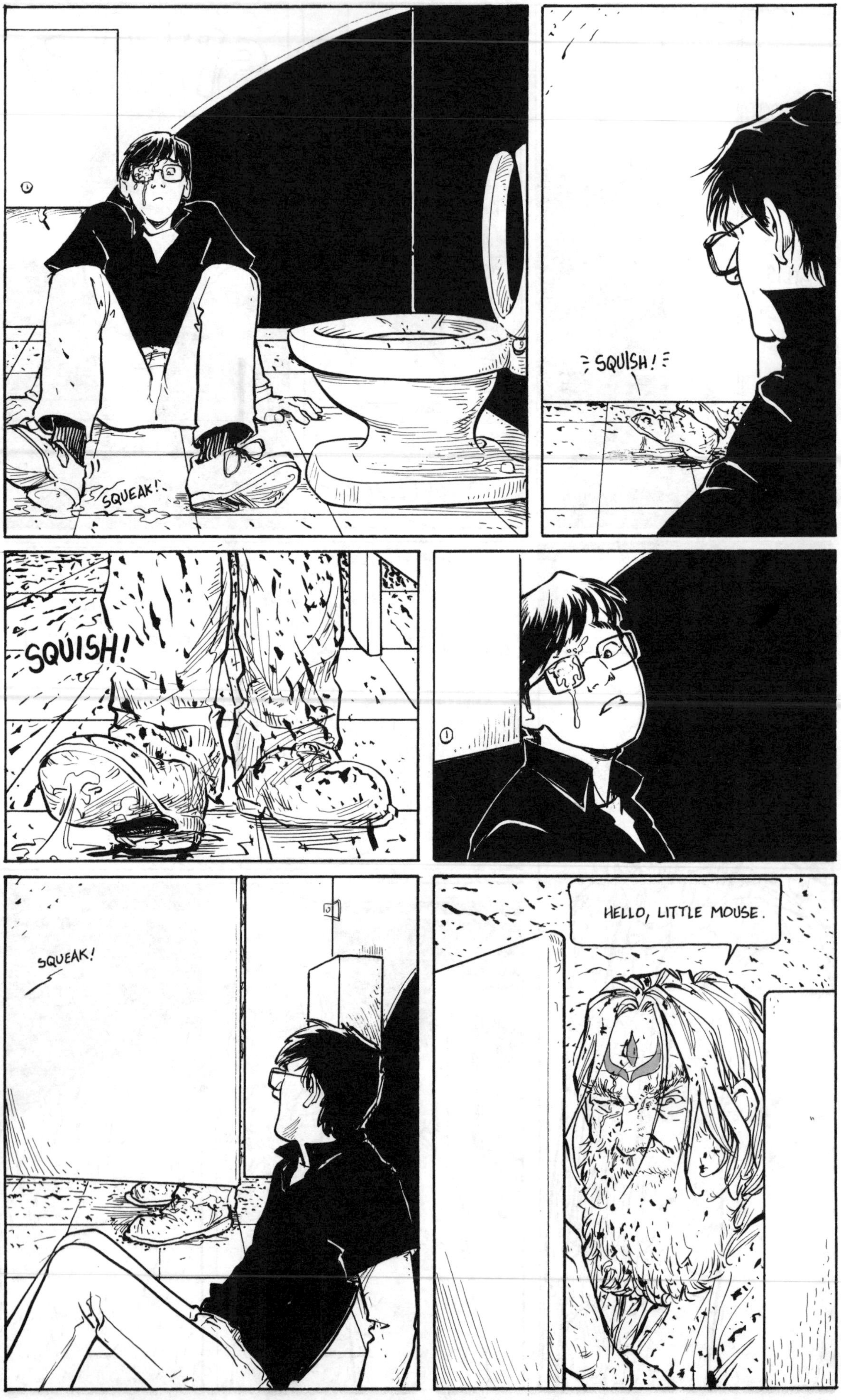
SQUEAK!
SQUISH!
SQUISH!
SQUEAK!
HELLO, LITTLE MOUSE.

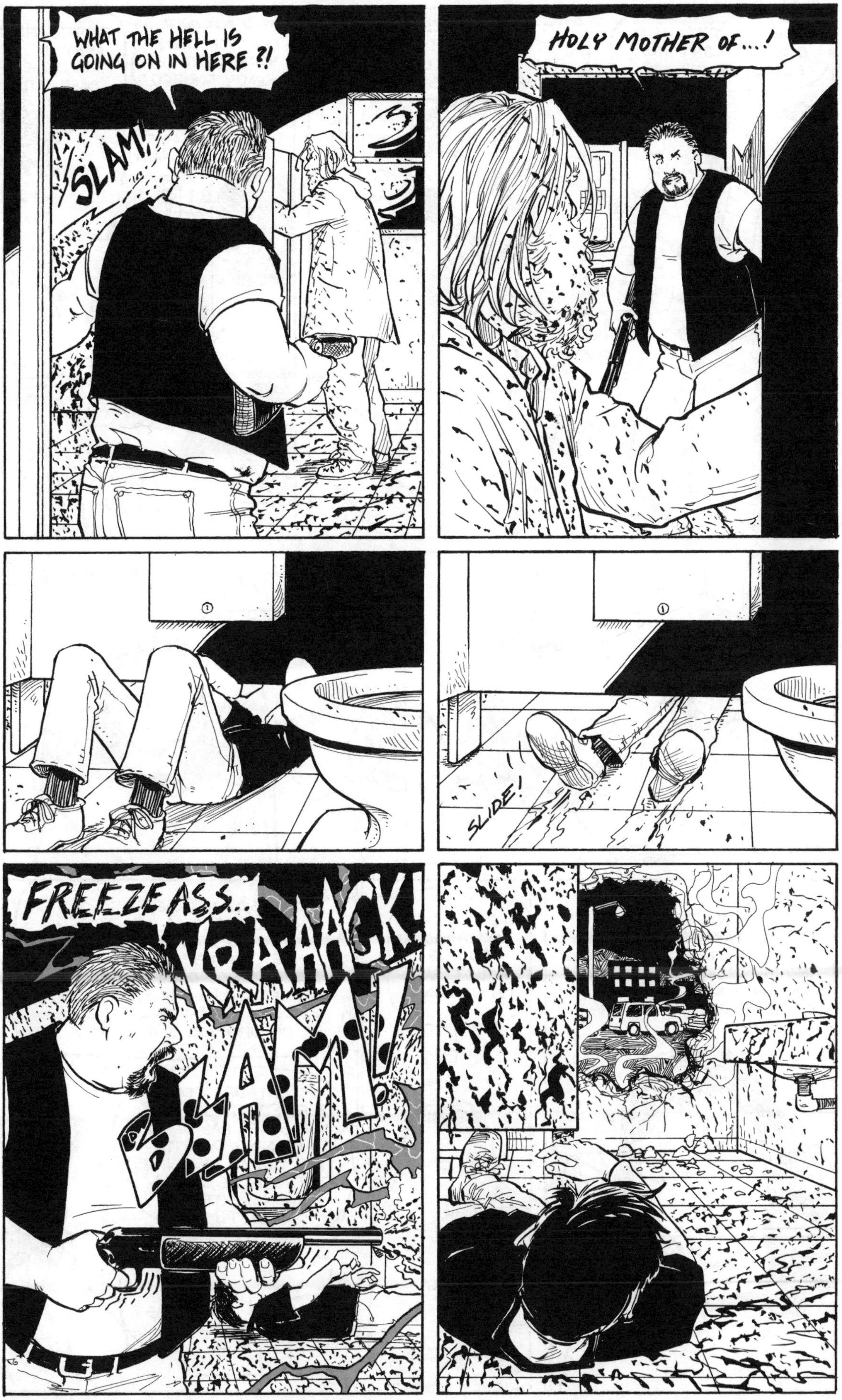
WHAT THE HELL IS GOING ON IN HERE ?!
SLAM!
HOLY MOTHER OF...!
SLIDE!
FREEZE ASS..
KRAAACK!
BLAM!

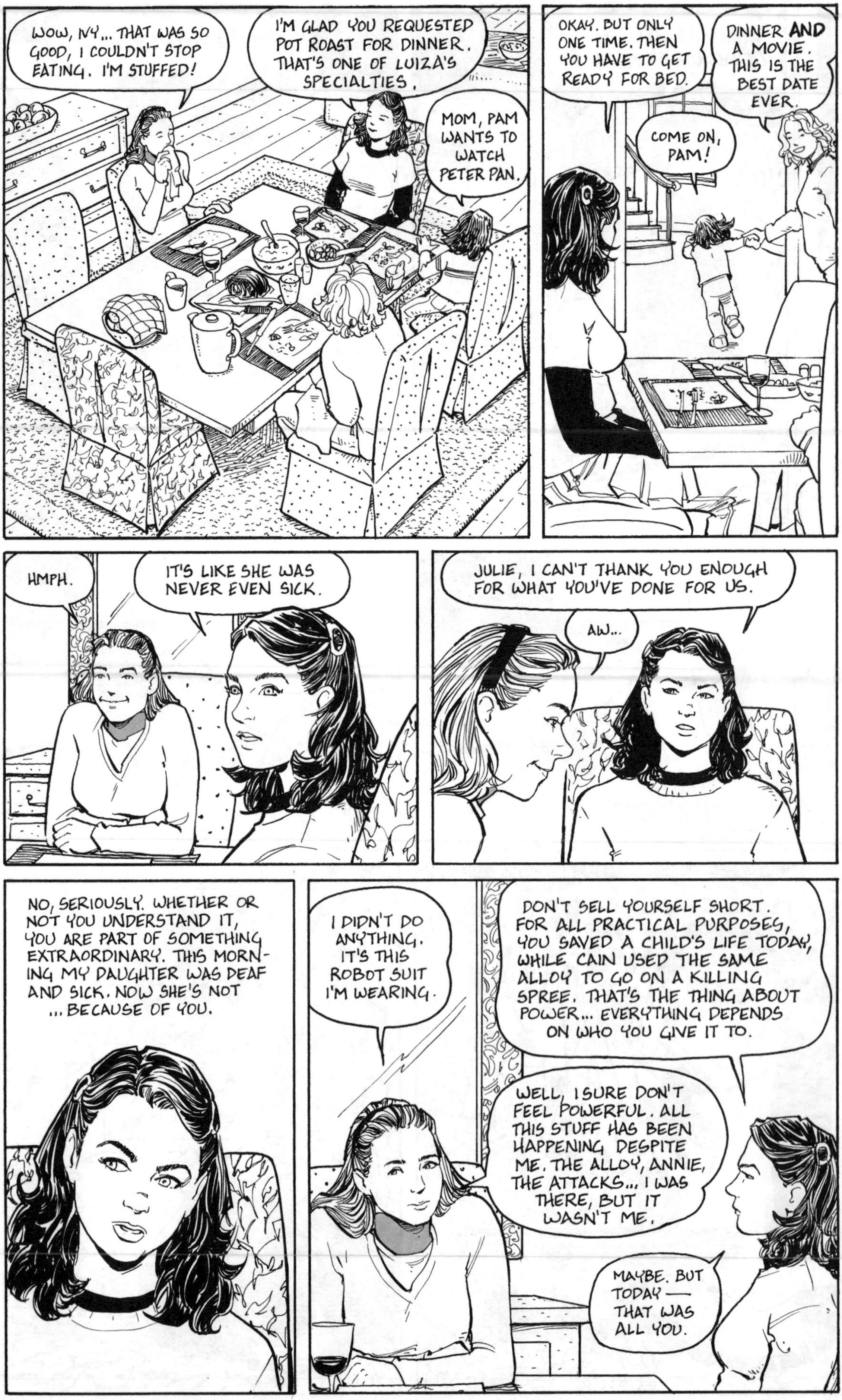
WOW, IVY... THAT WAS SO GOOD, I COULDN'T STOP EATING. I'M STUFFED!
I'M GLAD YOU REQUESTED POT ROAST FOR DINNER. THAT'S ONE OF LUIZA'S SPECIALTIES.
MOM, PAM WANTS TO WATCH PETER PAN.
OKAY. BUT ONLY ONE TIME. THEN YOU HAVE TO GET READY FOR BED.
DINNER **AND** A MOVIE. THIS IS THE BEST DATE EVER.
COME ON, PAM!
HMPH.
IT'S LIKE SHE WAS NEVER EVEN SICK.
JULIE, I CAN'T THANK YOU ENOUGH FOR WHAT YOU'VE DONE FOR US.
AW...
NO, SERIOUSLY. WHETHER OR NOT YOU UNDERSTAND IT, YOU ARE PART OF SOMETHING EXTRAORDINARY. THIS MORNING MY DAUGHTER WAS DEAF AND SICK. NOW SHE'S NOT ...BECAUSE OF YOU.
I DIDN'T DO ANYTHING. IT'S THIS ROBOT SUIT I'M WEARING.
DON'T SELL YOURSELF SHORT. FOR ALL PRACTICAL PURPOSES, YOU SAVED A CHILD'S LIFE TODAY, WHILE CAIN USED THE SAME ALLOY TO GO ON A KILLING SPREE. THAT'S THE THING ABOUT POWER... EVERYTHING DEPENDS ON WHO YOU GIVE IT TO.
WELL, I SURE DON'T FEEL POWERFUL. ALL THIS STUFF HAS BEEN HAPPENING DESPITE ME. THE ALLOY, ANNIE, THE ATTACKS... I WAS THERE, BUT IT WASN'T ME.
MAYBE. BUT TODAY — THAT WAS ALL YOU.

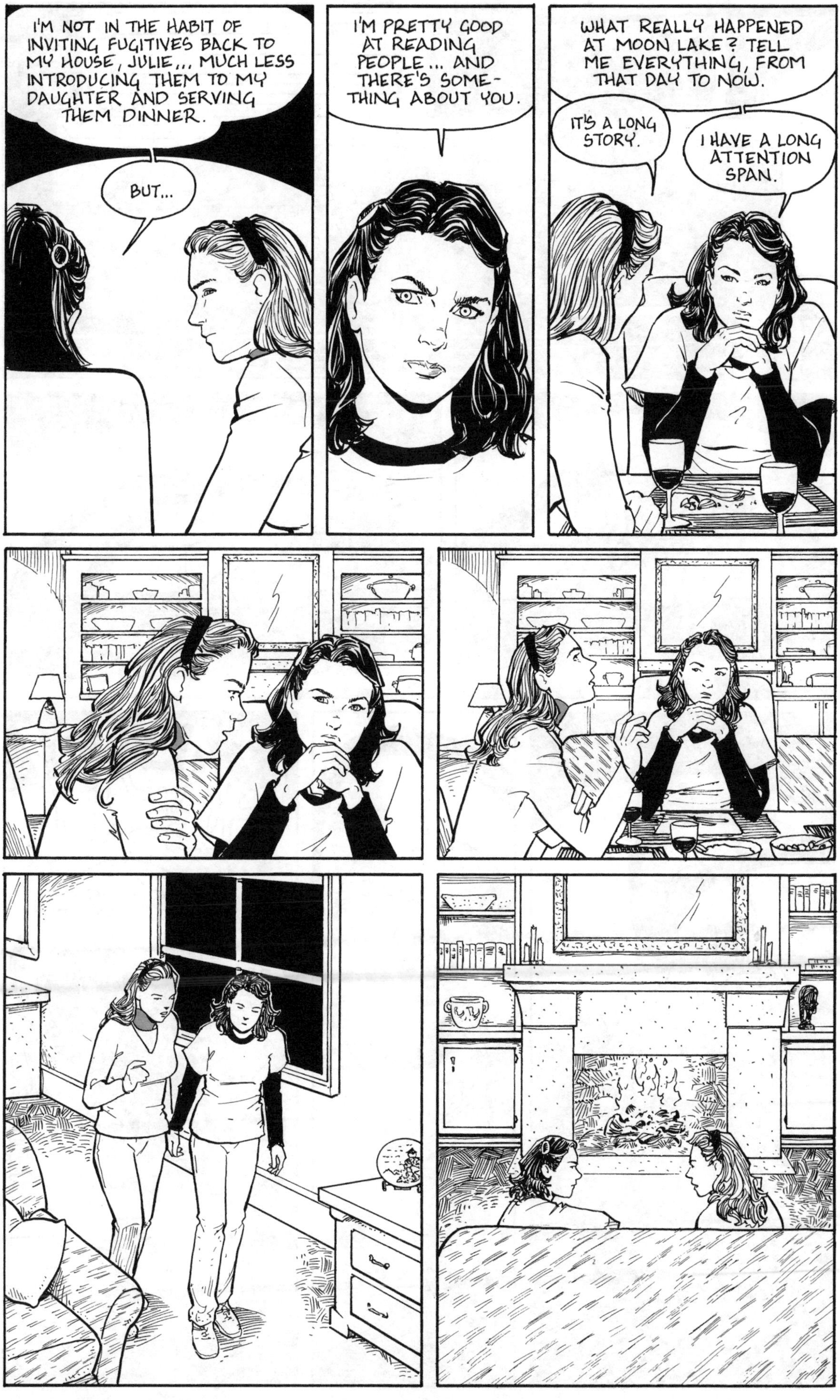
I'M NOT IN THE HABIT OF INVITING FUGITIVES BACK TO MY HOUSE, JULIE... MUCH LESS INTRODUCING THEM TO MY DAUGHTER AND SERVING THEM DINNER.
BUT...
I'M PRETTY GOOD AT READING PEOPLE... AND THERE'S SOMETHING ABOUT YOU.
WHAT REALLY HAPPENED AT MOON LAKE? TELL ME EVERYTHING, FROM THAT DAY TO NOW.
IT'S A LONG STORY.
I HAVE A LONG ATTENTION SPAN.

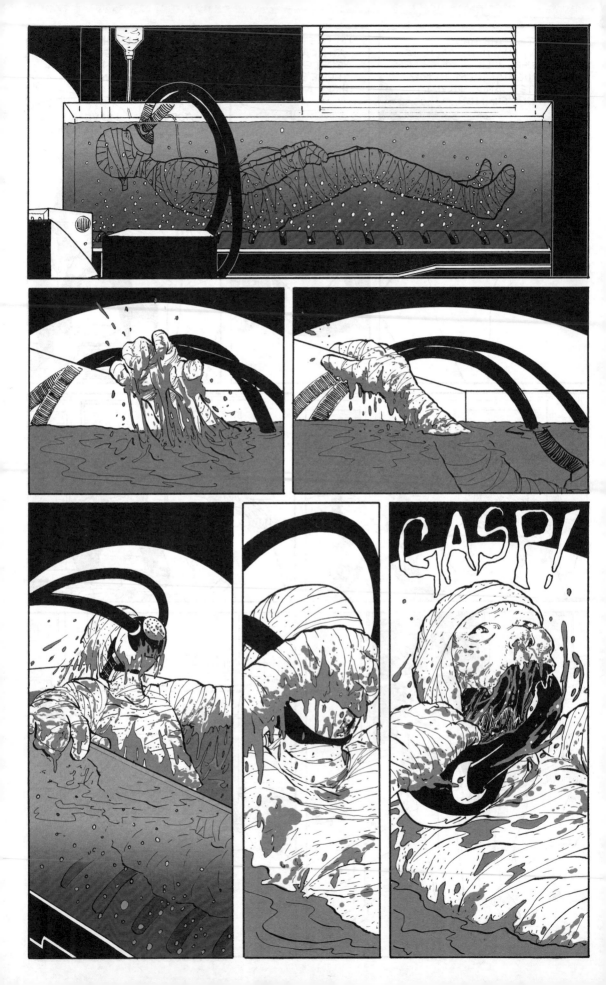

GASP!

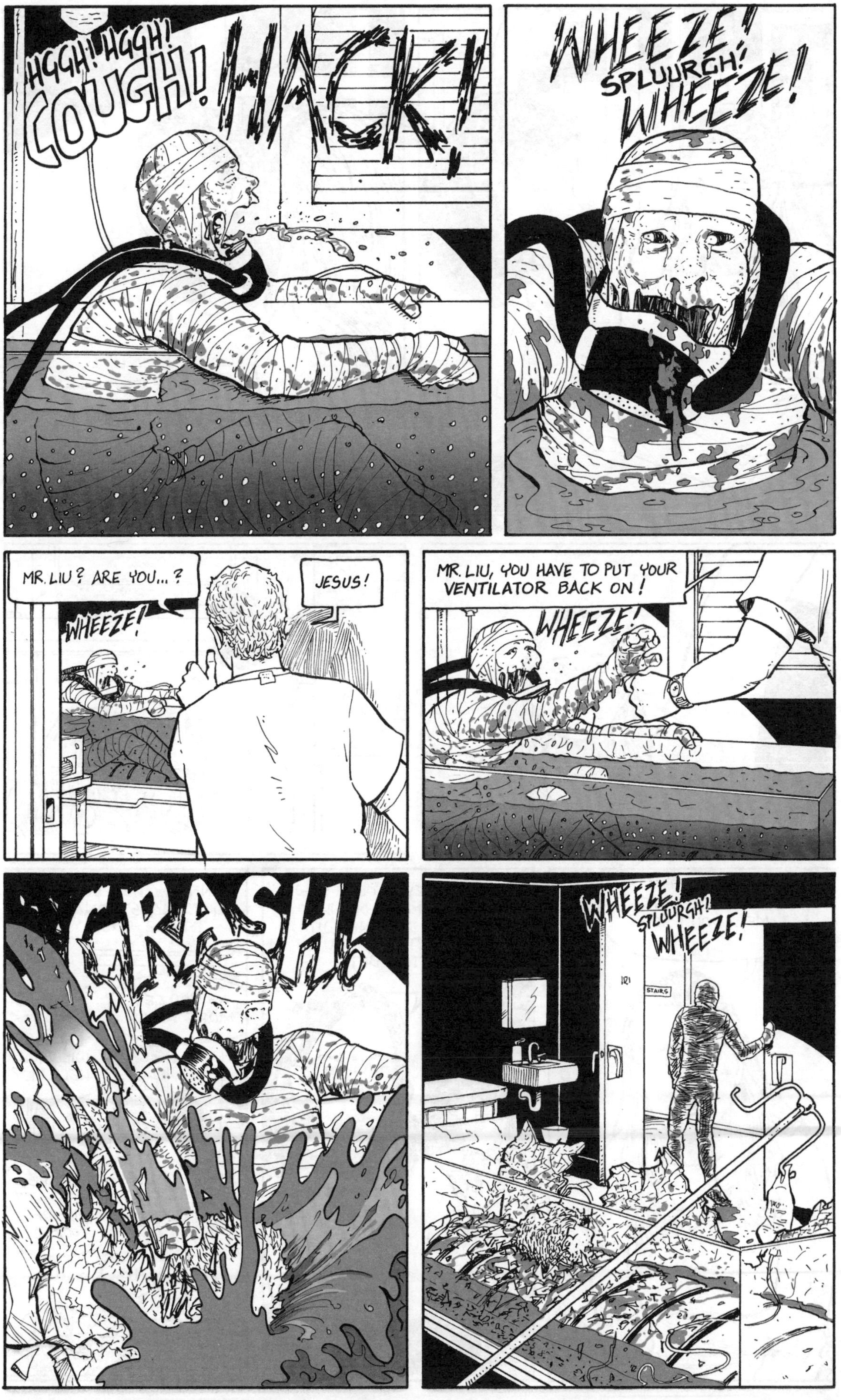
HGGH! HGGH!
COUGH!
HACK!
WHEEZE!
SPLUURGH!
WHEEZE!
MR. LIU? ARE YOU...?
WHEEZE!
JESUS!
MR. LIU, YOU HAVE TO PUT YOUR VENTILATOR BACK ON!
WHEEZE!
CRASH!
WHEEZE!
SPLUURGH!
WHEEZE!
STAIRS

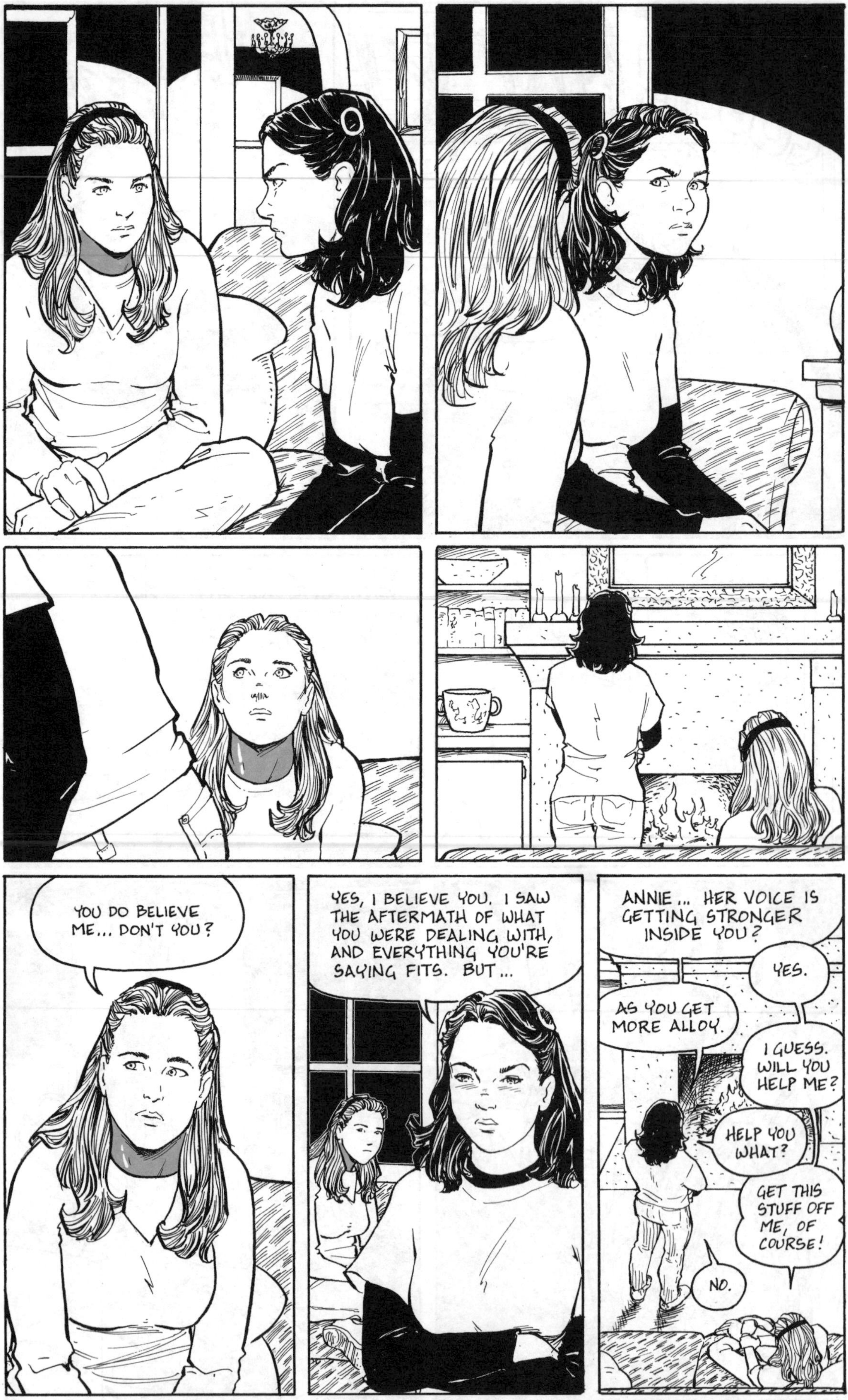
YOU DO BELIEVE ME... DON'T YOU?
YES, I BELIEVE YOU. I SAW THE AFTERMATH OF WHAT YOU WERE DEALING WITH, AND EVERYTHING YOU'RE SAYING FITS. BUT...
ANNIE... HER VOICE IS GETTING STRONGER INSIDE YOU?
YES.
AS YOU GET MORE ALLOY.
I GUESS. WILL YOU HELP ME?
HELP YOU WHAT?
GET THIS STUFF OFF ME, OF COURSE!
NO.

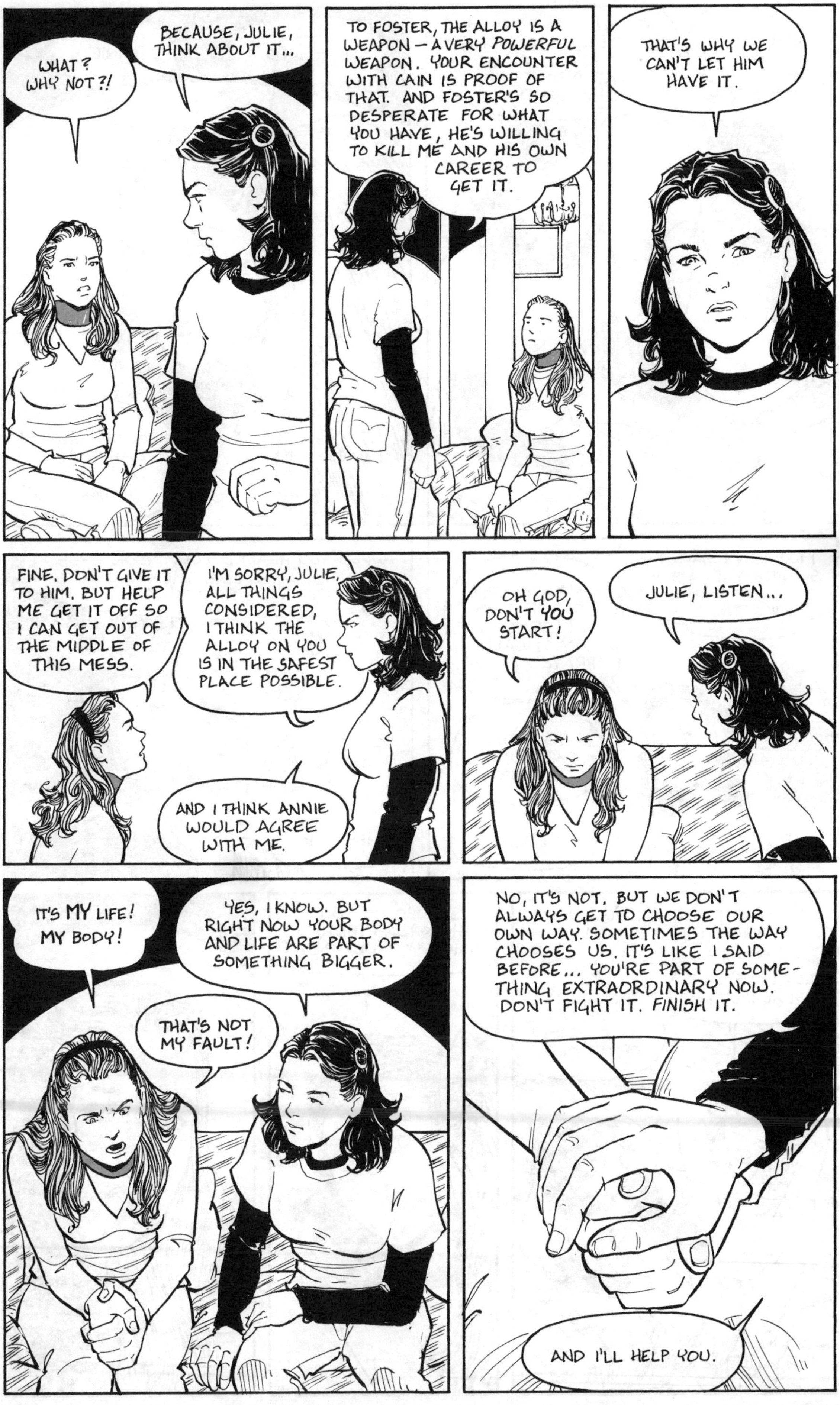

WHAT? WHY NOT?!
BECAUSE, JULIE, THINK ABOUT IT...
TO FOSTER, THE ALLOY IS A WEAPON — A VERY POWERFUL WEAPON. YOUR ENCOUNTER WITH CAIN IS PROOF OF THAT. AND FOSTER'S SO DESPERATE FOR WHAT YOU HAVE, HE'S WILLING TO KILL ME AND HIS OWN CAREER TO GET IT.
THAT'S WHY WE CAN'T LET HIM HAVE IT.
FINE. DON'T GIVE IT TO HIM. BUT HELP ME GET IT OFF SO I CAN GET OUT OF THE MIDDLE OF THIS MESS.
I'M SORRY, JULIE, ALL THINGS CONSIDERED, I THINK THE ALLOY ON YOU IS IN THE SAFEST PLACE POSSIBLE.
AND I THINK ANNIE WOULD AGREE WITH ME.
OH GOD, DON'T YOU START!
JULIE, LISTEN...
IT'S MY LIFE! MY BODY!
YES, I KNOW. BUT RIGHT NOW YOUR BODY AND LIFE ARE PART OF SOMETHING BIGGER.
THAT'S NOT MY FAULT!
NO, IT'S NOT. BUT WE DON'T ALWAYS GET TO CHOOSE OUR OWN WAY. SOMETIMES THE WAY CHOOSES US. IT'S LIKE I SAID BEFORE... YOU'RE PART OF SOMETHING EXTRAORDINARY NOW. DON'T FIGHT IT. FINISH IT.
AND I'LL HELP YOU.

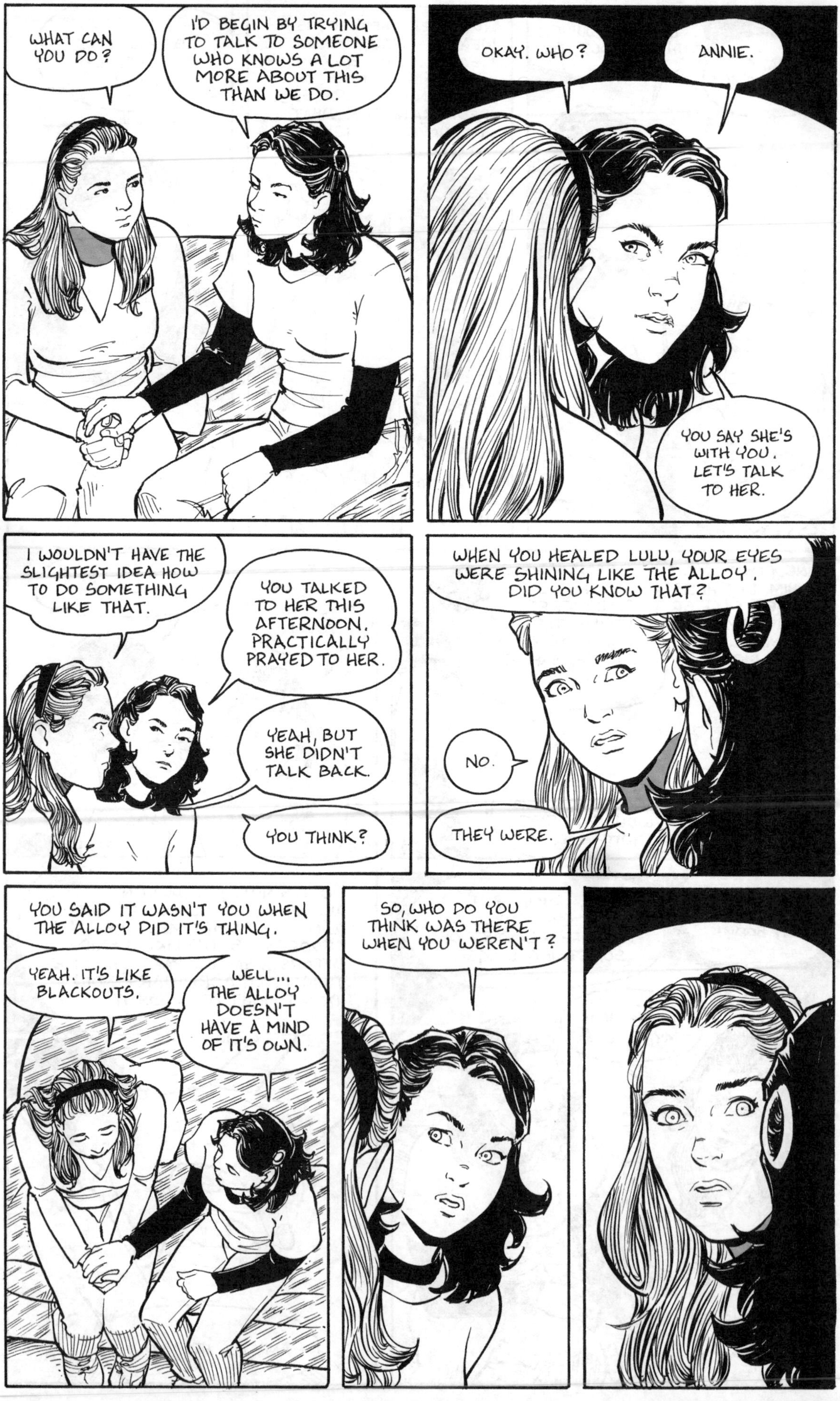
WHAT CAN YOU DO?
I'D BEGIN BY TRYING TO TALK TO SOMEONE WHO KNOWS A LOT MORE ABOUT THIS THAN WE DO.
OKAY. WHO?
ANNIE.
YOU SAY SHE'S WITH YOU. LET'S TALK TO HER.
I WOULDN'T HAVE THE SLIGHTEST IDEA HOW TO DO SOMETHING LIKE THAT.
YOU TALKED TO HER THIS AFTERNOON. PRACTICALLY PRAYED TO HER.
YEAH, BUT SHE DIDN'T TALK BACK.
YOU THINK?
WHEN YOU HEALED LULU, YOUR EYES WERE SHINING LIKE THE ALLOY. DID YOU KNOW THAT?
NO.
THEY WERE.
YOU SAID IT WASN'T YOU WHEN THE ALLOY DID IT'S THING.
YEAH. IT'S LIKE BLACKOUTS.
WELL... THE ALLOY DOESN'T HAVE A MIND OF IT'S OWN.
SO, WHO DO YOU THINK WAS THERE WHEN YOU WEREN'T?

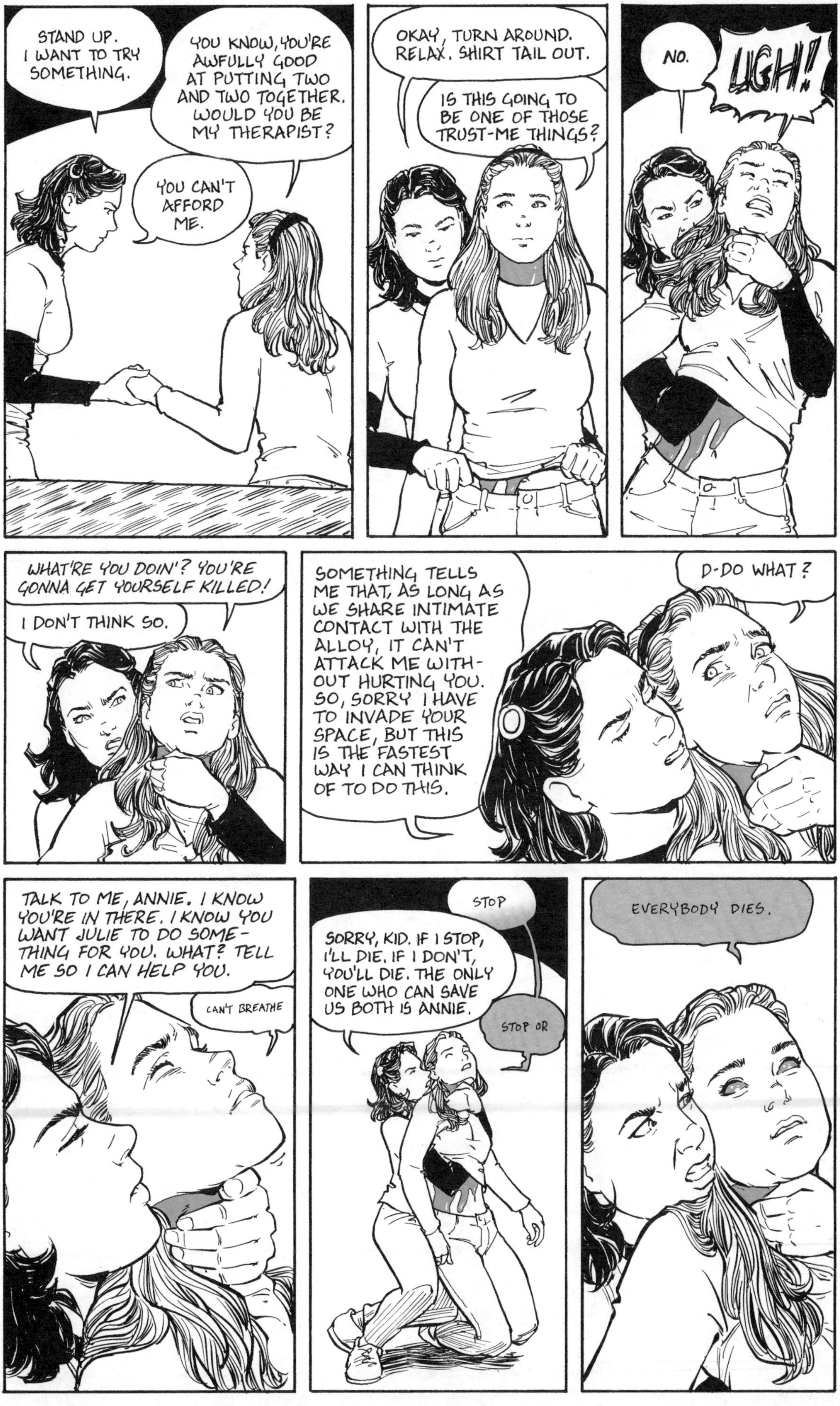
STAND UP. I WANT TO TRY SOMETHING.
YOU KNOW, YOU'RE AWFULLY GOOD AT PUTTING TWO AND TWO TOGETHER. WOULD YOU BE MY THERAPIST?
YOU CAN'T AFFORD ME.
OKAY, TURN AROUND. RELAX. SHIRT TAIL OUT.
IS THIS GOING TO BE ONE OF THOSE TRUST-ME THINGS?
NO.
UGH!
WHAT'RE YOU DOIN'? YOU'RE GONNA GET YOURSELF KILLED!
I DON'T THINK SO.
SOMETHING TELLS ME THAT, AS LONG AS WE SHARE INTIMATE CONTACT WITH THE ALLOY, IT CAN'T ATTACK ME WITH-OUT HURTING YOU. SO, SORRY I HAVE TO INVADE YOUR SPACE, BUT THIS IS THE FASTEST WAY I CAN THINK OF TO DO THIS.
D-DO WHAT?
TALK TO ME, ANNIE. I KNOW YOU'RE IN THERE. I KNOW YOU WANT JULIE TO DO SOME-THING FOR YOU. WHAT? TELL ME SO I CAN HELP YOU.
CAN'T BREATHE
STOP
SORRY, KID. IF I STOP, I'LL DIE. IF I DON'T, YOU'LL DIE. THE ONLY ONE WHO CAN SAVE US BOTH IS ANNIE.
STOP OR
EVERYBODY DIES.

"There is no hunting like the hunting of man,
and those who have hunted armed men long
enough and liked it, never care for anything
else thereafter."
—Ernest Hemingway

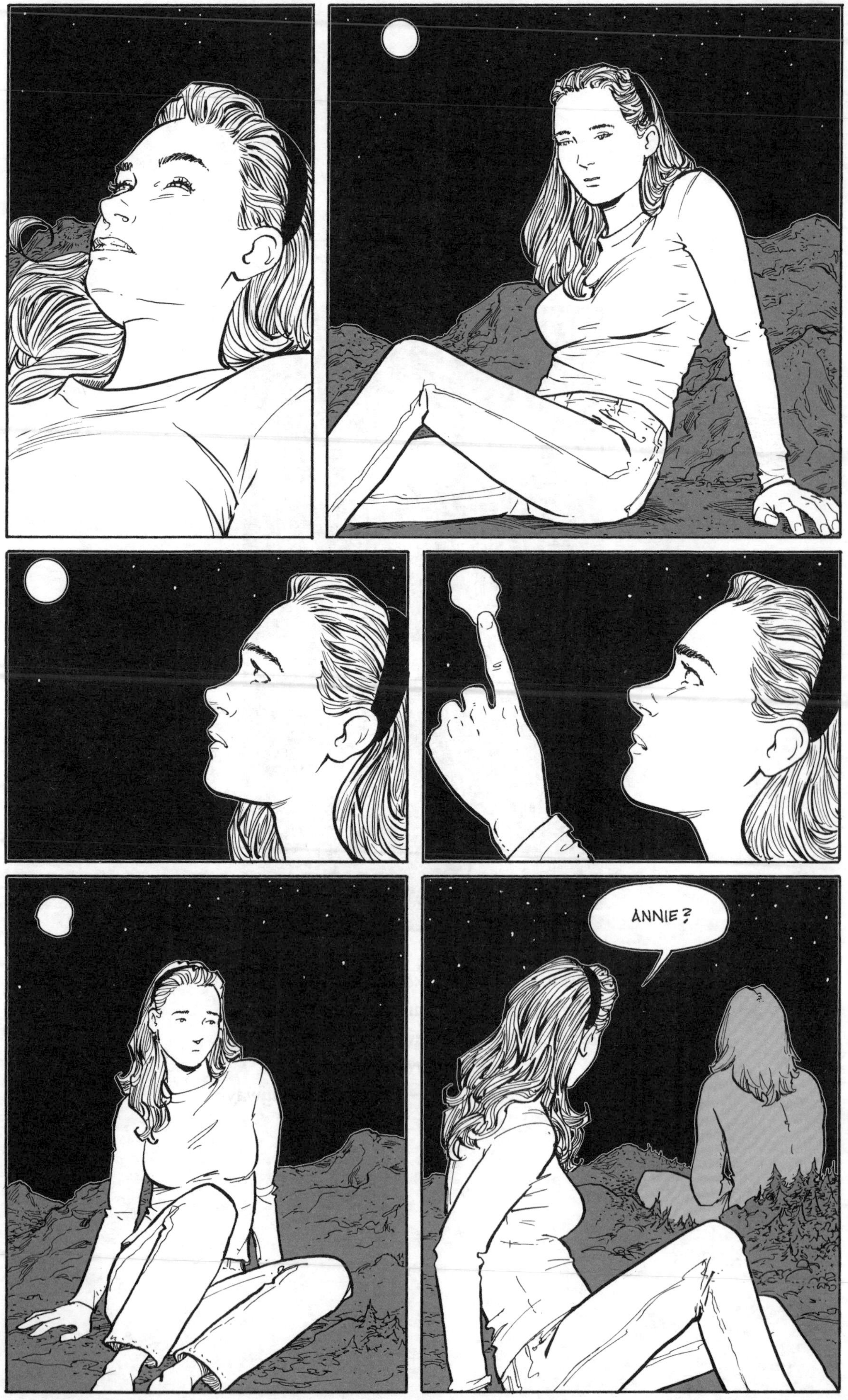
ANNIE?

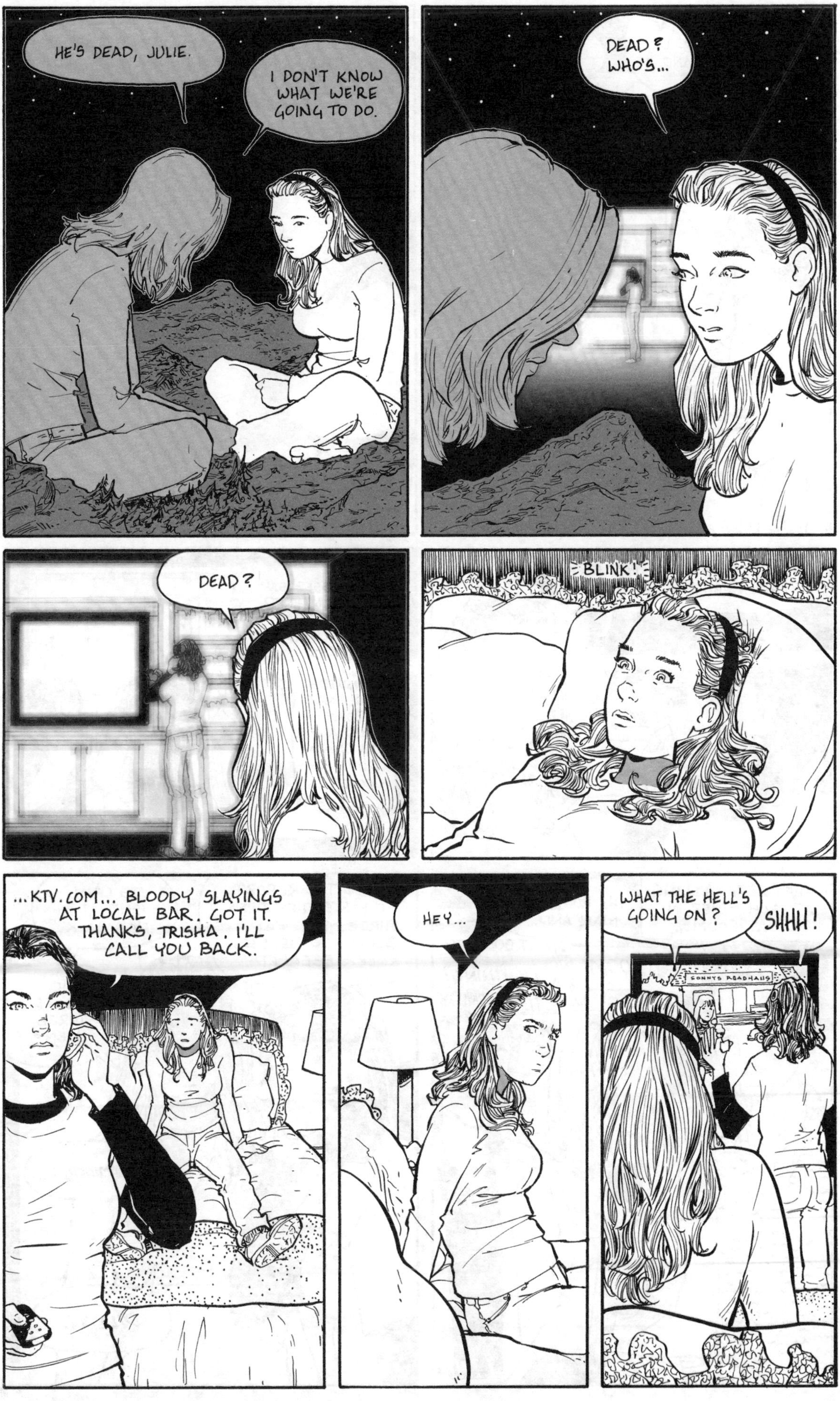
HE'S DEAD, JULIE.
I DON'T KNOW WHAT WE'RE GOING TO DO.
DEAD? WHO'S...
DEAD?
BLINK!
...KTV.COM... BLOODY SLAYINGS AT LOCAL BAR. GOT IT. THANKS, TRISHA. I'LL CALL YOU BACK.
HEY...
WHAT THE HELL'S GOING ON?
SHHH!
SONNYS ROADHAUS

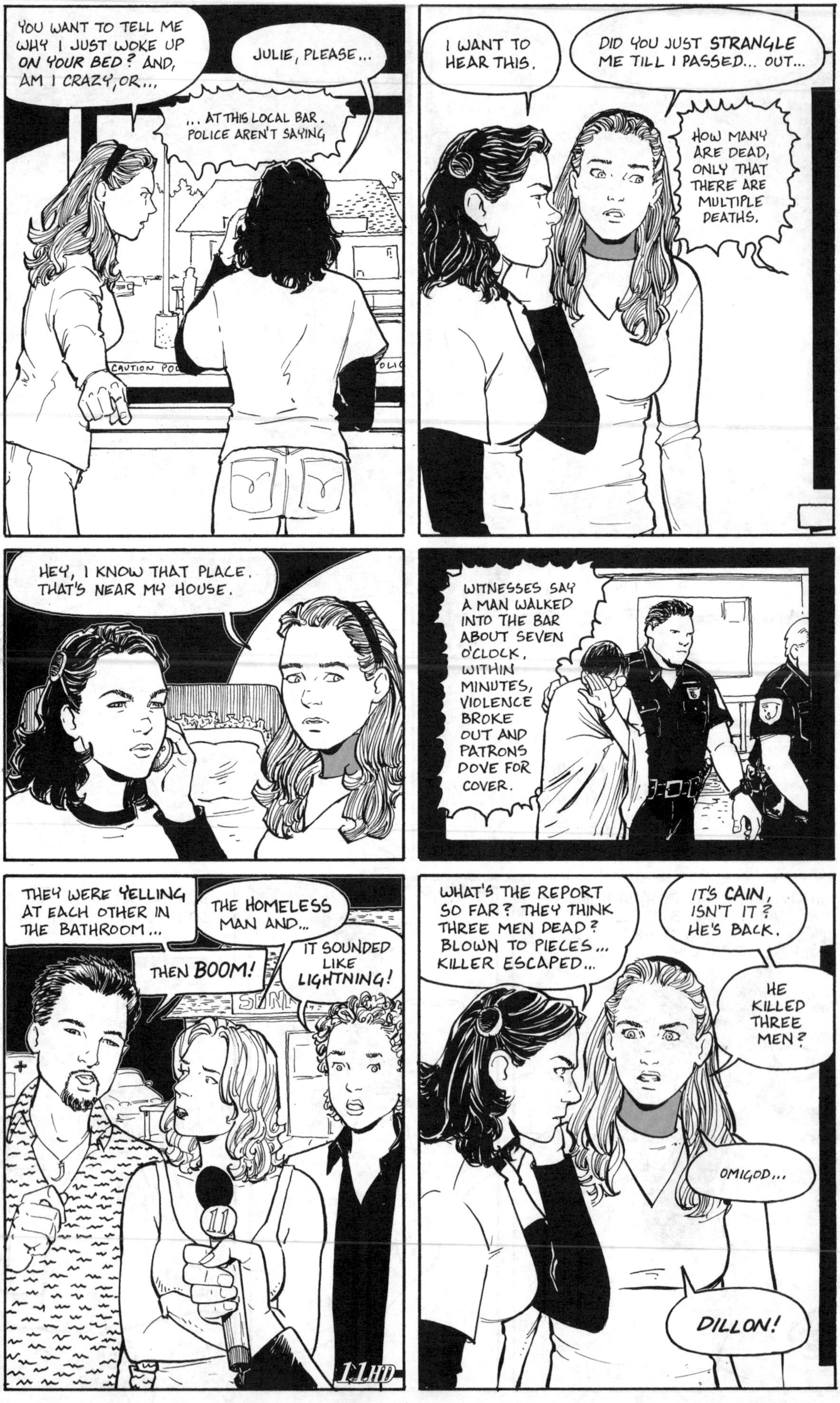
YOU WANT TO TELL ME WHY I JUST WOKE UP ON YOUR BED? AND, AM I CRAZY, OR...
JULIE, PLEASE...
... AT THIS LOCAL BAR. POLICE AREN'T SAYING
CAUTION PO
I WANT TO HEAR THIS.
DID YOU JUST STRANGLE ME TILL I PASSED... OUT...
HOW MANY ARE DEAD, ONLY THAT THERE ARE MULTIPLE DEATHS.
HEY, I KNOW THAT PLACE. THAT'S NEAR MY HOUSE.
WITNESSES SAY A MAN WALKED INTO THE BAR ABOUT SEVEN O'CLOCK. WITHIN MINUTES, VIOLENCE BROKE OUT AND PATRONS DOVE FOR COVER.
THEY WERE YELLING AT EACH OTHER IN THE BATHROOM...
THE HOMELESS MAN AND...
THEN BOOM!
IT SOUNDED LIKE LIGHTNING!
11
11HD
WHAT'S THE REPORT SO FAR? THEY THINK THREE MEN DEAD? BLOWN TO PIECES... KILLER ESCAPED...
IT'S CAIN, ISN'T IT? HE'S BACK.
HE KILLED THREE MEN?
OMIGOD...
DILLON!

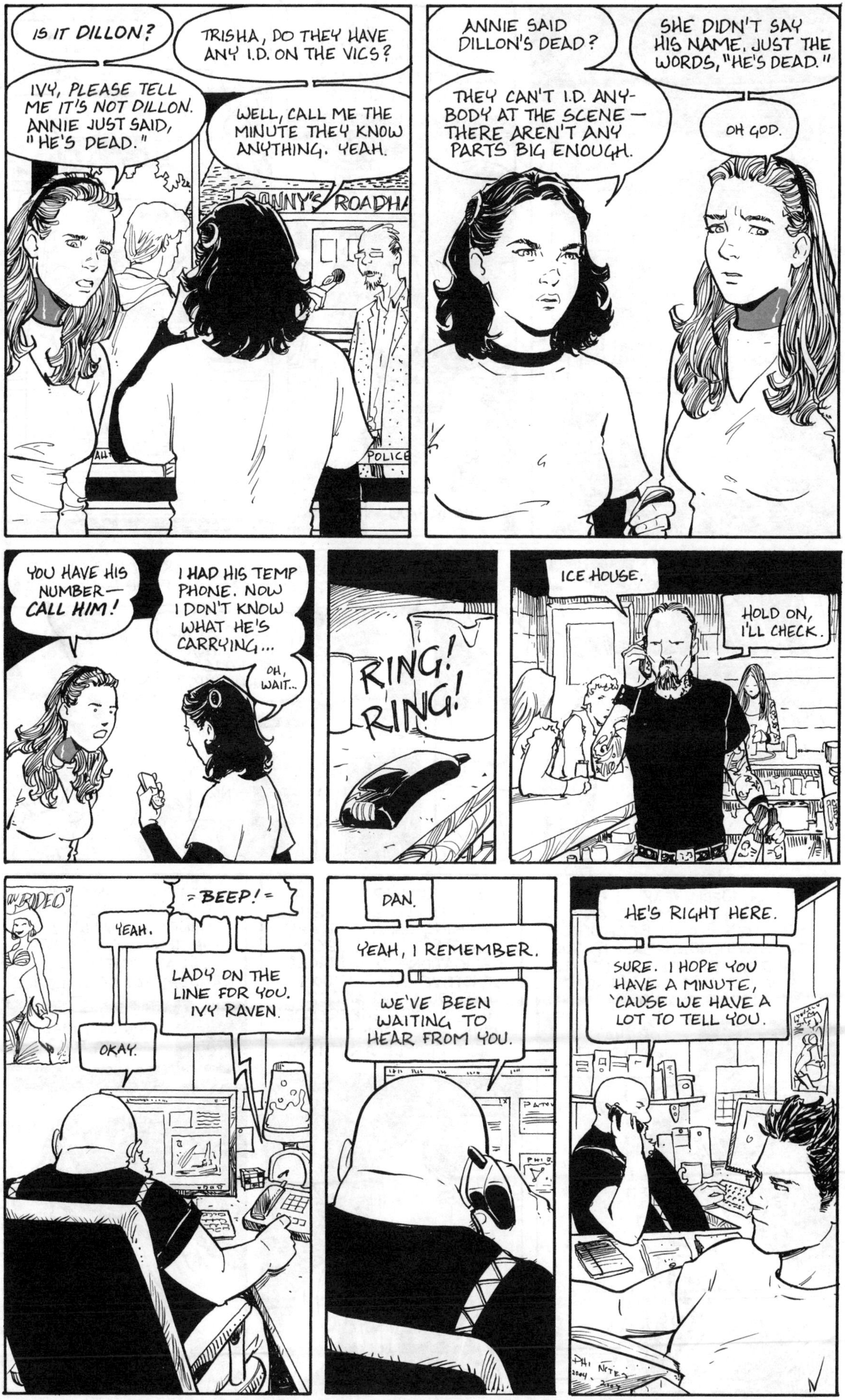
IS IT DILLON?
IVY, PLEASE TELL ME IT'S NOT DILLON. ANNIE JUST SAID, "HE'S DEAD."
TRISHA, DO THEY HAVE ANY I.D. ON THE VICS?
WELL, CALL ME THE MINUTE THEY KNOW ANYTHING. YEAH.
POLICE
ANNIE SAID DILLON'S DEAD?
THEY CAN'T I.D. ANYBODY AT THE SCENE — THERE AREN'T ANY PARTS BIG ENOUGH.
SHE DIDN'T SAY HIS NAME, JUST THE WORDS, "HE'S DEAD."
OH GOD.
YOU HAVE HIS NUMBER— CALL HIM!
I HAD HIS TEMP PHONE. NOW I DON'T KNOW WHAT HE'S CARRYING...
OH, WAIT...
RING! RING!
ICE HOUSE.
HOLD ON, I'LL CHECK.
YEAH.
=BEEP!=
LADY ON THE LINE FOR YOU. IVY RAVEN.
OKAY.
DAN.
YEAH, I REMEMBER.
WE'VE BEEN WAITING TO HEAR FROM YOU.
HE'S RIGHT HERE.
SURE. I HOPE YOU HAVE A MINUTE, 'CAUSE WE HAVE A LOT TO TELL YOU.

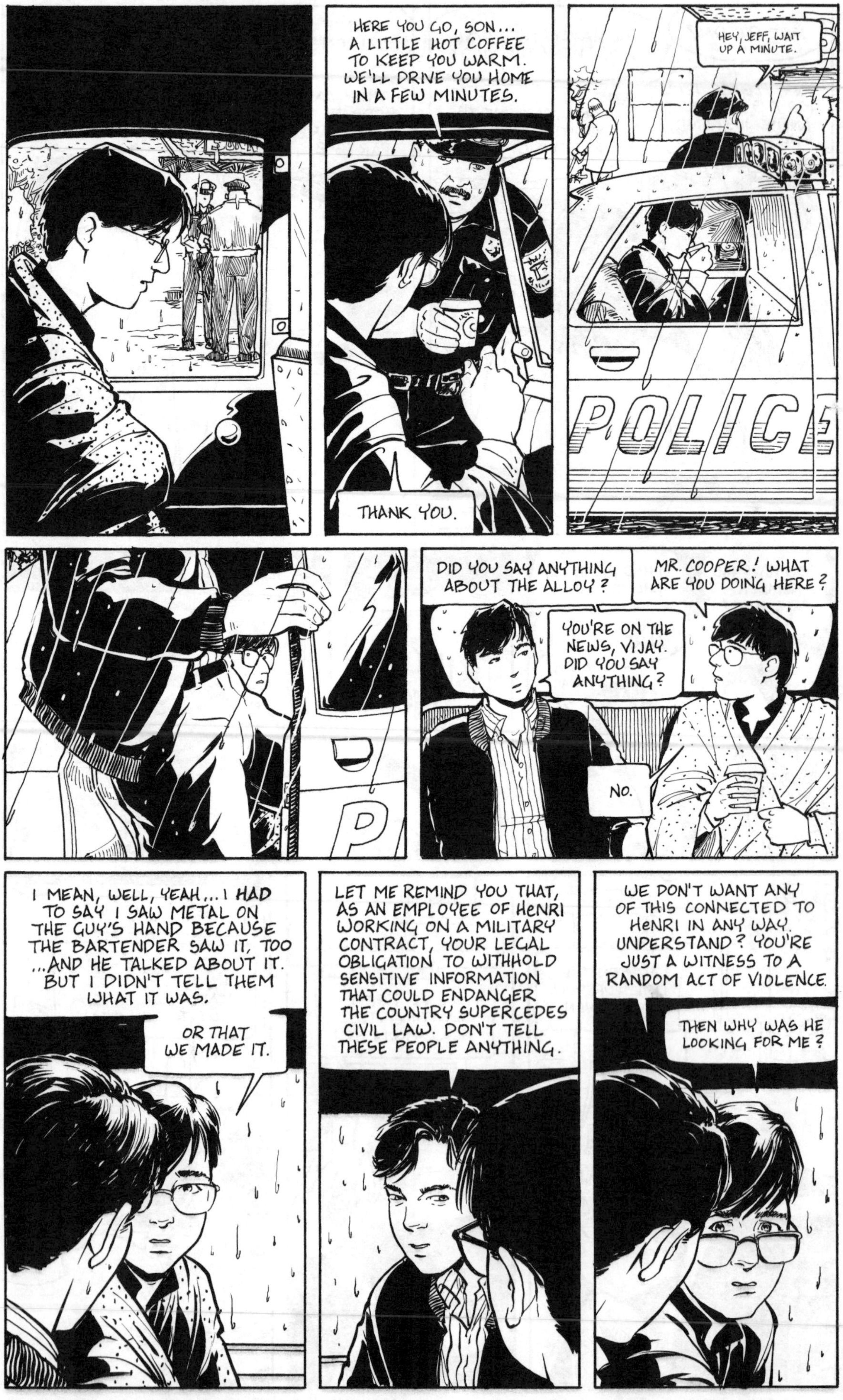
HERE YOU GO, SON... A LITTLE HOT COFFEE TO KEEP YOU WARM. WE'LL DRIVE YOU HOME IN A FEW MINUTES.
THANK YOU.
HEY, JEFF, WAIT UP A MINUTE.
POLICE
P
MR. COOPER! WHAT ARE YOU DOING HERE?
DID YOU SAY ANYTHING ABOUT THE ALLOY?
YOU'RE ON THE NEWS, VIJAY. DID YOU SAY ANYTHING?
NO.
I MEAN, WELL, YEAH... I HAD TO SAY I SAW METAL ON THE GUY'S HAND BECAUSE THE BARTENDER SAW IT, TOO ...AND HE TALKED ABOUT IT. BUT I DIDN'T TELL THEM WHAT IT WAS.
OR THAT WE MADE IT.
LET ME REMIND YOU THAT, AS AN EMPLOYEE OF HeNRI WORKING ON A MILITARY CONTRACT, YOUR LEGAL OBLIGATION TO WITHHOLD SENSITIVE INFORMATION THAT COULD ENDANGER THE COUNTRY SUPERCEDES CIVIL LAW. DON'T TELL THESE PEOPLE ANYTHING.
WE DON'T WANT ANY OF THIS CONNECTED TO HeNRI IN ANY WAY. UNDERSTAND? YOU'RE JUST A WITNESS TO A RANDOM ACT OF VIOLENCE.
THEN WHY WAS HE LOOKING FOR ME?

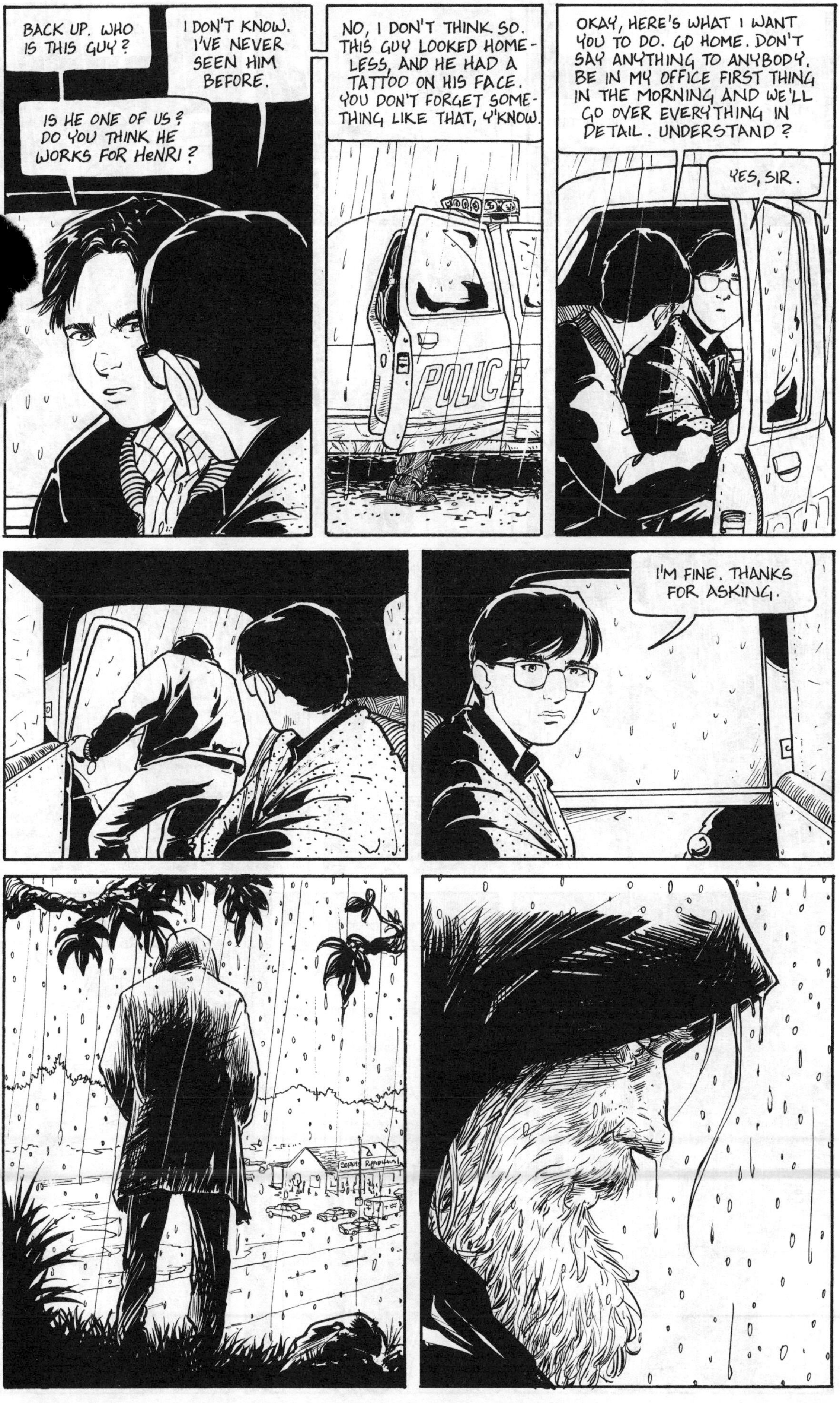
BACK UP. WHO IS THIS GUY?
IS HE ONE OF US? DO YOU THINK HE WORKS FOR HENRI?
I DON'T KNOW. I'VE NEVER SEEN HIM BEFORE.
NO, I DON'T THINK SO. THIS GUY LOOKED HOMELESS, AND HE HAD A TATTOO ON HIS FACE. YOU DON'T FORGET SOMETHING LIKE THAT, Y'KNOW.
POLICE
OKAY, HERE'S WHAT I WANT YOU TO DO. GO HOME. DON'T SAY ANYTHING TO ANYBODY. BE IN MY OFFICE FIRST THING IN THE MORNING AND WE'LL GO OVER EVERYTHING IN DETAIL. UNDERSTAND?
YES, SIR.
I'M FINE. THANKS FOR ASKING.

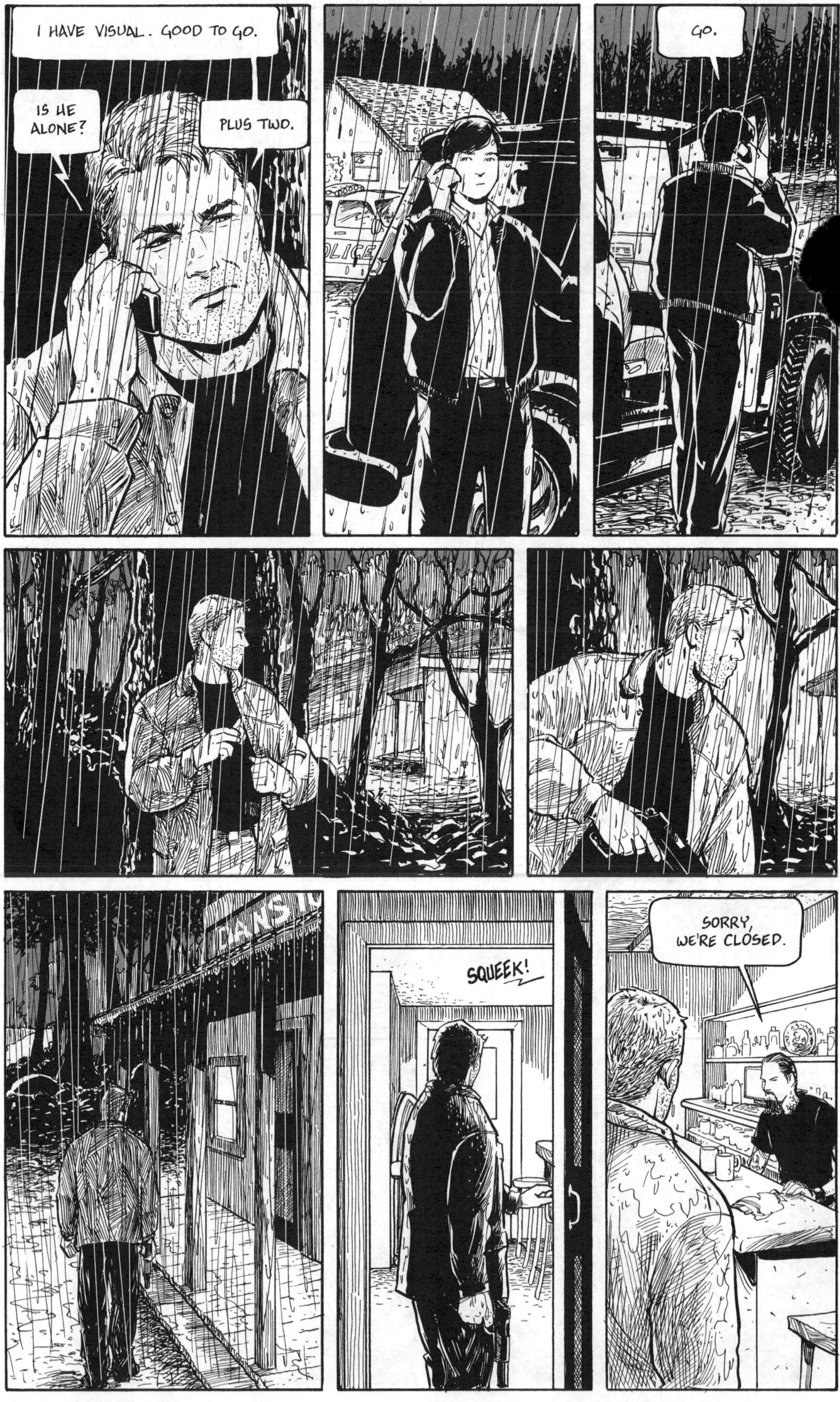
I HAVE VISUAL. GOOD TO GO.
IS HE ALONE?
PLUS TWO.
GO.
SQUEEK!
SORRY, WE'RE CLOSED.

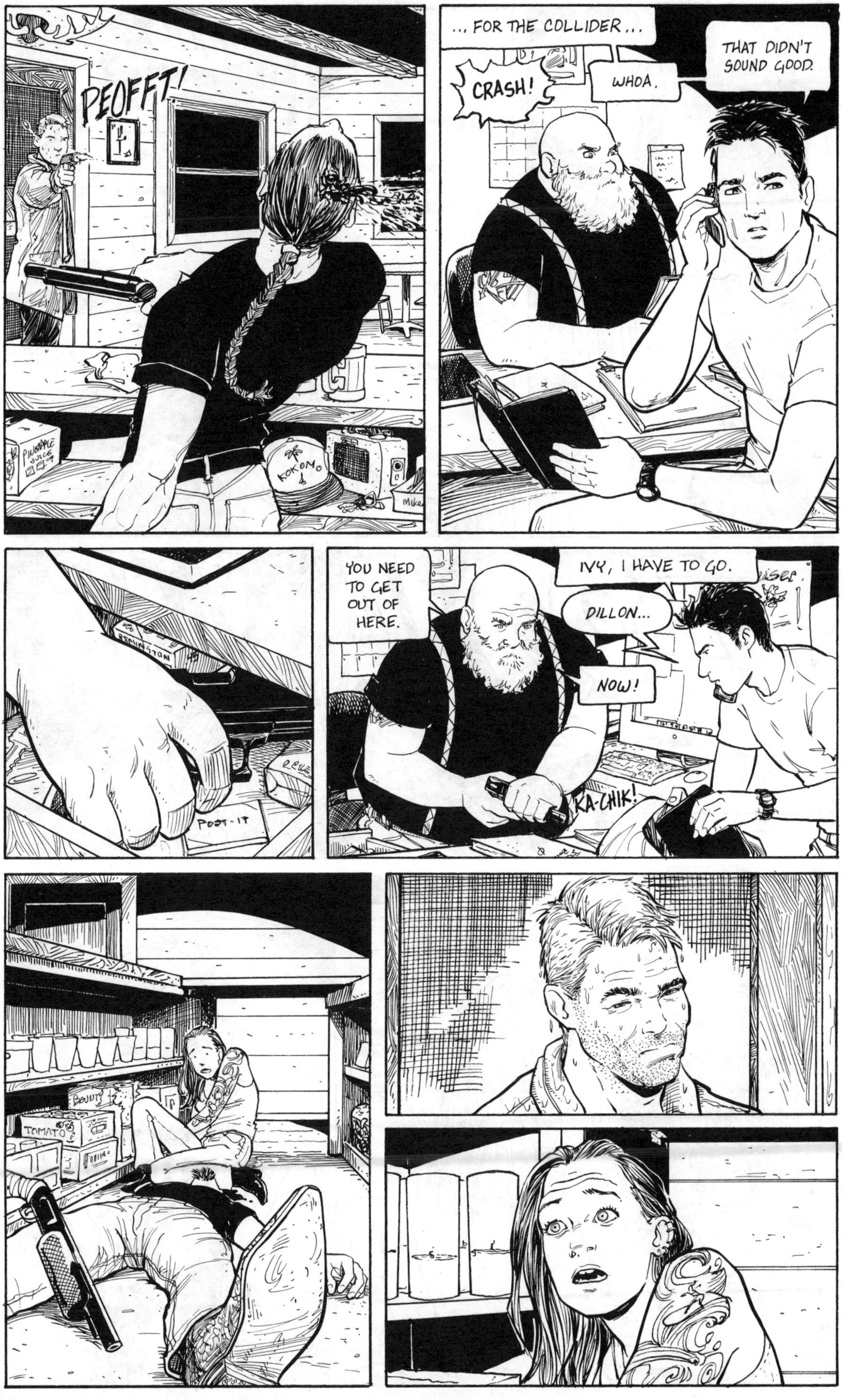
PEOFFT!
PINEAPPLE JUICE
KOKOMO
Mike
... FOR THE COLLIDER ...
CRASH!
WHOA.
THAT DIDN'T SOUND GOOD.
REMINGTON
POST-IT
YOU NEED TO GET OUT OF HERE.
IVY, I HAVE TO GO.
DILLON...
NOW!
KA-CHIK!
TOMATO

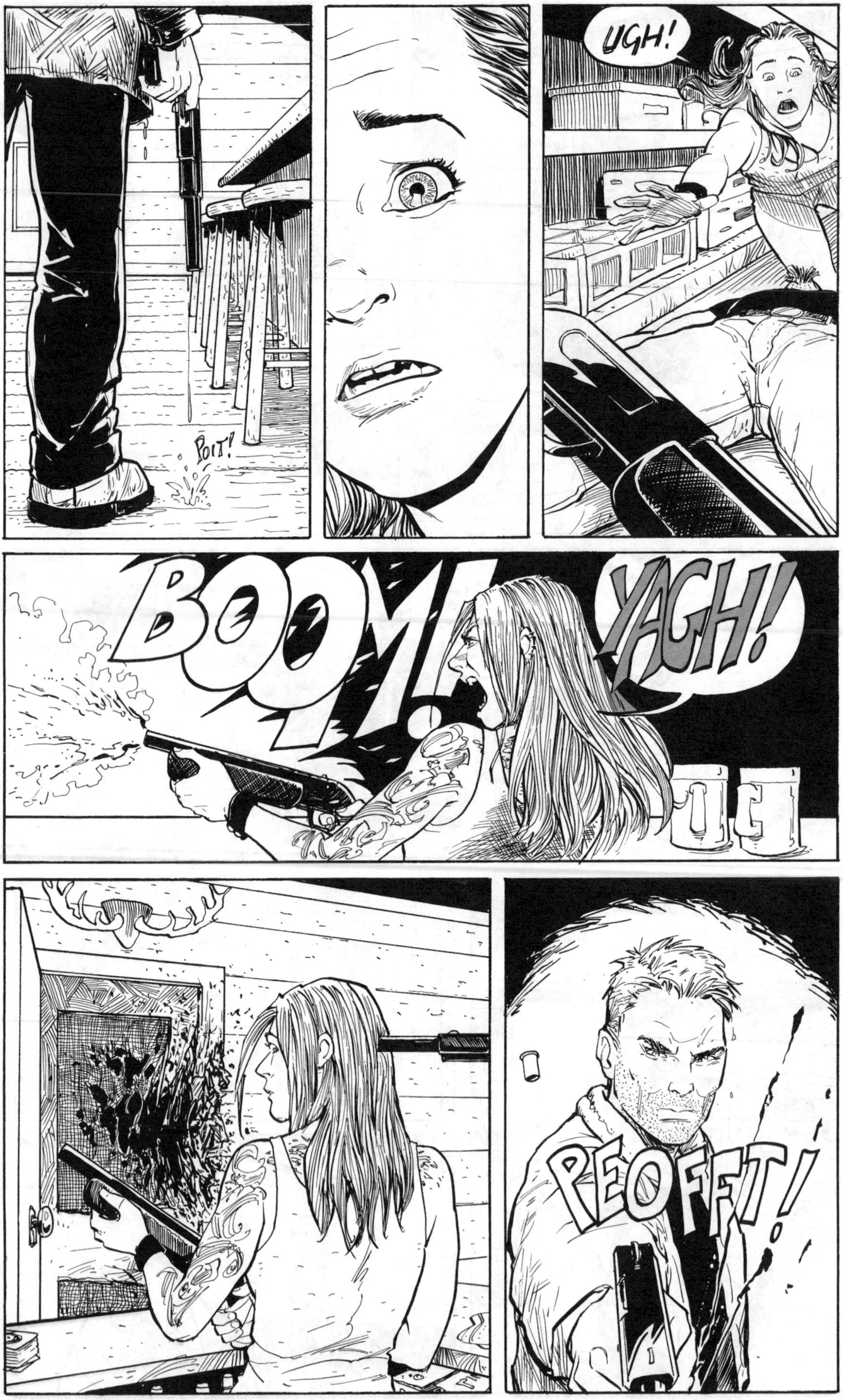
POIT!
UGH!
BOOM!
YAGH!
PEOFFT!

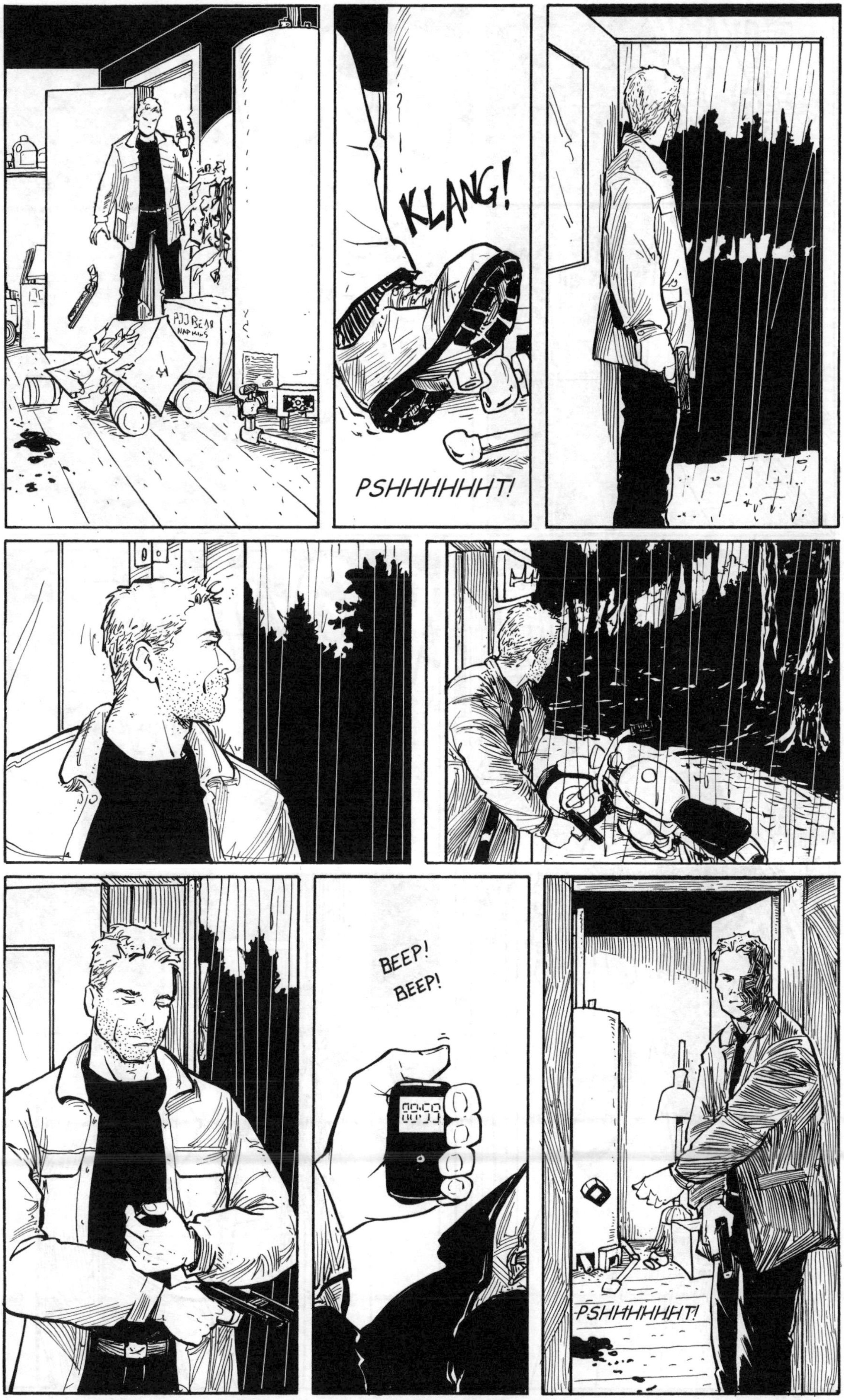
KLANG!
PSHHHHHHT!
BEEP!
BEEP!
PSHHHHHHT!

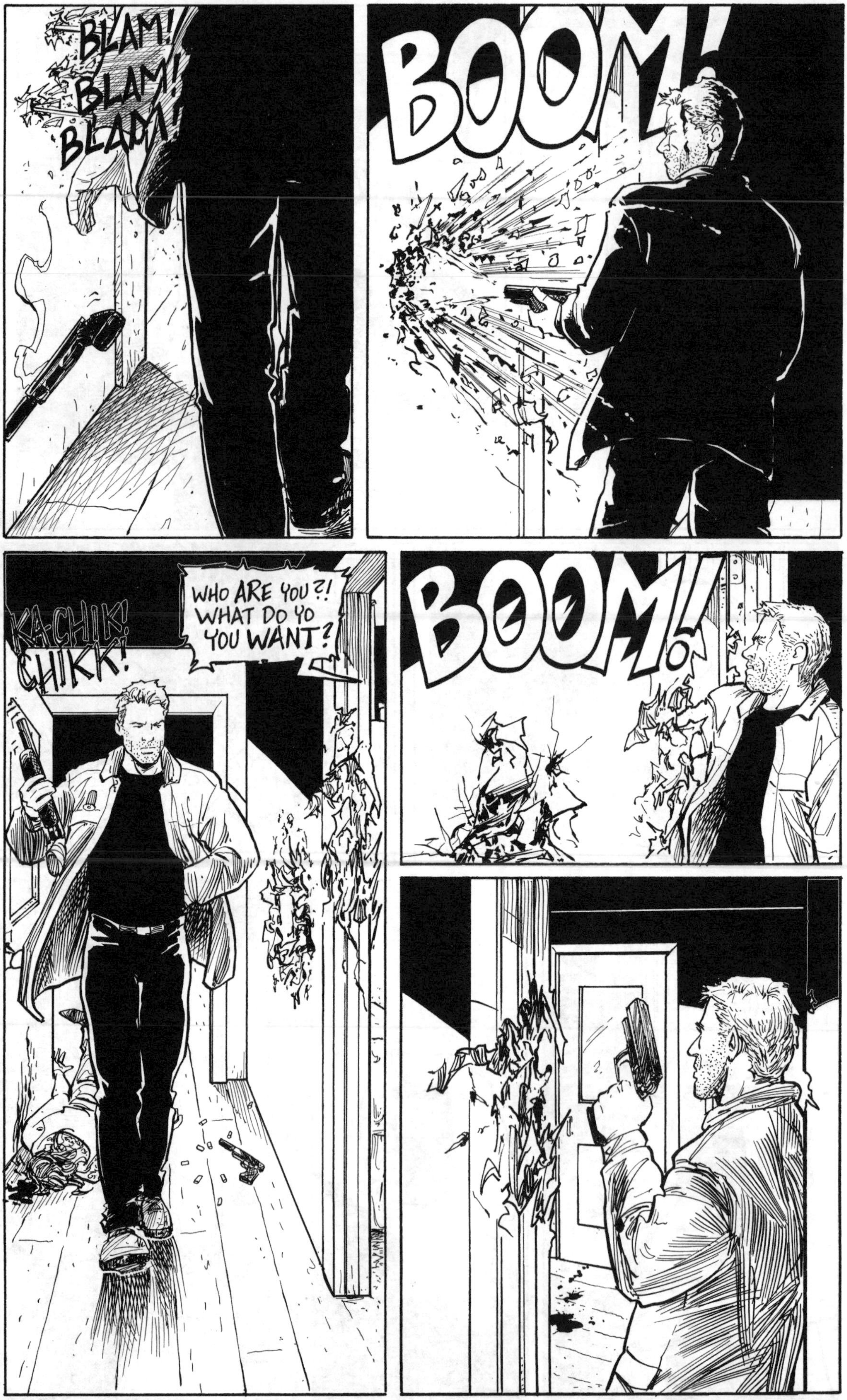
BLAM!
BLAM!
BLAM!
BOOM!
KA-CHIK!
CHIKK!
WHO ARE YOU?!
WHAT DO YO
YOU WANT?
BOOM!

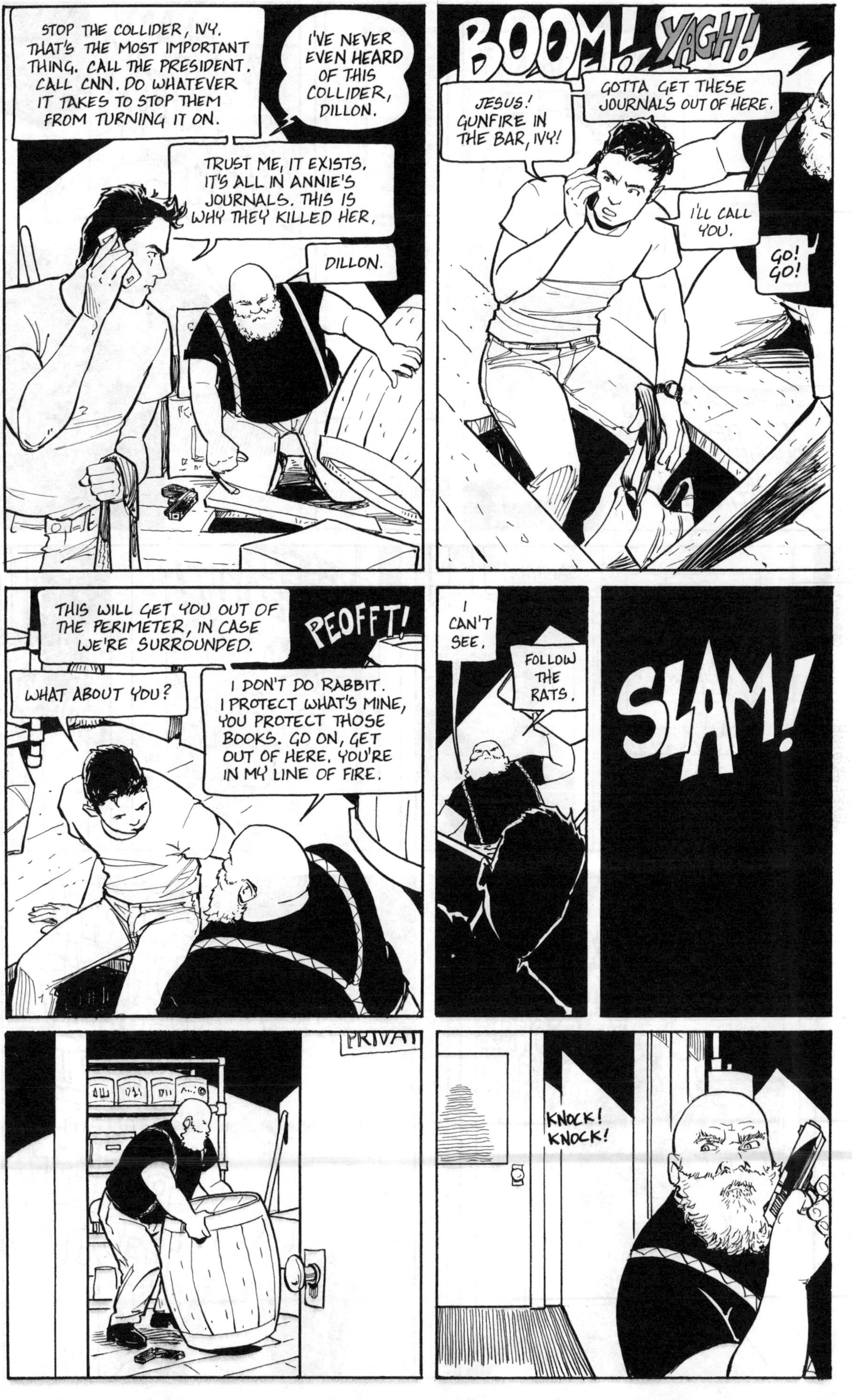
STOP THE COLLIDER, IVY. THAT'S THE MOST IMPORTANT THING. CALL THE PRESIDENT. CALL CNN. DO WHATEVER IT TAKES TO STOP THEM FROM TURNING IT ON.
I'VE NEVER EVEN HEARD OF THIS COLLIDER, DILLON.
TRUST ME, IT EXISTS. IT'S ALL IN ANNIE'S JOURNALS. THIS IS WHY THEY KILLED HER.
DILLON.
BOOM!
YAGH!
JESUS! GUNFIRE IN THE BAR, IVY!
GOTTA GET THESE JOURNALS OUT OF HERE.
I'LL CALL YOU.
GO! GO!
THIS WILL GET YOU OUT OF THE PERIMETER, IN CASE WE'RE SURROUNDED.
PEOFFT!
WHAT ABOUT YOU?
I DON'T DO RABBIT. I PROTECT WHAT'S MINE, YOU PROTECT THOSE BOOKS. GO ON, GET OUT OF HERE. YOU'RE IN MY LINE OF FIRE.
I CAN'T SEE.
FOLLOW THE RATS.
SLAM!
PRIVAT
KNOCK! KNOCK!

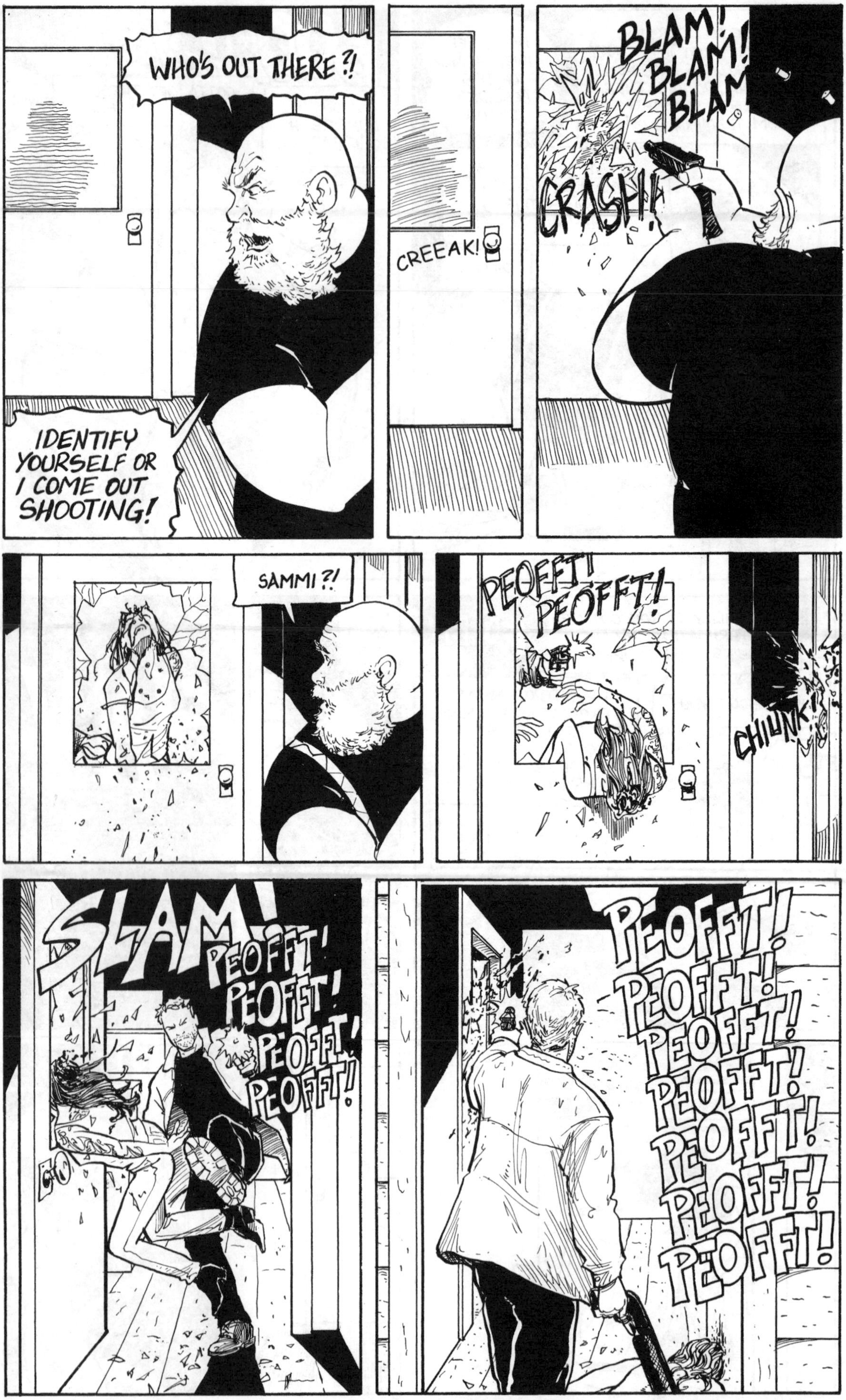
WHO'S OUT THERE ?!
IDENTIFY YOURSELF OR I COME OUT SHOOTING!
CREEAK!
BLAM! BLAM! BLAM!
CRASH!
SAMMI ?!
PEOFFT! PEOFFT!
CHUNK!
SLAM!
PEOFFT! PEOFFT! PEOFFT! PEOFFT!
PEOFFT! PEOFFT! PEOFFT! PEOFFT! PEOFFT! PEOFFT! PEOFFT!

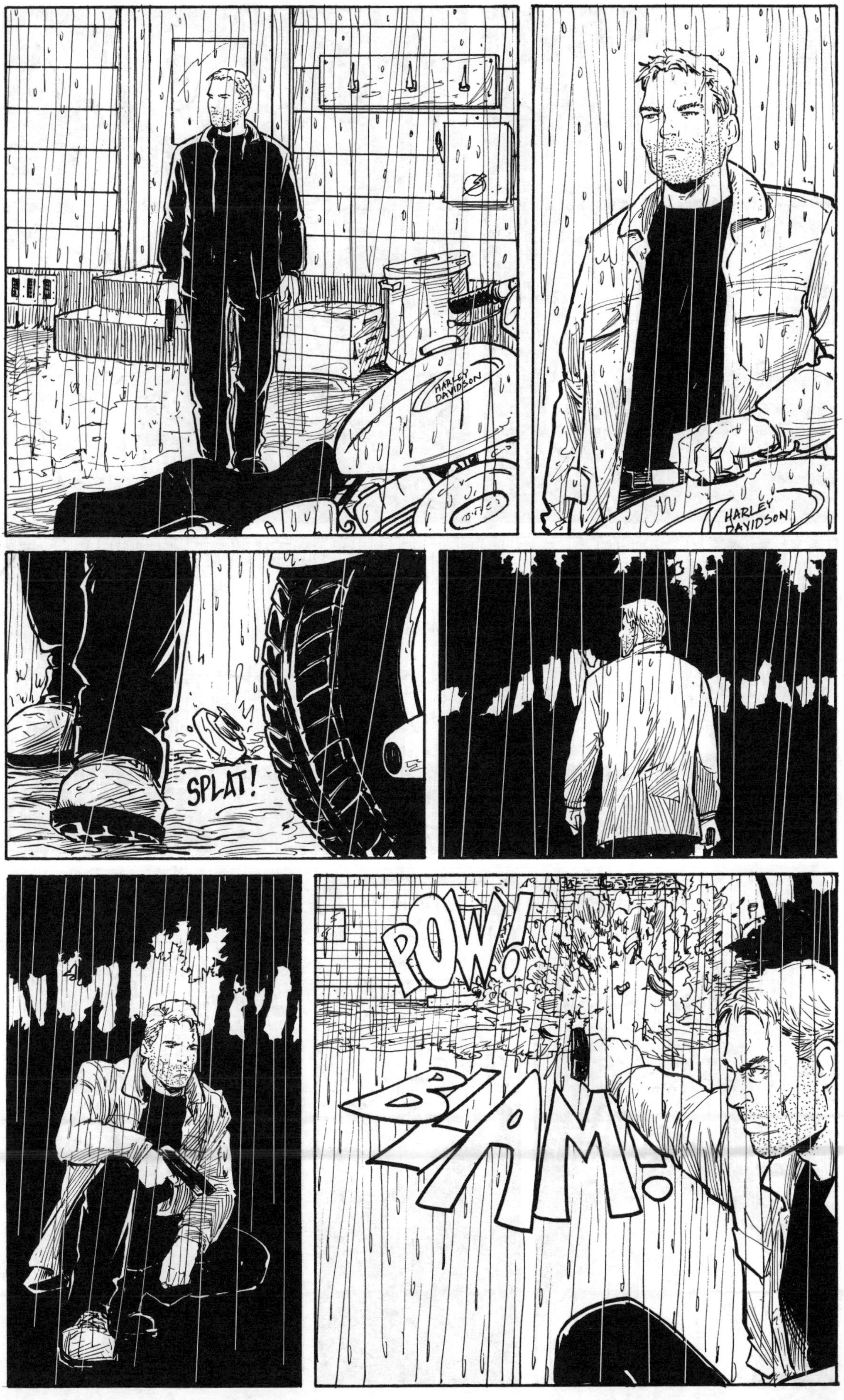
HARLEY DAVIDSON
HARLEY DAVIDSON
SPLAT!
POW!
BLAM!

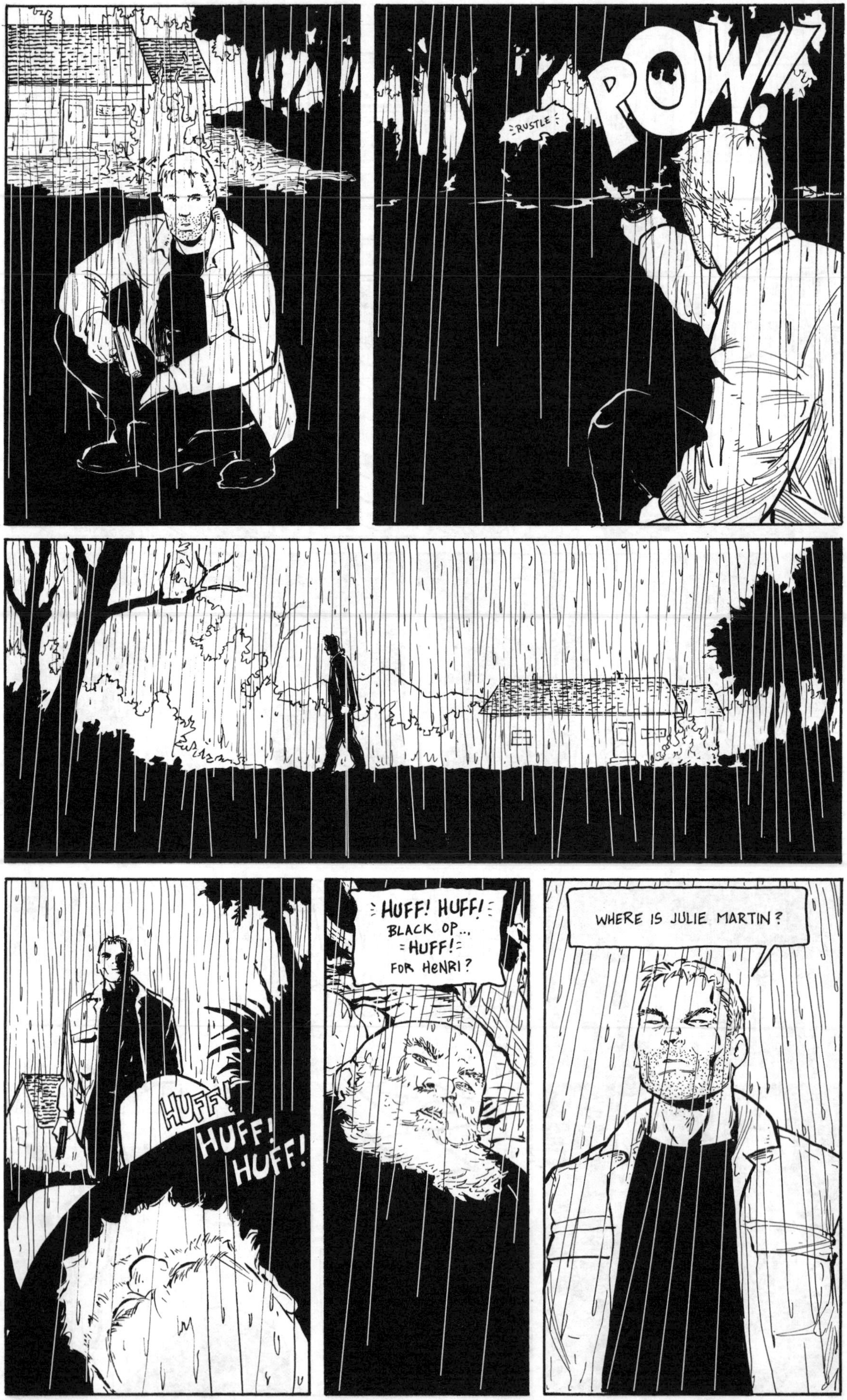
RUSTLE
POW!!
HUFF!
HUFF!
HUFF!
HUFF! HUFF!
BLACK OP...
HUFF!
FOR HENRI?
WHERE IS JULIE MARTIN?

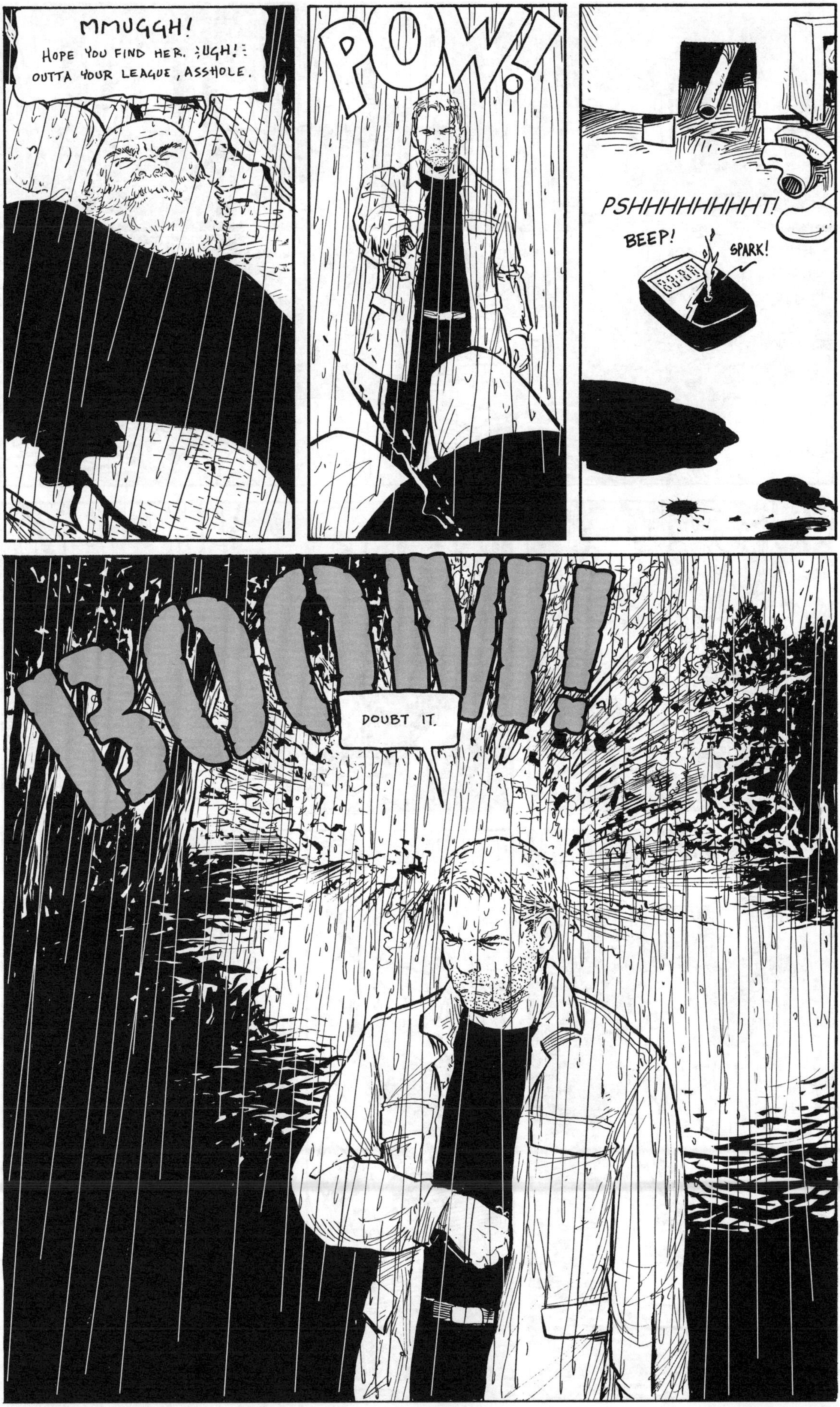
MMUGGH!
HOPE YOU FIND HER. ¡UGH!
OUTTA YOUR LEAGUE, ASSHOLE.
POW!
PSHHHHHHHHT!
BEEP!
SPARK!
BOOM!
DOUBT IT.

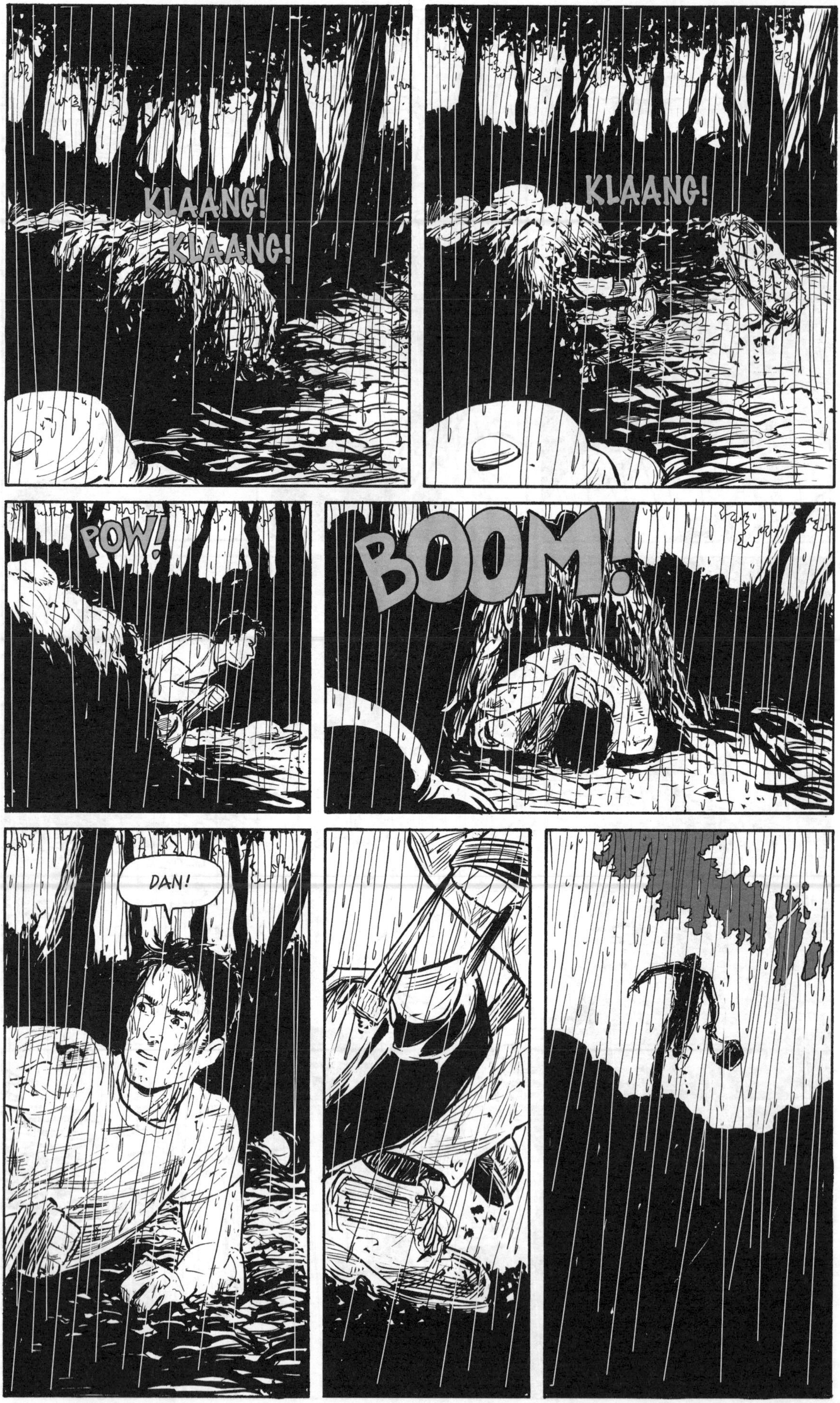
KLAANG!
KLAANG!
KLAANG!
POW!
BOOM!
DAN!

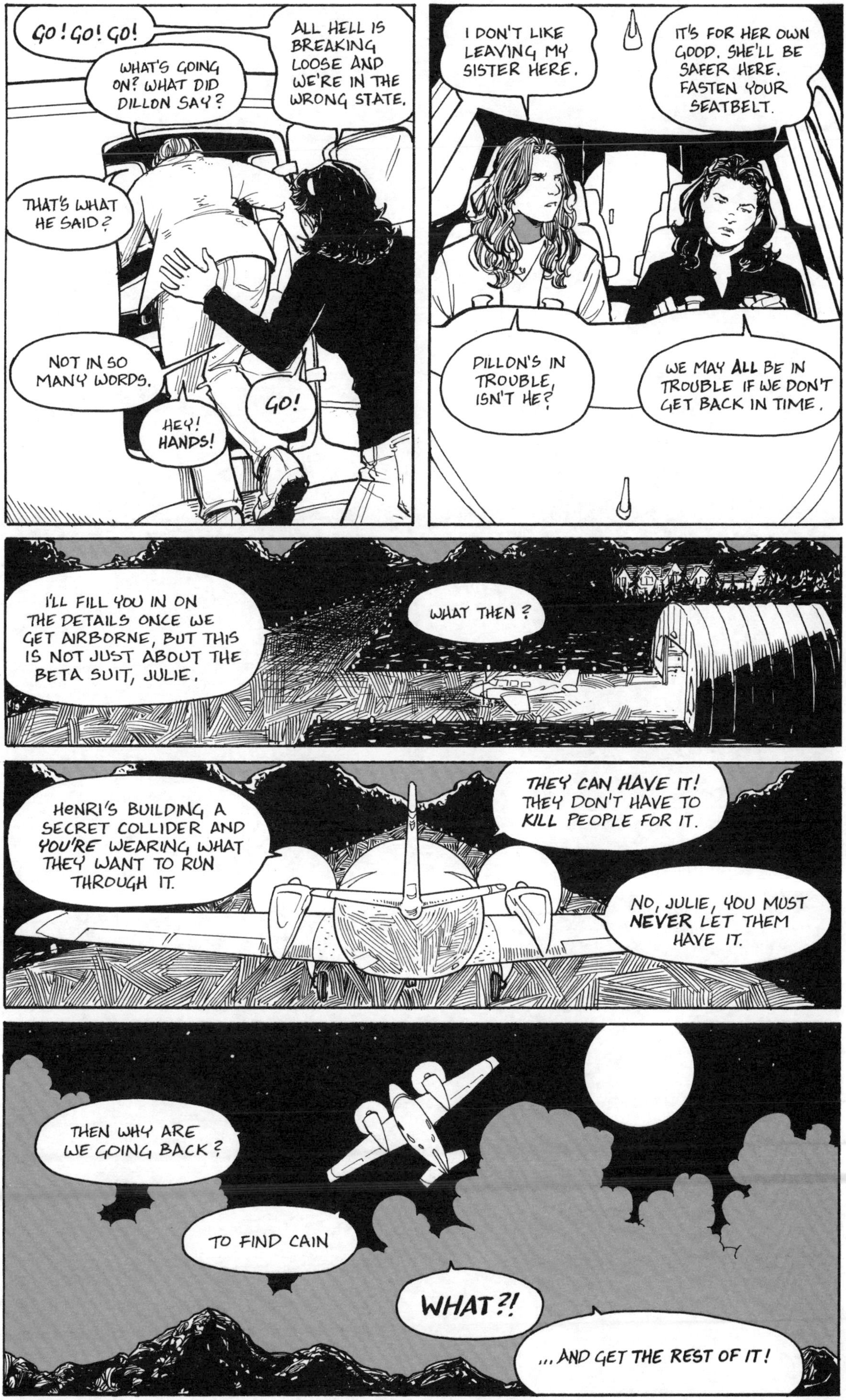
GO! GO! GO!
ALL HELL IS BREAKING LOOSE AND WE'RE IN THE WRONG STATE.
WHAT'S GOING ON? WHAT DID DILLON SAY?
THAT'S WHAT HE SAID?
NOT IN SO MANY WORDS.
HEY! HANDS!
GO!
I DON'T LIKE LEAVING MY SISTER HERE.
IT'S FOR HER OWN GOOD. SHE'LL BE SAFER HERE. FASTEN YOUR SEATBELT.
DILLON'S IN TROUBLE, ISN'T HE?
WE MAY ALL BE IN TROUBLE IF WE DON'T GET BACK IN TIME.
I'LL FILL YOU IN ON THE DETAILS ONCE WE GET AIRBORNE, BUT THIS IS NOT JUST ABOUT THE BETA SUIT, JULIE.
WHAT THEN?
HENRI'S BUILDING A SECRET COLLIDER AND YOU'RE WEARING WHAT THEY WANT TO RUN THROUGH IT.
THEY CAN HAVE IT! THEY DON'T HAVE TO KILL PEOPLE FOR IT.
NO, JULIE, YOU MUST NEVER LET THEM HAVE IT.
THEN WHY ARE WE GOING BACK?
TO FIND CAIN
WHAT?!
...AND GET THE REST OF IT!

"The past is never dead, it is not even past."
—William Faulkner

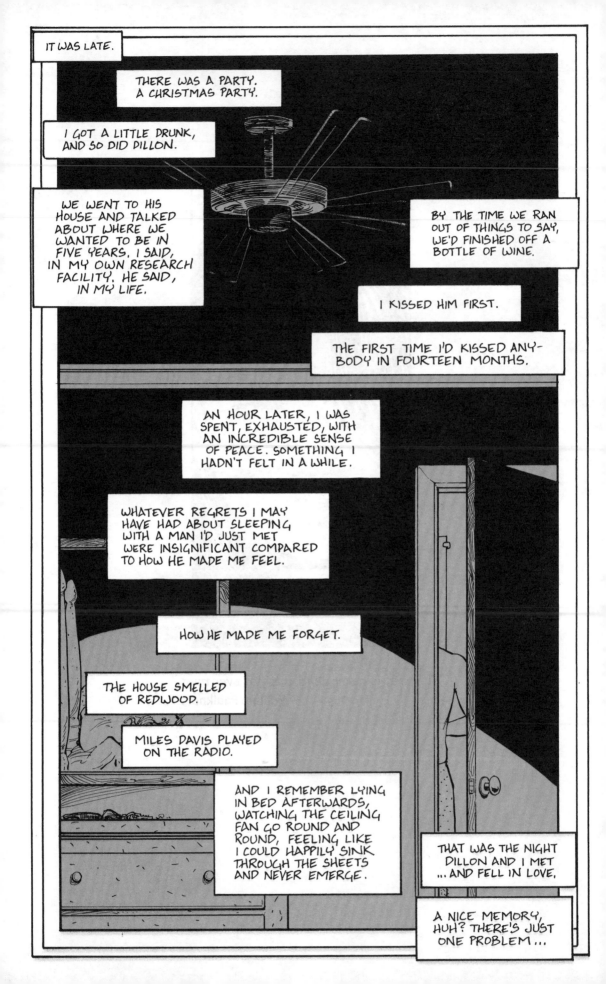

IT WAS LATE.

THERE WAS A PARTY. A CHRISTMAS PARTY.

I GOT A LITTLE DRUNK, AND SO DID DILLON.

WE WENT TO HIS HOUSE AND TALKED ABOUT WHERE WE WANTED TO BE IN FIVE YEARS. I SAID, IN MY OWN RESEARCH FACILITY. HE SAID, IN MY LIFE.

BY THE TIME WE RAN OUT OF THINGS TO SAY, WE'D FINISHED OFF A BOTTLE OF WINE.

I KISSED HIM FIRST.

THE FIRST TIME I'D KISSED ANY- BODY IN FOURTEEN MONTHS.

AN HOUR LATER, I WAS SPENT, EXHAUSTED, WITH AN INCREDIBLE SENSE OF PEACE. SOMETHING I HADN'T FELT IN A WHILE.

WHATEVER REGRETS I MAY HAVE HAD ABOUT SLEEPING WITH A MAN I'D JUST MET WERE INSIGNIFICANT COMPARED TO HOW HE MADE ME FEEL.

HOW HE MADE ME FORGET.

THE HOUSE SMELLED OF REDWOOD.

MILES DAVIS PLAYED ON THE RADIO.

AND I REMEMBER LYING IN BED AFTERWARDS, WATCHING THE CEILING FAN GO ROUND AND ROUND, FEELING LIKE I COULD HAPPILY SINK THROUGH THE SHEETS AND NEVER EMERGE.

THAT WAS THE NIGHT DILLON AND I MET ...AND FELL IN LOVE.

A NICE MEMORY, HUH? THERE'S JUST ONE PROBLEM...

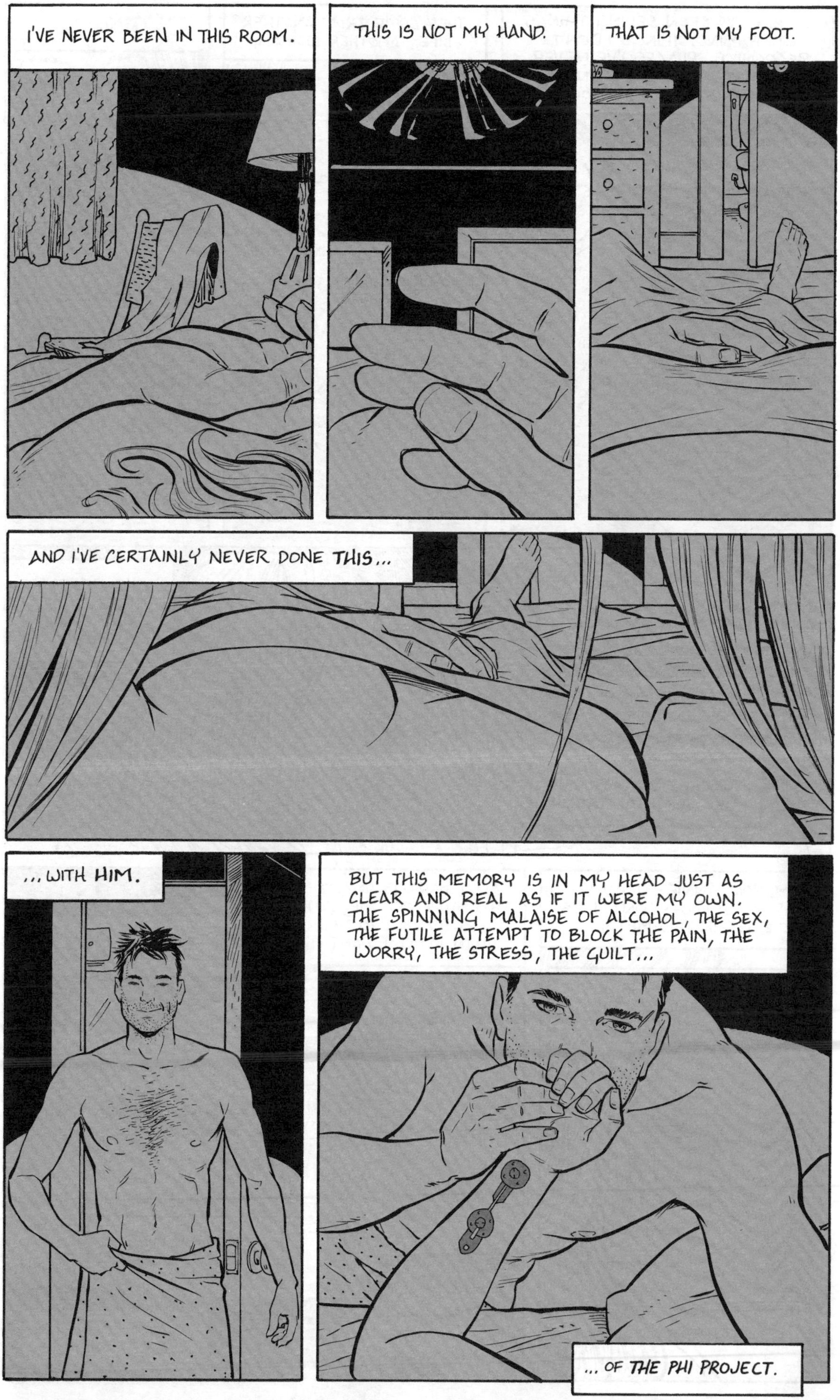
I'VE NEVER BEEN IN THIS ROOM.
THIS IS NOT MY HAND.
THAT IS NOT MY FOOT.
AND I'VE CERTAINLY NEVER DONE THIS...
...WITH HIM.
BUT THIS MEMORY IS IN MY HEAD JUST AS CLEAR AND REAL AS IF IT WERE MY OWN. THE SPINNING MALAISE OF ALCOHOL, THE SEX, THE FUTILE ATTEMPT TO BLOCK THE PAIN, THE WORRY, THE STRESS, THE GUILT...
... OF THE PHI PROJECT.

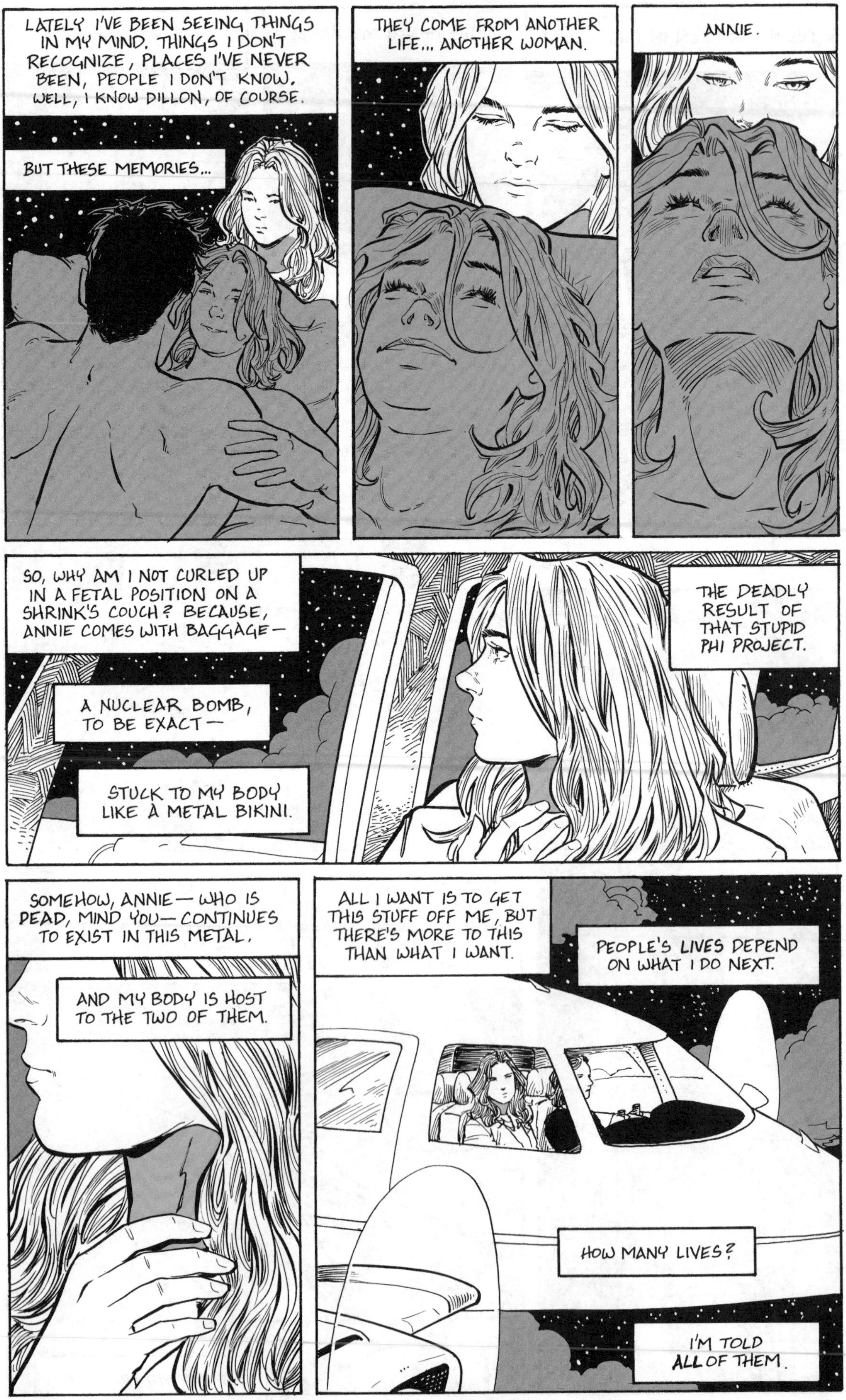
LATELY I'VE BEEN SEEING THINGS IN MY MIND. THINGS I DON'T RECOGNIZE, PLACES I'VE NEVER BEEN, PEOPLE I DON'T KNOW. WELL, I KNOW DILLON, OF COURSE.
BUT THESE MEMORIES...
THEY COME FROM ANOTHER LIFE... ANOTHER WOMAN.
ANNIE.
SO, WHY AM I NOT CURLED UP IN A FETAL POSITION ON A SHRINK'S COUCH? BECAUSE, ANNIE COMES WITH BAGGAGE—
A NUCLEAR BOMB, TO BE EXACT—
STUCK TO MY BODY LIKE A METAL BIKINI.
THE DEADLY RESULT OF THAT STUPID PHI PROJECT.
SOMEHOW, ANNIE— WHO IS DEAD, MIND YOU— CONTINUES TO EXIST IN THIS METAL.
AND MY BODY IS HOST TO THE TWO OF THEM.
ALL I WANT IS TO GET THIS STUFF OFF ME, BUT THERE'S MORE TO THIS THAN WHAT I WANT.
PEOPLE'S LIVES DEPEND ON WHAT I DO NEXT.
HOW MANY LIVES?
I'M TOLD ALL OF THEM.

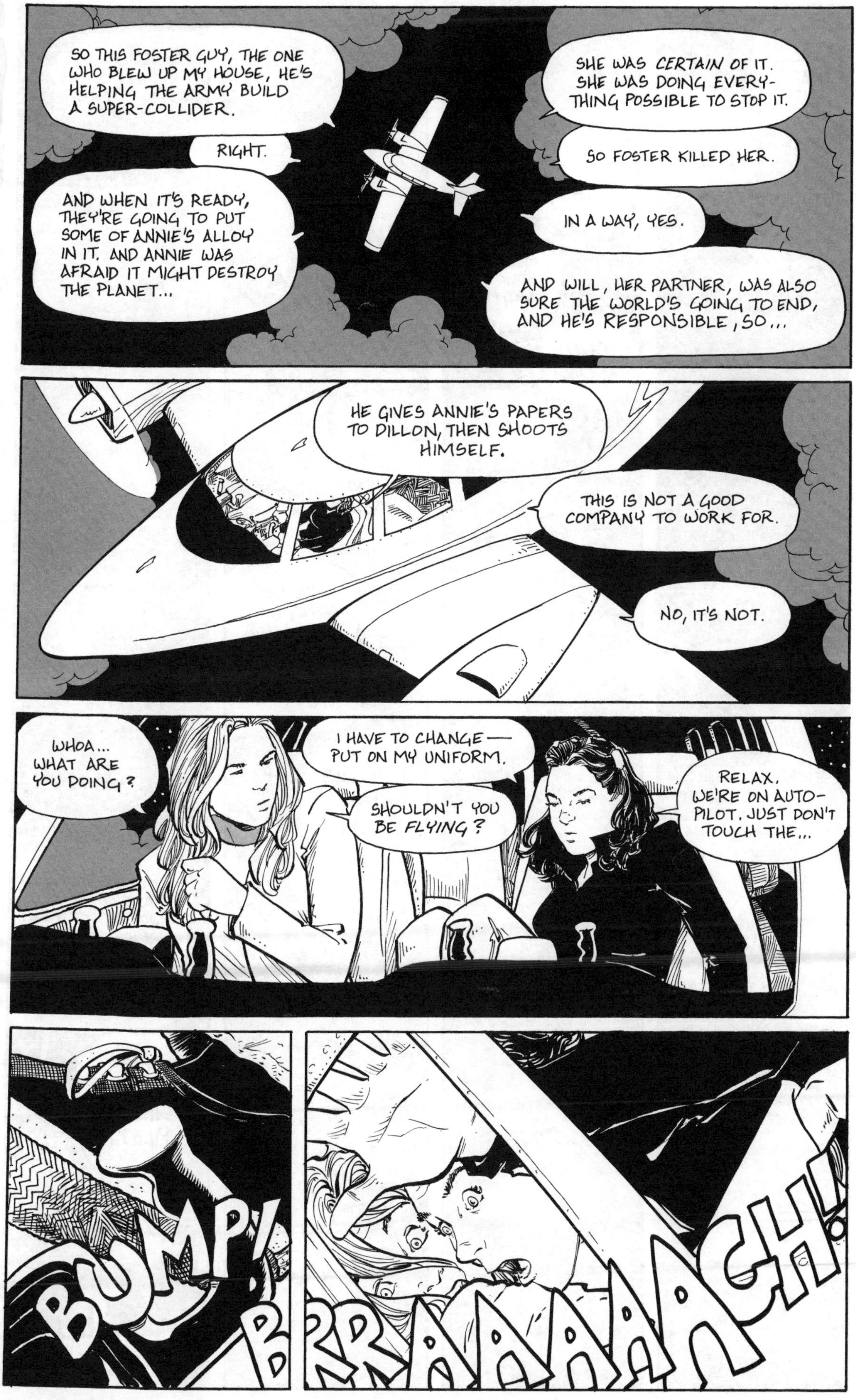
SO THIS FOSTER GUY, THE ONE WHO BLEW UP MY HOUSE, HE'S HELPING THE ARMY BUILD A SUPER-COLLIDER.
RIGHT.
AND WHEN IT'S READY, THEY'RE GOING TO PUT SOME OF ANNIE'S ALLOY IN IT. AND ANNIE WAS AFRAID IT MIGHT DESTROY THE PLANET...
SHE WAS CERTAIN OF IT. SHE WAS DOING EVERYTHING POSSIBLE TO STOP IT.
SO FOSTER KILLED HER.
IN A WAY, YES.
AND WILL, HER PARTNER, WAS ALSO SURE THE WORLD'S GOING TO END, AND HE'S RESPONSIBLE, SO...
HE GIVES ANNIE'S PAPERS TO DILLON, THEN SHOOTS HIMSELF.
THIS IS NOT A GOOD COMPANY TO WORK FOR.
NO, IT'S NOT.
WHOA... WHAT ARE YOU DOING?
I HAVE TO CHANGE— PUT ON MY UNIFORM.
SHOULDN'T YOU BE FLYING?
RELAX. WE'RE ON AUTO-PILOT. JUST DON'T TOUCH THE...
BUMP!
BRRAAAAAACH!!

AAGH! MAKE IT STOP!
WELL... MMPH LET GO OF MY...
GET BACK ON YOUR SIDE!
MOVE YOUR LEG!
OW! BOOBS!
SORRY.
HURRY, WE'RE CRASHING!
WE'RE NOT GOING TO CRASH, FOR PETE'S SAKE... WE'RE 23,000 FEET UP IN THE...
FLY THE FRIKKIN' PLANE!
LOOK, IF YOU AND I ARE GOING TO WORK TOGETHER, WE'RE GOING TO HAVE TO HAVE SOME MEASURE OF MUTUAL RESPECT...
YOU'RE A SHITTY PILOT!

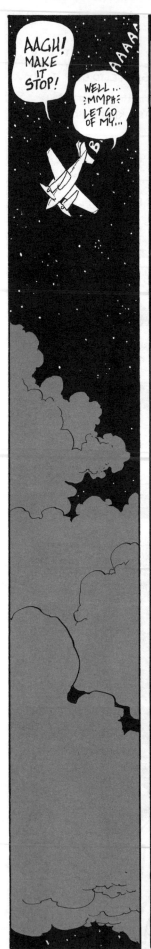

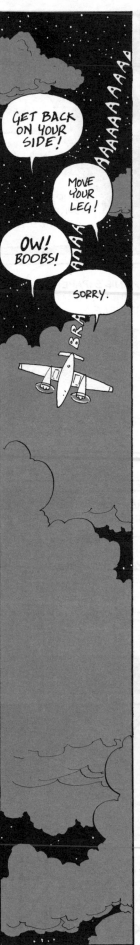

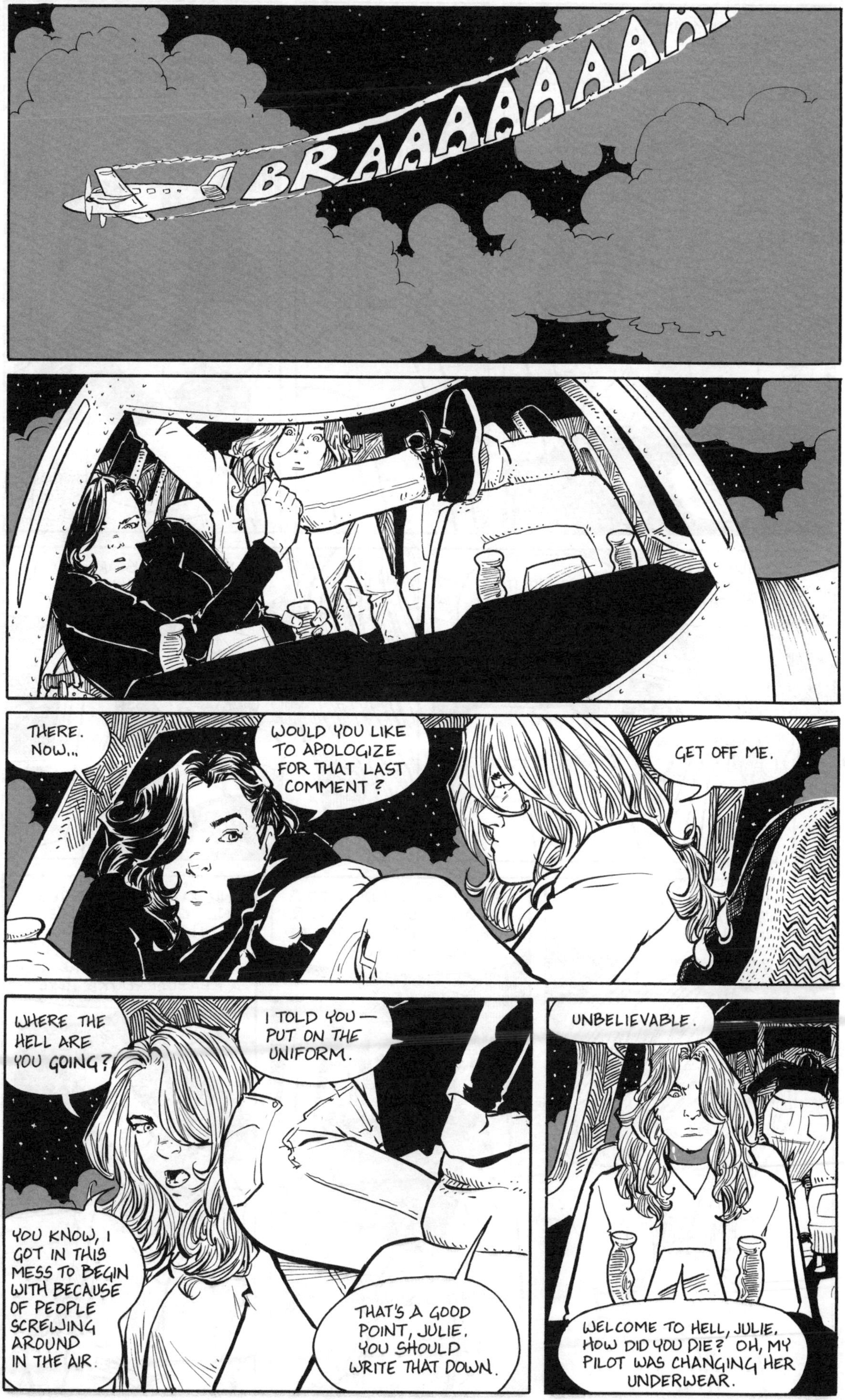
BRAAAAAAAAAH
THERE. NOW...
WOULD YOU LIKE TO APOLOGIZE FOR THAT LAST COMMENT?
GET OFF ME.
WHERE THE HELL ARE YOU GOING?
I TOLD YOU — PUT ON THE UNIFORM.
YOU KNOW, I GOT IN THIS MESS TO BEGIN WITH BECAUSE OF PEOPLE SCREWING AROUND IN THE AIR.
THAT'S A GOOD POINT, JULIE. YOU SHOULD WRITE THAT DOWN.
UNBELIEVABLE.
WELCOME TO HELL, JULIE. HOW DID YOU DIE? OH, MY PILOT WAS CHANGING HER UNDERWEAR.

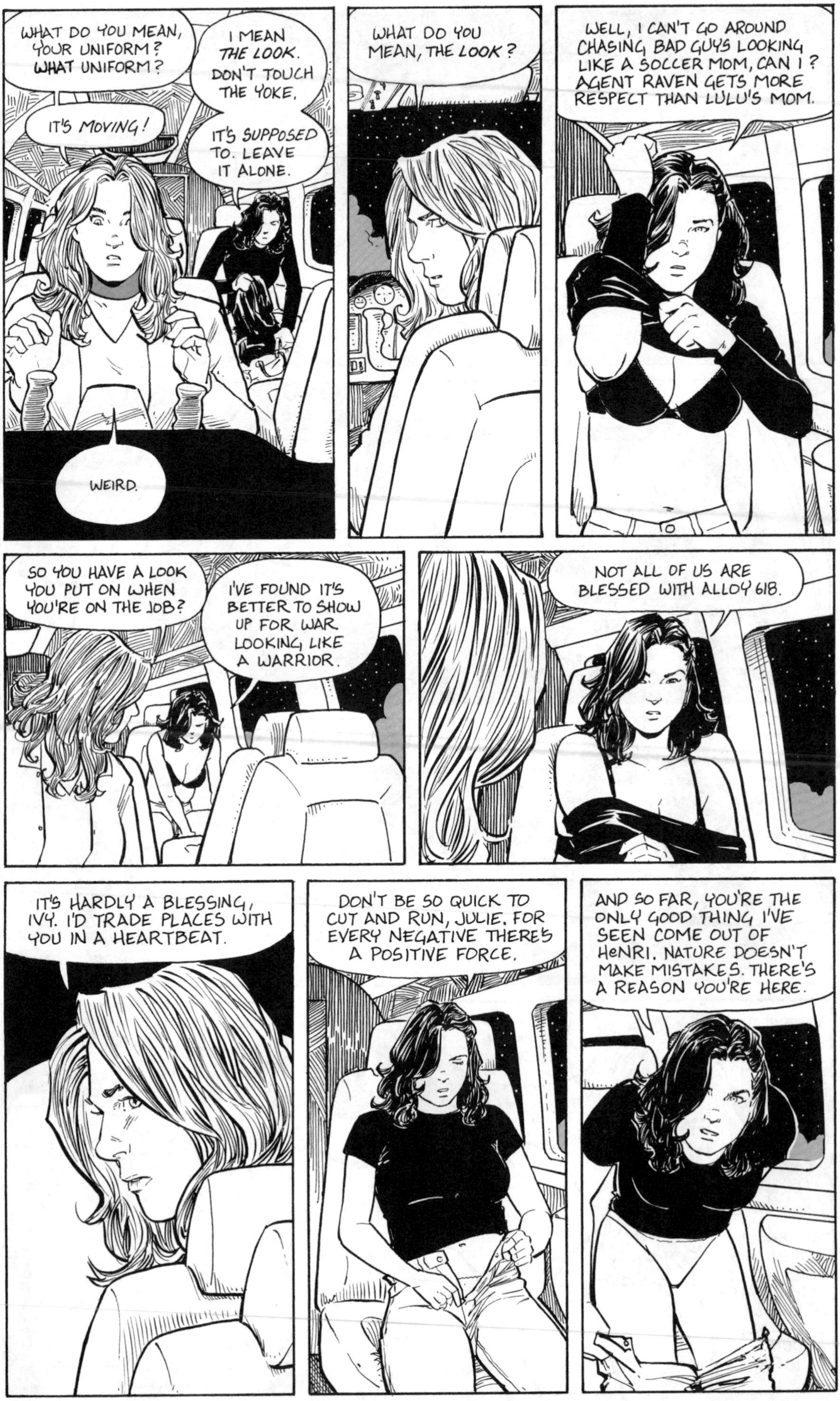
WHAT DO YOU MEAN, YOUR UNIFORM? WHAT UNIFORM?
I MEAN THE LOOK. DON'T TOUCH THE YOKE.
IT'S MOVING!
IT'S SUPPOSED TO. LEAVE IT ALONE.
WEIRD.
WHAT DO YOU MEAN, THE LOOK?
WELL, I CAN'T GO AROUND CHASING BAD GUYS LOOKING LIKE A SOCCER MOM, CAN I? AGENT RAVEN GETS MORE RESPECT THAN LULU'S MOM.
SO YOU HAVE A LOOK YOU PUT ON WHEN YOU'RE ON THE JOB?
I'VE FOUND IT'S BETTER TO SHOW UP FOR WAR LOOKING LIKE A WARRIOR.
NOT ALL OF US ARE BLESSED WITH ALLOY 618.
IT'S HARDLY A BLESSING, IVY. I'D TRADE PLACES WITH YOU IN A HEARTBEAT.
DON'T BE SO QUICK TO CUT AND RUN, JULIE. FOR EVERY NEGATIVE THERE'S A POSITIVE FORCE.
AND SO FAR, YOU'RE THE ONLY GOOD THING I'VE SEEN COME OUT OF HeNRI. NATURE DOESN'T MAKE MISTAKES. THERE'S A REASON YOU'RE HERE.

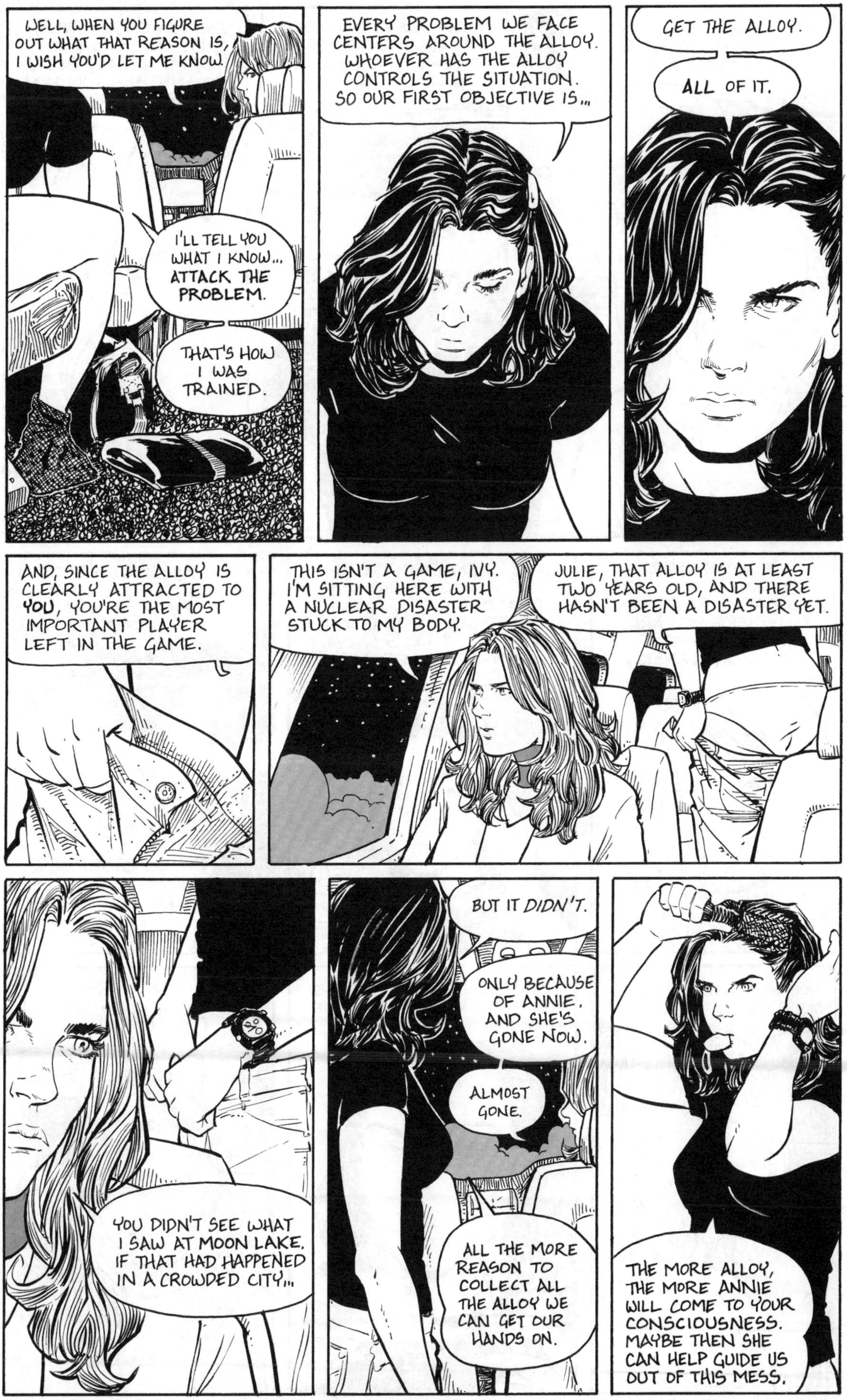
WELL, WHEN YOU FIGURE OUT WHAT THAT REASON IS, I WISH YOU'D LET ME KNOW.
I'LL TELL YOU WHAT I KNOW... ATTACK THE PROBLEM.
THAT'S HOW I WAS TRAINED.
EVERY PROBLEM WE FACE CENTERS AROUND THE ALLOY. WHOEVER HAS THE ALLOY CONTROLS THE SITUATION. SO OUR FIRST OBJECTIVE IS...
GET THE ALLOY.
ALL OF IT.
AND, SINCE THE ALLOY IS CLEARLY ATTRACTED TO YOU, YOU'RE THE MOST IMPORTANT PLAYER LEFT IN THE GAME.
THIS ISN'T A GAME, IVY. I'M SITTING HERE WITH A NUCLEAR DISASTER STUCK TO MY BODY.
JULIE, THAT ALLOY IS AT LEAST TWO YEARS OLD, AND THERE HASN'T BEEN A DISASTER YET.
YOU DIDN'T SEE WHAT I SAW AT MOON LAKE. IF THAT HAD HAPPENED IN A CROWDED CITY...
BUT IT DIDN'T.
ONLY BECAUSE OF ANNIE. AND SHE'S GONE NOW.
ALMOST GONE.
ALL THE MORE REASON TO COLLECT ALL THE ALLOY WE CAN GET OUR HANDS ON.
THE MORE ALLOY, THE MORE ANNIE WILL COME TO YOUR CONSCIOUSNESS. MAYBE THEN SHE CAN HELP GUIDE US OUT OF THIS MESS.

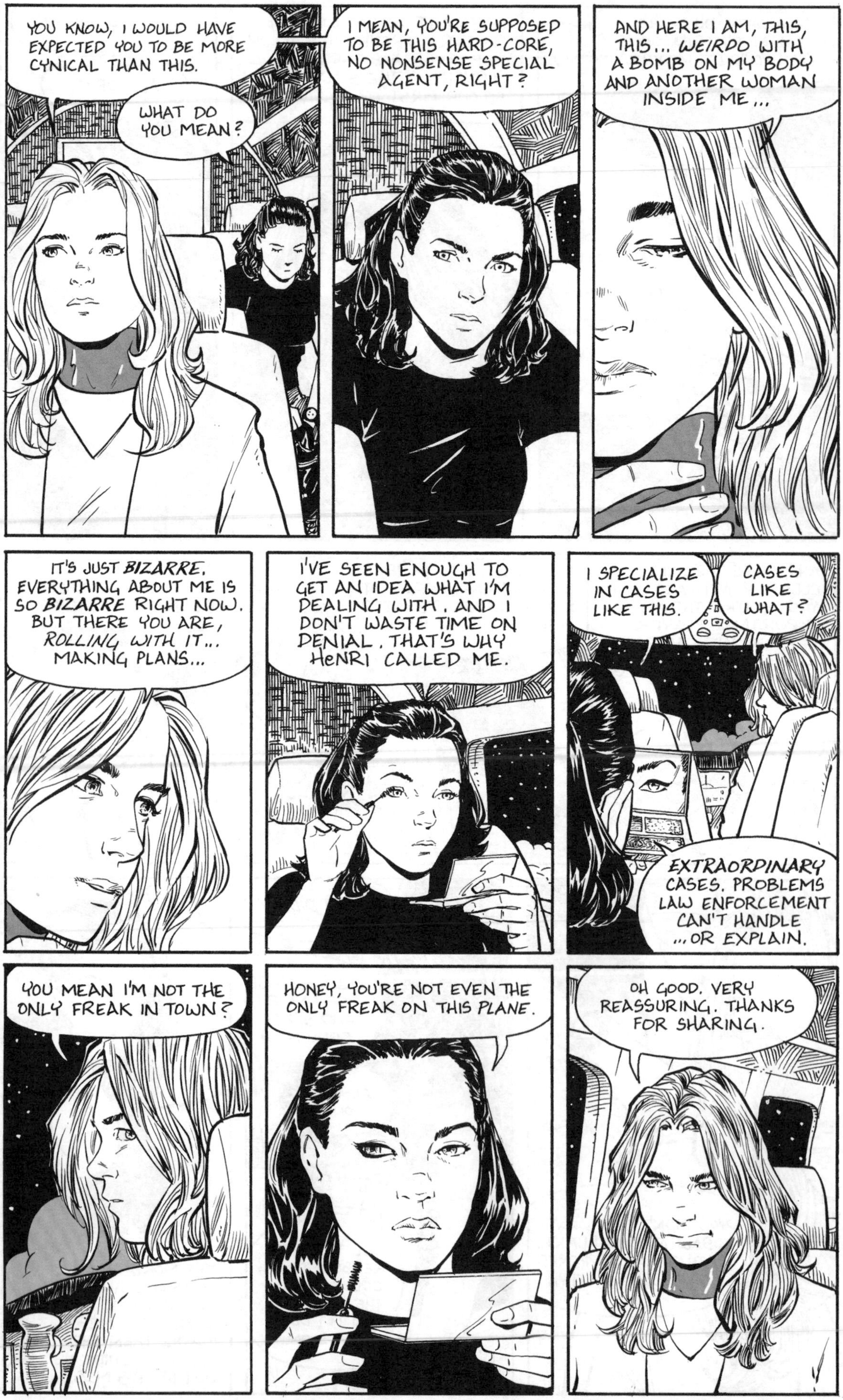
YOU KNOW, I WOULD HAVE EXPECTED YOU TO BE MORE CYNICAL THAN THIS.
WHAT DO YOU MEAN?
I MEAN, YOU'RE SUPPOSED TO BE THIS HARD-CORE, NO NONSENSE SPECIAL AGENT, RIGHT?
AND HERE I AM, THIS, THIS... WEIRDO WITH A BOMB ON MY BODY AND ANOTHER WOMAN INSIDE ME...
IT'S JUST BIZARRE. EVERYTHING ABOUT ME IS SO BIZARRE RIGHT NOW. BUT THERE YOU ARE, ROLLING WITH IT... MAKING PLANS...
I'VE SEEN ENOUGH TO GET AN IDEA WHAT I'M DEALING WITH. AND I DON'T WASTE TIME ON DENIAL. THAT'S WHY HENRI CALLED ME.
I SPECIALIZE IN CASES LIKE THIS.
CASES LIKE WHAT?
EXTRAORDINARY CASES. PROBLEMS LAW ENFORCEMENT CAN'T HANDLE ...OR EXPLAIN.
YOU MEAN I'M NOT THE ONLY FREAK IN TOWN?
HONEY, YOU'RE NOT EVEN THE ONLY FREAK ON THIS PLANE.
OH GOOD. VERY REASSURING. THANKS FOR SHARING.

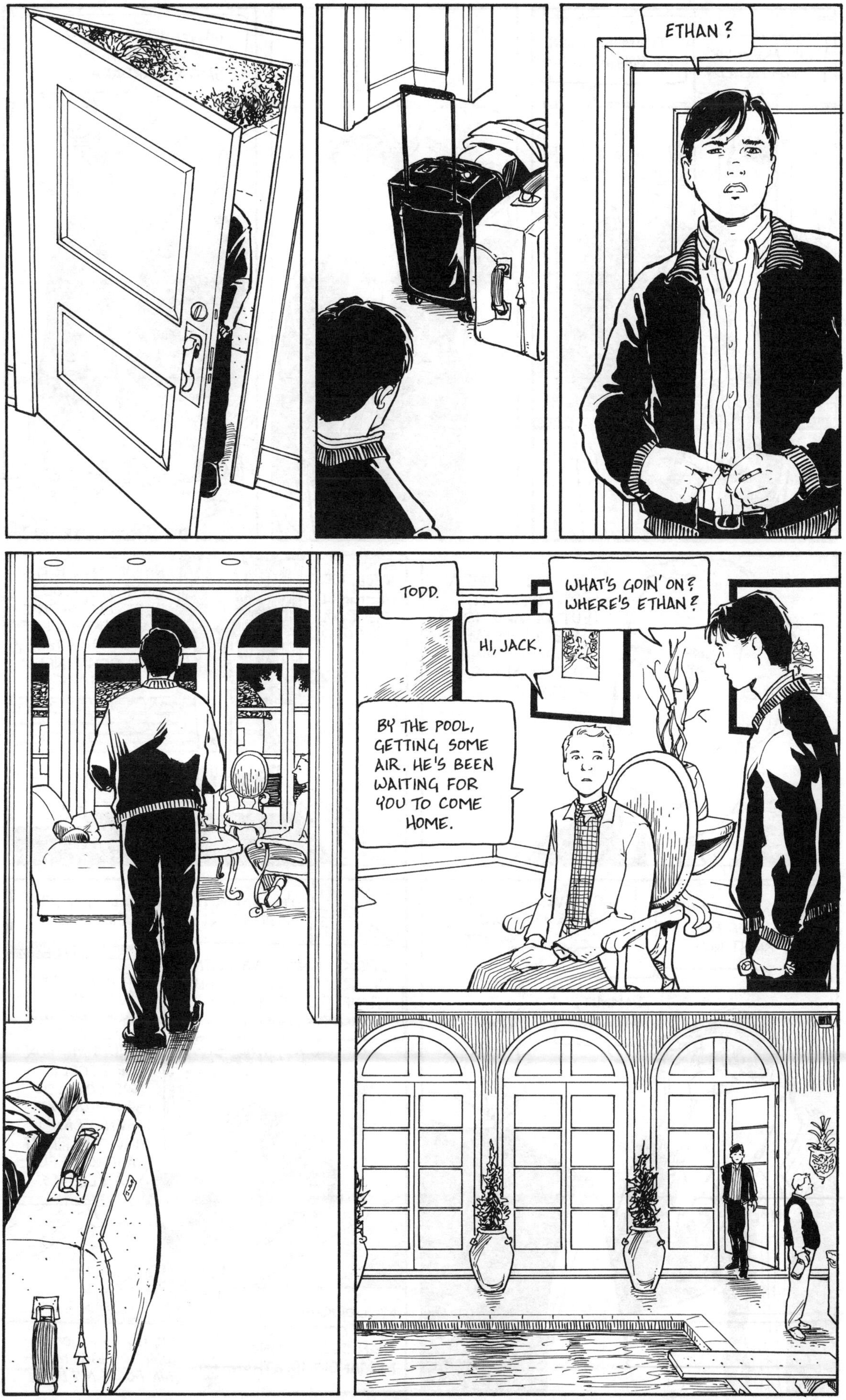
ETHAN?
TODD.
WHAT'S GOIN' ON? WHERE'S ETHAN?
HI, JACK.
BY THE POOL, GETTING SOME AIR. HE'S BEEN WAITING FOR YOU TO COME HOME.

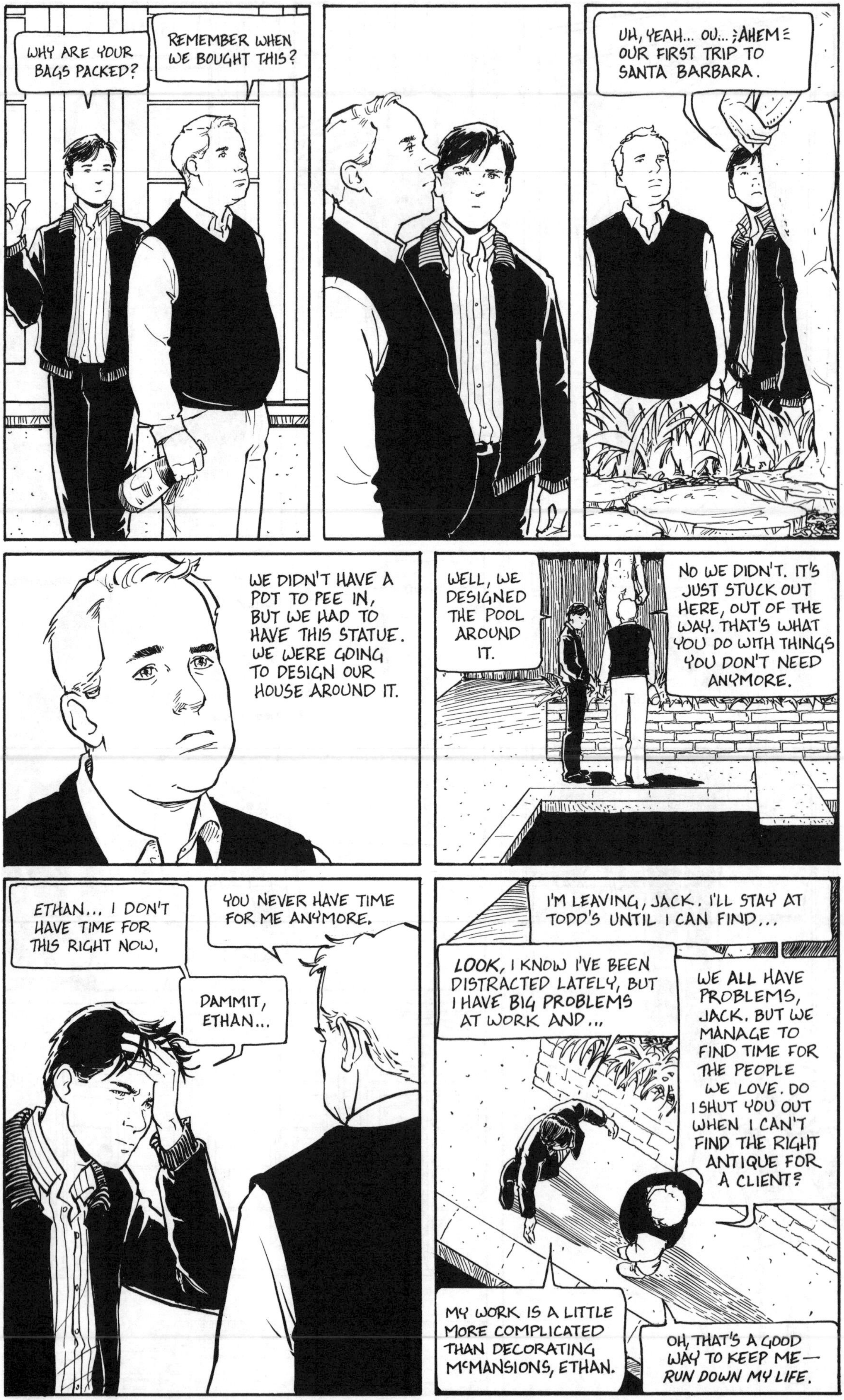
WHY ARE YOUR BAGS PACKED?
REMEMBER WHEN WE BOUGHT THIS?
UH, YEAH... OU... AHEM OUR FIRST TRIP TO SANTA BARBARA.
WE DIDN'T HAVE A POT TO PEE IN, BUT WE HAD TO HAVE THIS STATUE. WE WERE GOING TO DESIGN OUR HOUSE AROUND IT.
WELL, WE DESIGNED THE POOL AROUND IT.
NO WE DIDN'T. IT'S JUST STUCK OUT HERE, OUT OF THE WAY. THAT'S WHAT YOU DO WITH THINGS YOU DON'T NEED ANYMORE.
ETHAN... I DON'T HAVE TIME FOR THIS RIGHT NOW.
YOU NEVER HAVE TIME FOR ME ANYMORE.
DAMMIT, ETHAN...
I'M LEAVING, JACK. I'LL STAY AT TODD'S UNTIL I CAN FIND...
LOOK, I KNOW I'VE BEEN DISTRACTED LATELY, BUT I HAVE BIG PROBLEMS AT WORK AND...
WE ALL HAVE PROBLEMS, JACK. BUT WE MANAGE TO FIND TIME FOR THE PEOPLE WE LOVE. DO I SHUT YOU OUT WHEN I CAN'T FIND THE RIGHT ANTIQUE FOR A CLIENT?
MY WORK IS A LITTLE MORE COMPLICATED THAN DECORATING McMANSIONS, ETHAN.
OH, THAT'S A GOOD WAY TO KEEP ME— RUN DOWN MY LIFE.

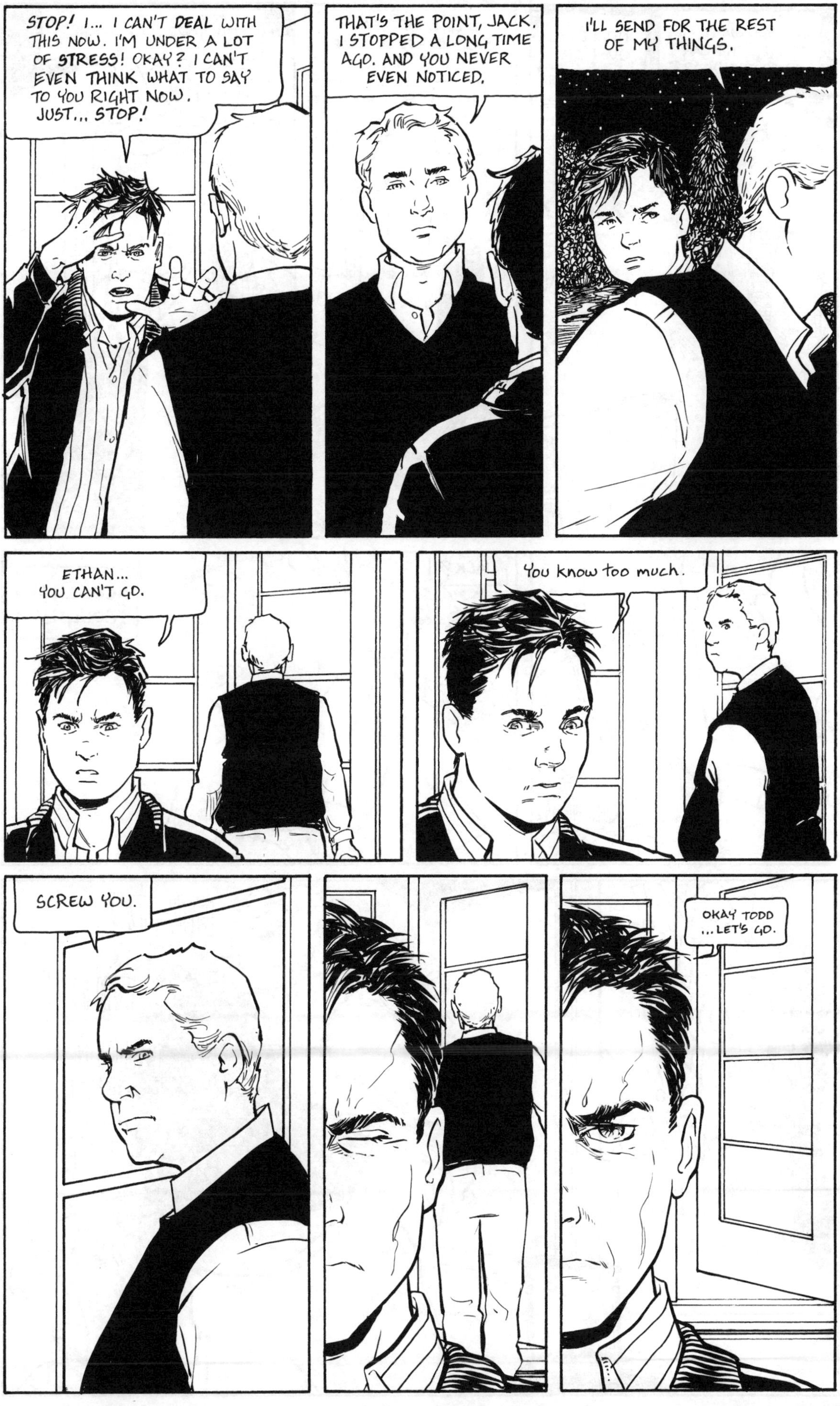
STOP! I... I CAN'T DEAL WITH THIS NOW. I'M UNDER A LOT OF STRESS! OKAY? I CAN'T EVEN THINK WHAT TO SAY TO YOU RIGHT NOW. JUST... STOP!
THAT'S THE POINT, JACK. I STOPPED A LONG TIME AGO. AND YOU NEVER EVEN NOTICED.
I'LL SEND FOR THE REST OF MY THINGS.
ETHAN... YOU CAN'T GO.
You know too much.
SCREW YOU.
OKAY TODD ...LET'S GO.

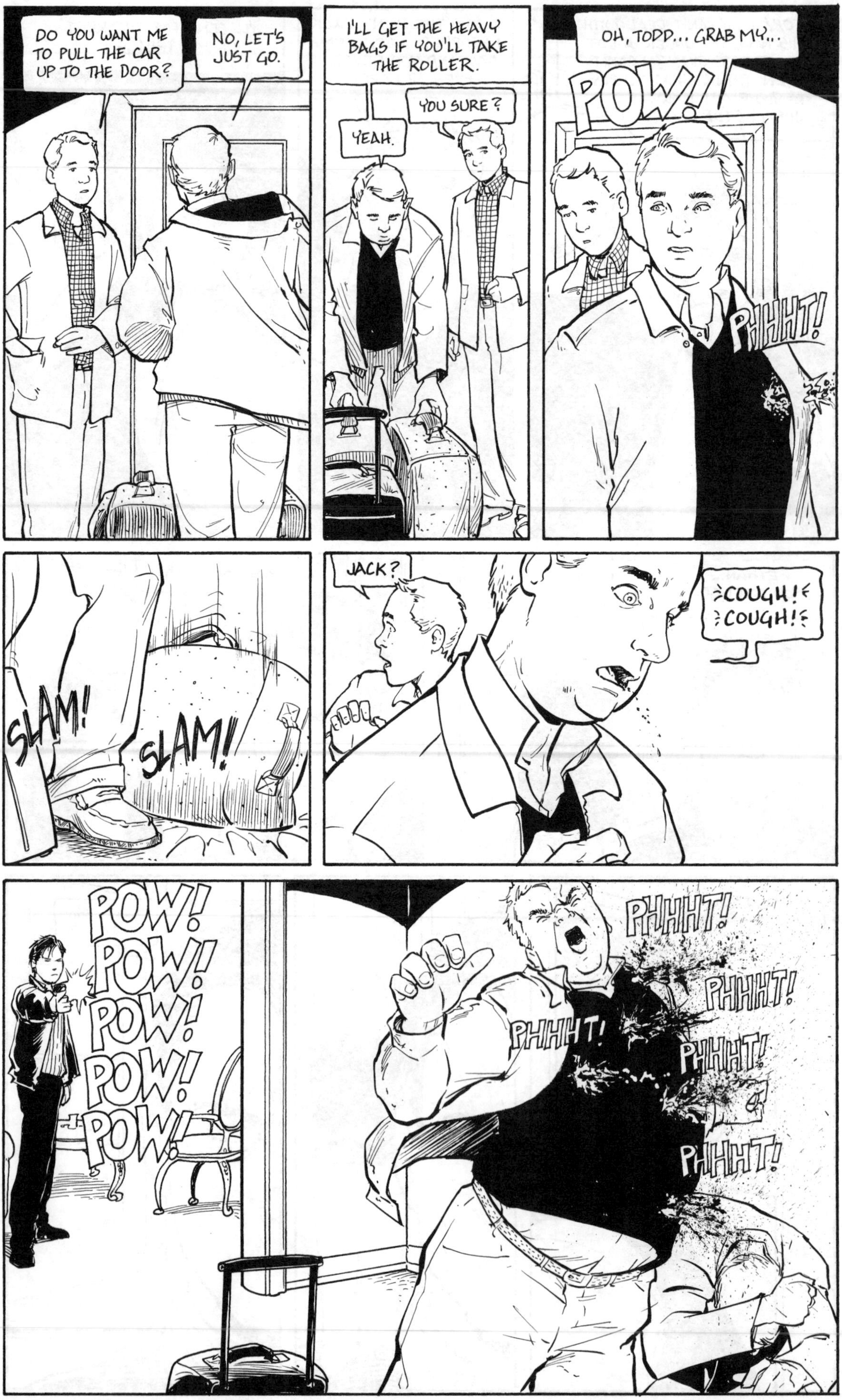
DO YOU WANT ME TO PULL THE CAR UP TO THE DOOR?
NO, LET'S JUST GO.
I'LL GET THE HEAVY BAGS IF YOU'LL TAKE THE ROLLER.
YOU SURE?
YEAH.
OH, TODD... GRAB MY...
POW!
PHHHT!
SLAM!
SLAM!
JACK?
COUGH! COUGH!
POW!
POW!
POW!
POW!
POW!
PHHHT!
PHHHT!
PHHHT!
PHHHT!
PHHHT!

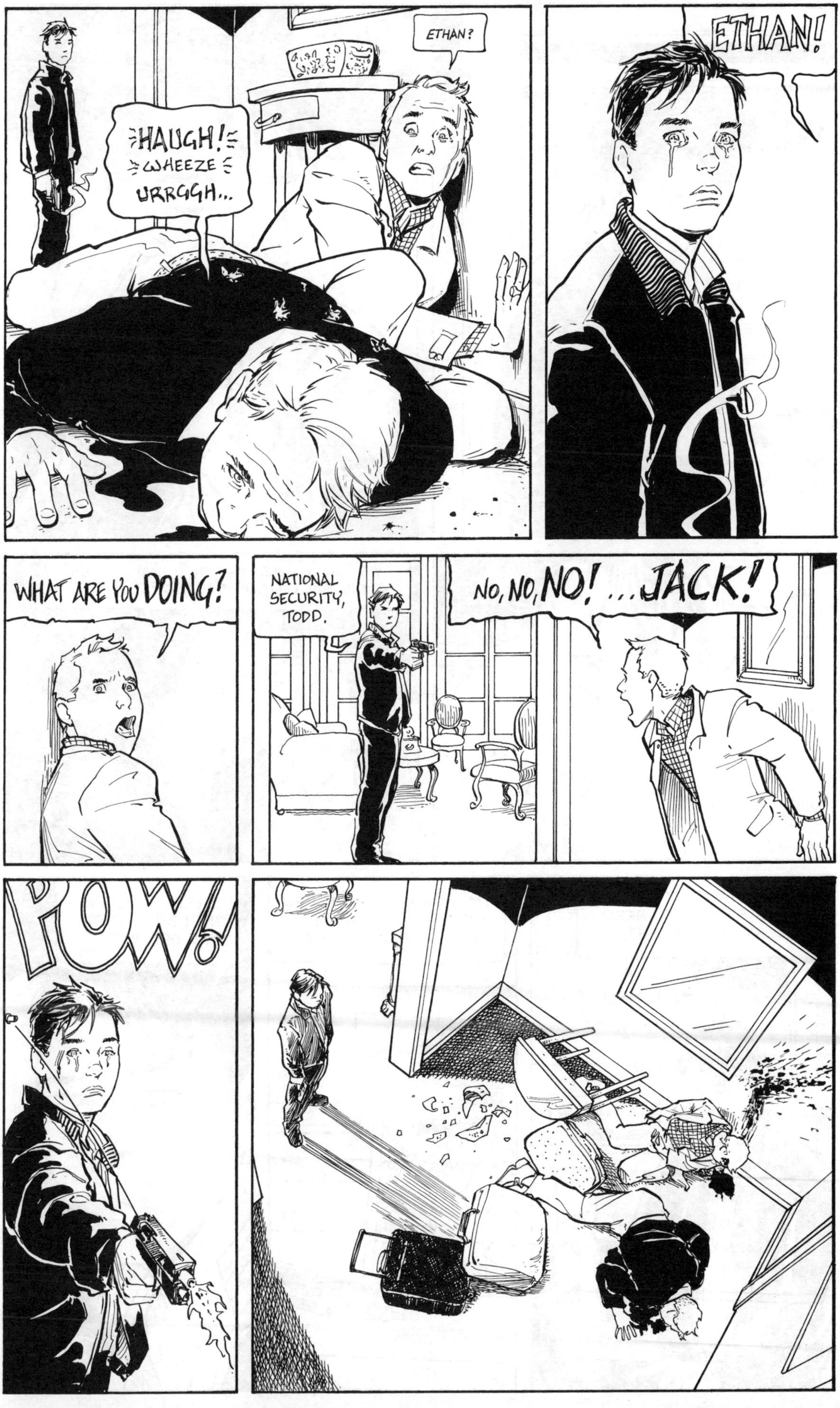
ETHAN?
HAUGH! WHEEZE URRGGH...
ETHAN!
WHAT ARE YOU DOING?
NATIONAL SECURITY, TODD.
NO, NO, NO! ...JACK!
POW!

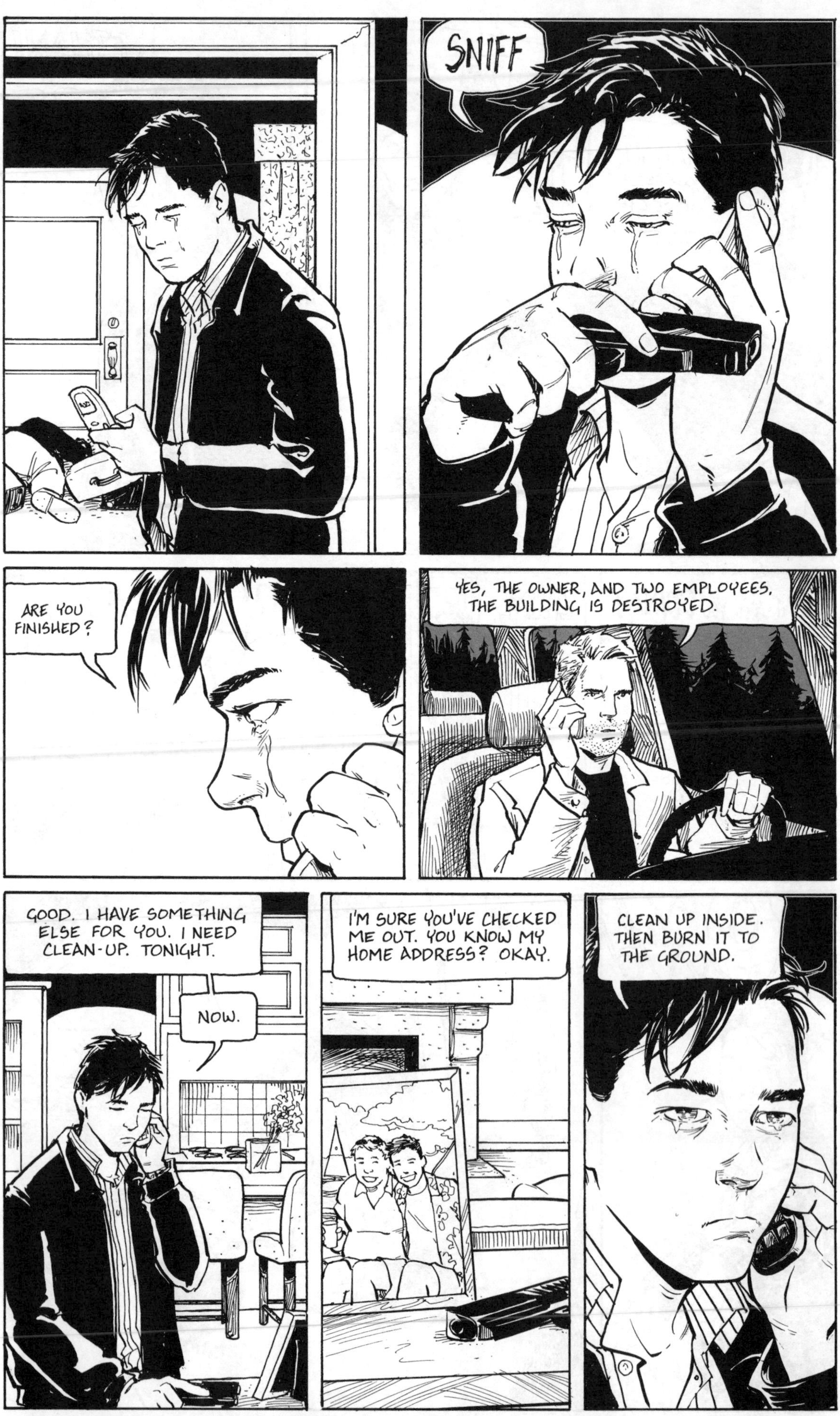
SNIFF
ARE YOU FINISHED?
YES, THE OWNER, AND TWO EMPLOYEES. THE BUILDING IS DESTROYED.
GOOD. I HAVE SOMETHING ELSE FOR YOU. I NEED CLEAN-UP. TONIGHT.
NOW.
I'M SURE YOU'VE CHECKED ME OUT. YOU KNOW MY HOME ADDRESS? OKAY.
CLEAN UP INSIDE. THEN BURN IT TO THE GROUND.

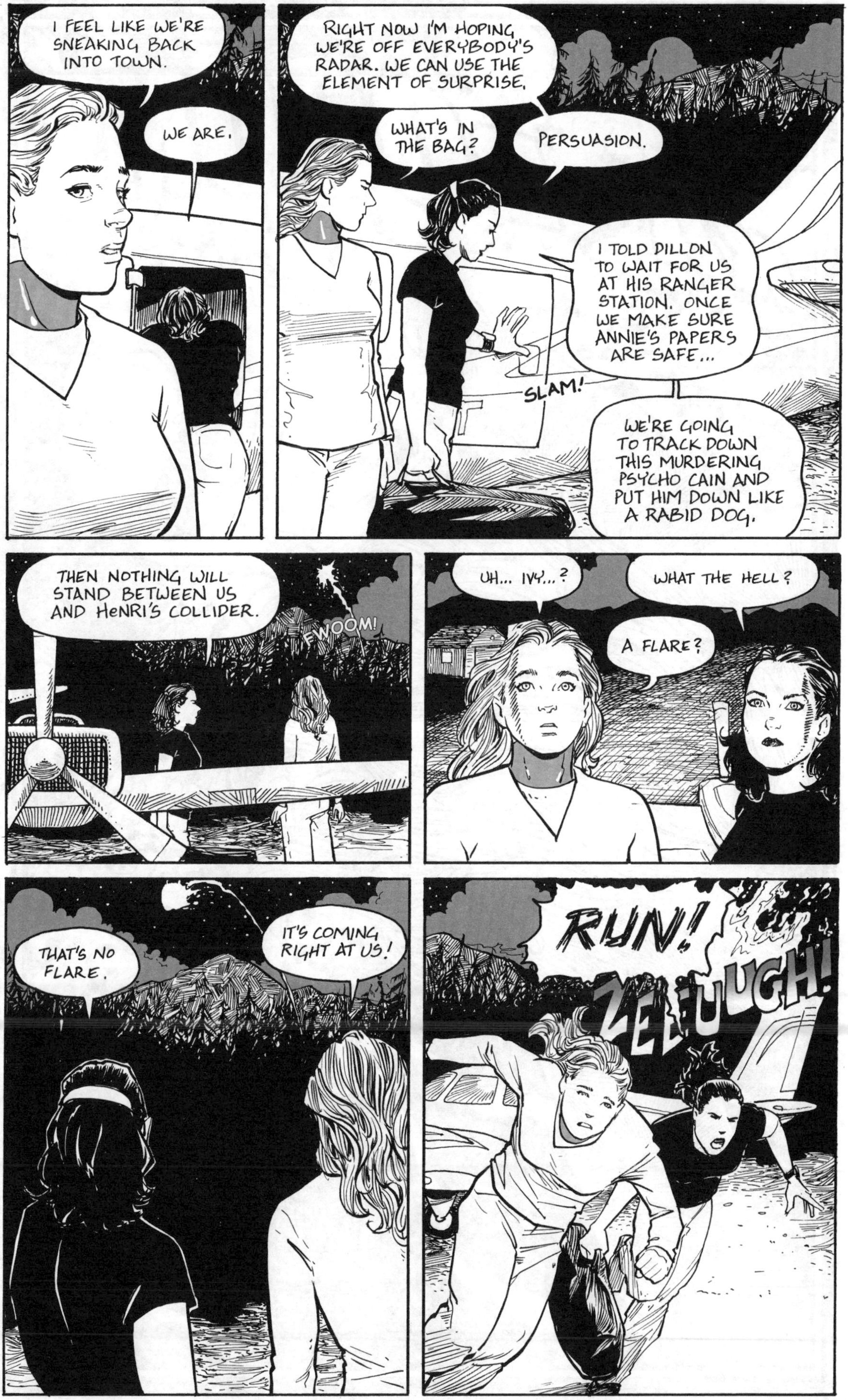
I FEEL LIKE WE'RE SNEAKING BACK INTO TOWN.
WE ARE.
RIGHT NOW I'M HOPING WE'RE OFF EVERYBODY'S RADAR. WE CAN USE THE ELEMENT OF SURPRISE.
WHAT'S IN THE BAG?
PERSUASION.
I TOLD DILLON TO WAIT FOR US AT HIS RANGER STATION. ONCE WE MAKE SURE ANNIE'S PAPERS ARE SAFE...
SLAM!
WE'RE GOING TO TRACK DOWN THIS MURDERING PSYCHO CAIN AND PUT HIM DOWN LIKE A RABID DOG.
THEN NOTHING WILL STAND BETWEEN US AND HeNRI'S COLLIDER.
FWOOM!
UH... IVY...?
WHAT THE HELL?
A FLARE?
THAT'S NO FLARE.
IT'S COMING RIGHT AT US!
RUN!
ZELUUGH!

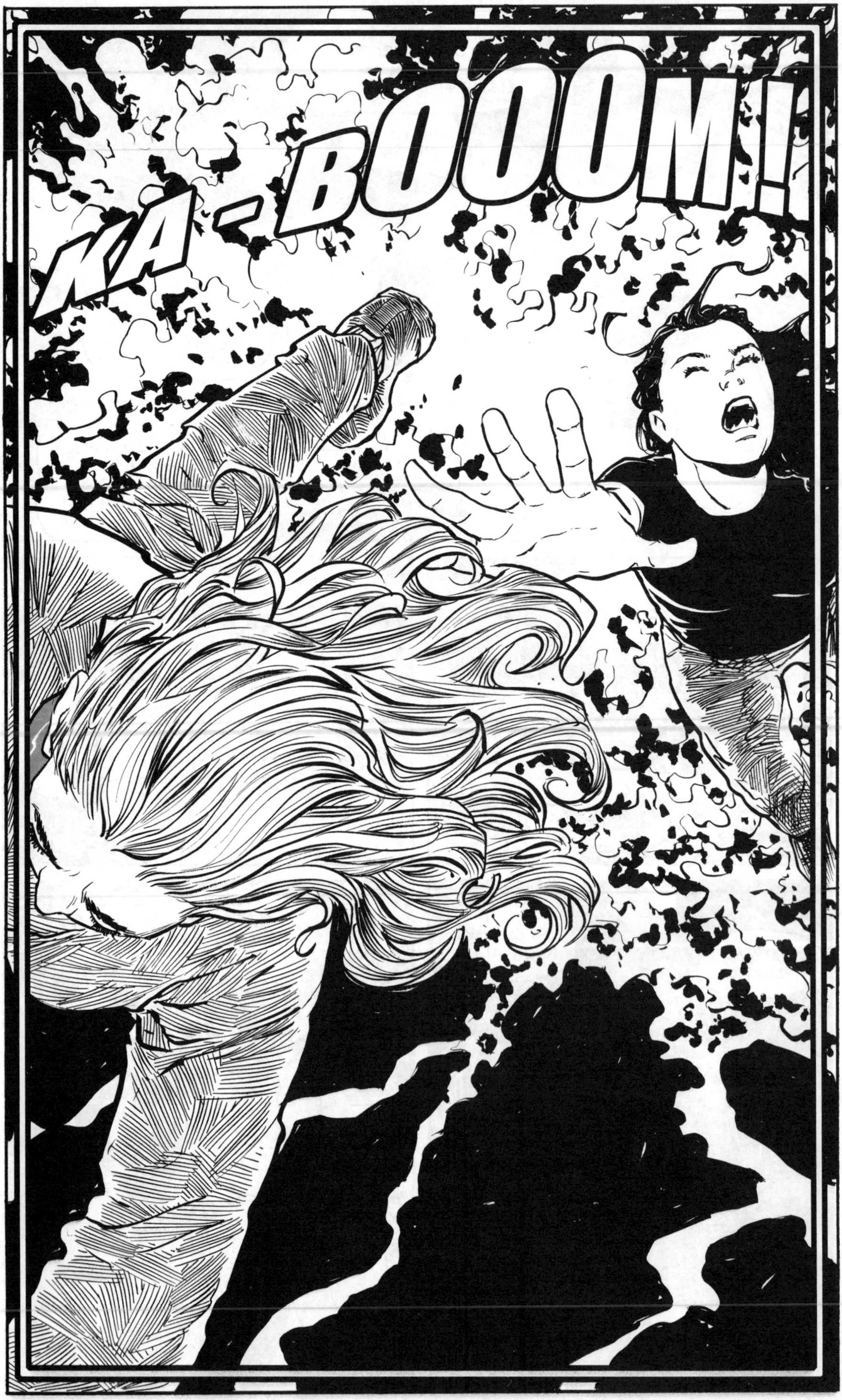
KA-BOOOOM!!

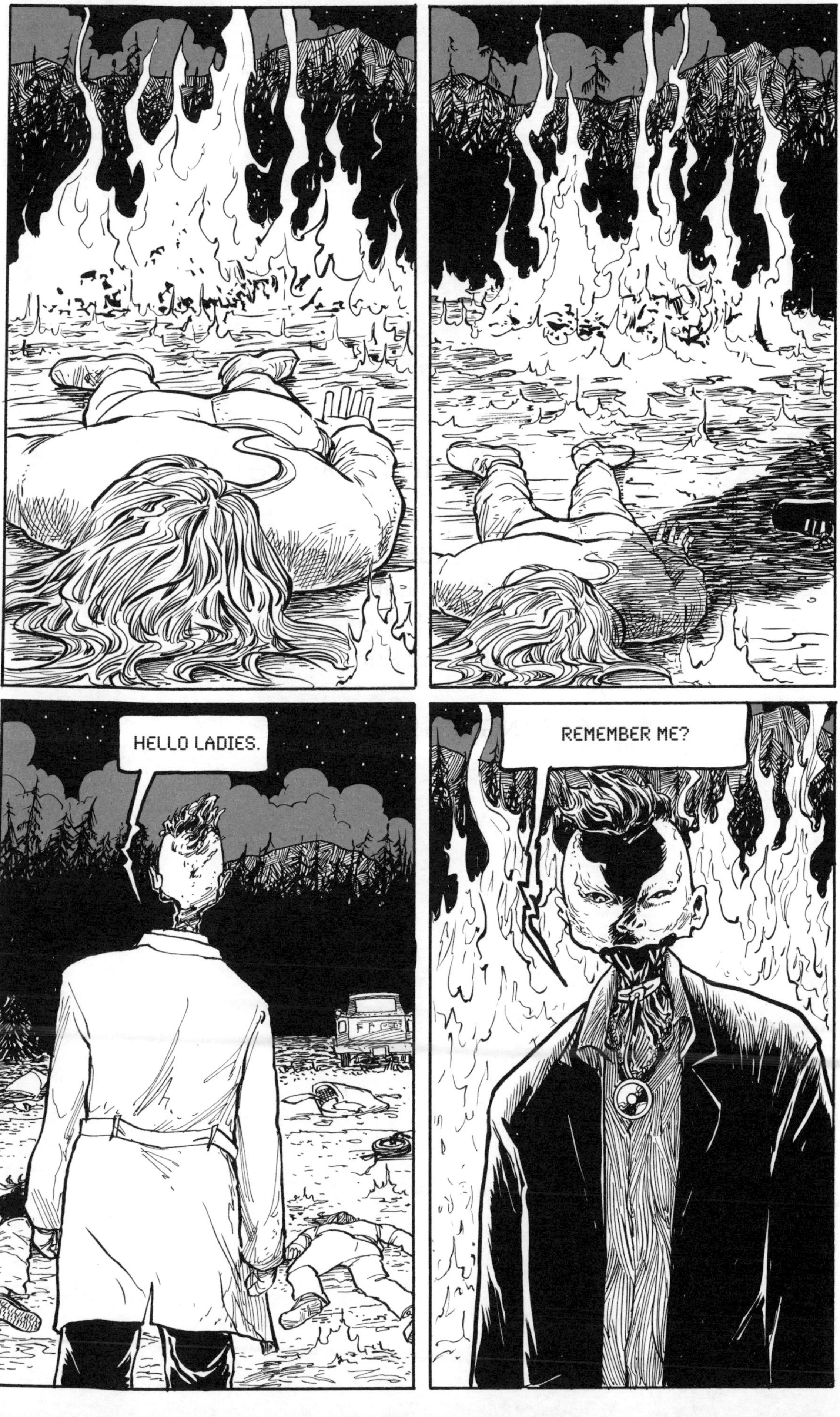
HELLO LADIES.
REMEMBER ME?

Books by Terry Moore

ECHO
Moon Lake
Atomic Dreams
Desert Run

STRANGERS IN PARADISE